The changing nature of democracy

The changing nature of democracy

Edited by Takashi Inoguchi,
Edward Newman, and John Keane

United Nations
University Press

TOKYO · NEW YORK · PARIS

© The United Nations University, 1998

The views expressed in this publication are those of the authors and do not necessarily reflect the views of the United Nations University.

United Nations University Press
The United Nations University, 53-70, Jingumae 5-chome, Shibuya-ku, Tokyo 150-8925, Japan
Tel: (03) 3499-2811   Fax: (03) 3406-7345
E-mail: mbox@hq.unu.edu

UNU Office in North America
2 United Nations Plaza, Room DC2-1462-70, New York, NY 10017
Tel: (212) 963-6387   Fax: (212) 371-9454   Telex: 422311 UN UI

United Nations University Press is the publishing division of the United Nations University.

Cover design by Joyce C. Weston

Printed in the United States of America

UNUP-1005
ISBN 92-808-1005-7

Library of Congress Cataloging-in-Publication Data

The changing nature of democracy / edited by Takashi Inoguchi, Edward Newman, and John Keane.
    p.   cm.
  Includes bibliographical references and index.
  ISBN 9280810057 (pbk.)
  1. Democracy—History—20th century.   I. Inoguchi, Takashi.
II. Newman, Edward, 1970–   III. Keane, John, 1949–
  JC421.C43   1998
  321.8–ddc21   98-9061
                                                          CIP

Contents

1

Introduction: The changing nature of democracy

Takashi Inoguchi, Edward Newman, and John Keane

Democracy is widely advocated and sought, but its meaning is widely contested. At a time when democracy is proliferating geographically it is appropriate to re-examine the perennial debates of established democracies and the tensions and opportunities evident in transitional societies as they embrace democratic institutions and norms. Is democracy fulfilling its promise both in established democracies and in transitional societies? A re-examination is timely also because the nature of democracy is diversifying as it proliferates and is conditioned by cultural and political differences and varying stages of economic and social development. In turn, as democracy evolves in this way, a standard definition or model of democracy is increasingly elusive. Furthermore, as the global political, economic, and technological environments rapidly change, we need to examine how these changes have affected the nature of democracy.

The language and aspirations of democracy are increasingly seen within the context of an emerging global ethos which purports to find points of unity in the human condition and perhaps even a fledgling global citizenship. Transparency, accountability, and performance more than ever before form the benchmark for authority, legitimacy, and "good governance," promoted by global media and communications. Subsequently, democracy is recognized as the primary vehicle for the fulfilment of individual and collective aspirations, the articulation of interests, and the nurturing of civil society. In turn, the fulfilment of human material and spiritual aspirations is increasingly seen to underpin both domestic and international peace and security. The wider conception of peace and security embraces all spheres of

1

life – economic, political, social, and environmental in addition to territorial and military security – and democracy is increasingly seen as an integral part of this matrix. Autocratic authority has been challenged across the globe in a "worldwide movement toward democracy."[1] As a part of the same process, the concept of democracy has been internationalized as never before, as state boundaries permeate issues that cause repercussions on all spheres of life across the globe. In addition to the geographic widening of democracy as a political system, there is a debate concerning its sphere of applicability. What areas of life are, or should be, subject to democracy and to the nonviolent controversies about power within public spheres of debate and controversy?

Definitions and criteria

Democracy and democratic theory are largely conditional on differing conceptions of citizenship, social needs, and human nature. These conceptions are in turn the result of social, cultural, and ideological variables. Clearly, the world reflects great diversity: the definition and criteria of democracy represent a major problem. Even the notion of a "definition" is contentious: should such foundational criteria be based upon procedural factors and institutions, or abstract outcomes? Yet, without an accepted definition of democracy, there will be no consensus in identifying problems associated with democracy and democratization. Without solid measures or concepts of democracy, the processes of democratization and democratic consolidation cannot be effectively monitored. However elusive and context dependent a definition of democracy is, the chapter by Juan Linz and Alfred Stepan on democratic consolidation (ch. 4) argues that certain general conditions must exist for a political system to be reasonably described as democratic. From the time of the Greek city democracies, perennial tensions have existed in trying to apply the ideal of government by the people: individual freedom and rights, collective goods, state cohesion, minority rights, and social justice all compete in this. Indeed, the central dialectic is the achievement of collective public goods and the aggregation of common values without threatening private individual rights and freedoms. Yet, what is the "common good"? Where does the balance lie between efficiency and representation and legitimacy? The balance between these values represents a significant challenge for many political societies, as Bernard Crick's "Meditation on Democracy" (ch. 16) observes.

Moreover, the presence of identity groups – such as ethnicity and nationality – within many democratic polities exerts strains over and above these perennial democratic paradoxes.

The history of democratic theory and practice has reflected a number of political models, often categorized as direct participatory democracy, one-party people's democracy, social democracy, and liberal representative democracy. In the immediate post-Cold War context and with the ethos of the "end" of ideological history, the widely held assumption, especially in the West, has been that liberal democracy in the free-market context is the most efficient and equitable organizing principle of modern society. Social and people's democracies have effectively ceased to be contenders in the democracy debate in the post-Cold War world, and the demise of Keynesian welfare economics is now terminable. However, Claus Offe's contribution on social order and political agency (ch. 3) argues that the "neo-liberal" environment is not necessarily conducive to equal access to public goods, opportunities, or democratic processes. In an attempt to address this problem, Ian Marsh (ch. 9) examines the tension between democratic values – particularly representation – and economic competitiveness in the hope of achieving a synthesis.

Specifically, it is possible to question the extent to which liberal democratic institutions and norms hold all the answers for transitional and fledgling democratic societies. Post-communist, post-conflict, and other developing societies have been undergoing two symbiotic processes – the transition to political democracy, and the transition to the free market as the primary mechanism of economic production and distribution. These societies are also balancing domestic and international pressures. In considering experiences of democracy worldwide, especially within this post-Cold War ethos, there is also a danger of ethnocentrism in the West. The liberal, atomistic, and pluralist conception of democracy stresses individual freedom and safeguards against excessive governmental control and power. Accordingly, civil and political rights, in a free-market economic context, have greater emphasis than more communitarian ideas of duty and social justice. Yet this does not have universal acceptance.

Something of a paradox exists. Democracy is recognized as the prerequisite for legitimate authority and governance, and democracy covers an unprecedented geographic area of the world. The number of countries worldwide that might reasonably be described as meeting basic democratic criteria has jumped from 10 in 1896 to roughly

3

100 in 1996. Leaps of technology in electronic communication – some might even suggest a communications revolution – provide new opportunities for the transference of ideas and information and, perhaps, even opportunities for a revival of some form of direct participatory democracy. Simultaneously, however, a certain amount of disillusionment and stagnation has been observed in the structures and practices of the oldest democracies. While more and more countries in the developing world are moving toward democratic governance, old democracies have increasingly revealed their own deficiencies. In particular, the substance and scope of democracy appear to be thinning. As democracy prospers, so it declines.

Democracy is the political machinery that translates public preference into public policy. Without active participation on the part of citizens, democratic institutions cannot produce intended policy results. In many leading democratic countries, however, public disenchantment with politics and government has noticeably grown, seriously hampering the performance of political institutions. As the participants in democratic politics increase, a number of factors have emerged that have contributed to the undermining of democratic mechanisms. First, universal suffrage has reduced the incentives for privileged élites to participate in democratic politics. As economic globalization accelerates, the incentives for transnational businesses to voice their discontent in the national political arena diminish. Secondly, narrowing party cleavages and programme differences, and corruption, have rendered party competition less meaningful and even, in some cases, outright controversial or irrelevant.

"Old" democratic countries in Europe and North America, as well as Japan, have recently experienced tremendous electoral volatility as political parties are abandoned for new formations and leaders. The established democratic institutions and party systems of the old democracies have been put into question and even challenged by electorates and extra-constitutional groups; the liberal democratic premise of government of the people, by the people, and for the people must be examined anew. Low turnouts in elections, declining membership for political parties and a general dealignment of established political structures, and an increased resort to private local associations may reflect a waning of democratic vitality. The advancement of international communications has made political leaders more vulnerable to public opinion controversies. On the positive side, instant electronic communication has contributed to undermining authoritarian regimes by exposing their deficiencies and weaknesses.

4

Elihu Katz's chapter on mass media and participatory democracy (ch. 6) shows the historical impact of the various media upon the nature of public and private discourse and the modalities of democracy, offering a mixed conclusion about the relationship. CNN-style live coverage has reduced the efficacy of outdated propaganda and eroded the ability of political leaders to manipulate public opinion, while activating grass-roots movements all around the world. On the negative side, however, oversimplified, biased, distorted mass-media coverage has flourished, making political leaders today increasingly vulnerable to public moods.

Within the system, vested interests have become deeply institutionalized in entangled webs of bureaucracies that can hamper effective policy implementation. Moreover, the rise of global market forces has weakened the central role of the domestic body politic. Popular apathy and cynicism towards politics have subsequently grown. In a number of cases, unaccountable and unresponsive bureaucracies and institutionalized interests could lead one to conclude that the democratic process involves little more than a legitimizing of élites. Two decades ago, Theodore J. Lowi presented a critical analysis of America's interest group politics and bureaucratic expansion in his seminal book *The End of Liberalism: The Second Republic of the United States*. Despite repeated attempts to downsize government and undertake privatization, government bureaucracies remain major obstacles to reform and to new policy initiatives at the national, state, and local levels in the United States. There and elsewhere, government bureaucracies were originally designed to implement public policy in the most efficient way, but have taken on a life of their own and represent entrenched interests. In newly democratizing countries, the complex bureaucratic structures nurtured over decades under undemocratic regimes likewise pose a formidable challenge to political leaders. As many democratic institutions fail to perform around the world, the efficacy of political systems has become an important issue. Even democratically elected leaders often cannot implement their policies, owing to political gridlock between the executive and legislative branches, continuous bureaucratic intensification, and bargaining between parties and interest groups. In highly institutionalized societies, political efficacy has become harder to attain. In some quarters, it is observed that democracy is not necessarily an efficient political system.

Under these circumstances, the performance of political institutions inevitably will be called into question. However, there are clearly methodological problems in testing the "declining democracy" thesis, in terms of identifying tangible indicators. Party membership and electoral support are convenient quantitative indicators. However, they do not convey attitudinal factors or illustrate a distinction between levels of support for parties, personalities, and policies and support for democratic processes and structures themselves. A distinction should also be made between the institutions and procedures of democracy – such as elections, freedom of speech, the rule of law – and the content or substance of democracy. In any situation, the emphasis should be not just on the institutional criteria of democracy but on the results. Does it serve to fulfil the aspirations of citizenship – whatever these are defined as – and does it serve peace, respect for human rights, and development?

One can approach these problems by focusing on legitimacy and efficacy – two components of democratic governance, according to Seymour Martin Lipset. Currently, the most fashionable definition of democracy is a minimalist one, which merely requires holding free elections in a multi-party setting. This has been more or less achieved recently in a number of countries, including Cambodia and Bosnia. Yet, such a minimal democratic requirement has conflicting consequences for political legitimization: it renders the process of democratization easy in the first instance but more difficult to sustain in a meaningful and substantive way in the long term; it both requires the sociopolitical preconditions of democracy and understates the extent to which democracy is an unfinished, never-ending, political project.

Regional characteristics of democracy and democratic transition

The prevailing global movement is clearly towards liberal-democratic procedures. However, do transitional societies have the social and cultural prerequisites necessary to support a participatory or representative democratic process? Can the alienation that existed amongst many sections of post-communist societies and those racked by (un)civil war be reversed in such a way as to cultivate a culture of civic competence and democratic empowerment? In the wake of overwhelming state intervention in post-communist societies, can social movements and the ethos of civil society fill the vacuum as the state recedes? In former communist societies there tends to be a lack of networks of non-state associations and movements of civil society that define citizenship and the community in a participatory and voluntary manner. This is not to suggest that post-communist societies have no traditions of civil society; more, that this tradition was muted and suppressed for many years in its relationship with the state and the one-party system. Indeed, in the Cold War context, civil society represented a vehicle of opposition in some situations and it is now being rediscovered as part of the fabric of citizenship in a more harmonious relationship with the state.

However, simply having elections and a constitution, and other such "top-down" mechanisms, does not necessarily create this culture of democracy where there has been a negative relationship between civil society and the state over a prolonged period of time. "Bottom-up" private associations, local democracy, and civil society evolve through a process of political socialization over many years. In societies where such activities have been stifled, the freedom and opportunities of liberal democracy may not necessarily be taken up, because the norms of civic activism and responsibility must be (re)learned. Similarly, there may not be a tradition of "loyal opposition" akin to the "Westminster model" of democracy. In post-conflict societies and former colonies, opposition has often been based on a tradition of extra-constitutional (and sometimes violent) forms of activism. In some contexts, opposition is reflected in street demonstrations and even riots, which can border on the anti-constitutional. This can represent an obstacle to the consolidation of fledgling democracy, which requires support from government and opposition alike. Thus, public politics in transitional societies may not always reflect the moderate mainstream – it may reflect the extremes. In such a context, the normalization of procedures and social norms – the institutionalization of both uncertainty and certainty, according to Philippe Schmitter's concept of democratic consolidation (ch. 2) – is the primary challenge.

Clearly, post-communist and post-conflict societies experience the dilemmas of competing agendas. A paradox exists: there are often parallel paths to market economics and democracy, yet the insecurities of economic transition can threaten and distort fledgling democratic structures. None the less, demands for effective public administration have continued to grow as the relationship between the state and the market has been turning towards the latter's favour. In many respects, the tyranny of the market seems much stronger than the tyranny of the state these days. Moreover, the relationship between the state and civil society has been changing towards the latter's favour as well. In transitional societies, security and economic development must be balanced against political freedom and social welfare. The role of the state in this balance is debatable: it can nurture public dialogue and organize the modalities of transition at the same time as bargaining between competing domestic and international interests. In economic terms, the liberal thesis of Friedrich Hayek is often the guiding light of prosperity and development, but the economic rewards of this approach may not filter down evenly. The rolling back of public structures and uneven economic development have not been conducive to the consolidation of social cohesion and civic unity, in many societies. Moreover, the tenets of liberal democracy – an informed and motivated citizenship, a progressive party system, and a loyal opposition – have been slow to take root. Mihály Simai's chapter, "The Democratization Process and the Market" (ch. 8), explores these tensions in the post-communist states of Eastern and Central Europe, highlighting numerous fragilities.

Subsequently, some elements of post-communist societies look back to earlier and more secure times, to a paternalistic command economy that at least offered a modicum of security. Arguably, many voters in Russia were attracted to the Communist Party during national elections in 1996 as a result of the uncertainties inherent in the symbiotic transition to democracy and the market. As an extension of this, democracy can promote instability and even extremism; parallels can be made with the volatility of the interwar period in Europe. In transitional contexts there must also be a balance between the rural and urban societies. The social repercussions of economic and political transition have exacerbated the disjuncture between town and countryside, at the cost of the latter. Again, this is not conducive to social cohesion or the distribution of prosperity and can accelerate the alienation and regression of rural life. The consequences of modernization – of which democracy is an integral part – are not beneficial to all sections of society.

In many spheres of life, our conception of political space is defying the traditional state-centric enclosure. Within this context, democracy increasingly is a concept that extends beyond the domestic polity, partly as a condition of the globalizing trends of ideas and interaction. The internationalization of human rights and ideas of "good governance," in addition to the belief that the spread of democracy will underpin international peace and stability, have made democracy a legitimate issue of international relations. This can be seen as an evolution beyond the Westphalian conception of an international society of states: the classical criteria of sovereign state legitimacy did not specify any domestic conditions of governance. The post-Cold War language of multilateralism has often reflected the belief in an inexorable march, even a crusade, towards liberal political democracy as if it is a universal human right. However, there has clearly been resistance to the universalization of a cosmopolitan, liberal conception of human rights and democracy, especially in some non-Western cultures. A sensitivity to neocolonial, paternalist, or hegemonic designs has accompanied the internationalization of democracy. Some groups have rejected this crusade as an ethnocentric and paternalistic – perhaps arrogant – scheme of the West, with manipulative overtones. Rudyard Kipling's idea of the "White man's burden," a civilizing mission with superior pretensions, has been conjured up in this respect. Non-Western voices have certainly expressed concern towards the interventionist connotations attached to ideas of "good governance" and democracy, especially when these are seen as a pretext for interference or intervention. Takashi Inoguchi's chapter (ch. 11) explores the cultural dimension of democracy in an analysis of "Asian" norms and values, yet questions the validity of an East–West cultural dichotomy and its application to democracy.

This controversy threatens to distort the democracy debate. It is, therefore, essential to recognize that, beyond certain minimum criteria, there are different, even diverse, models of democracy, with equal worth. On the basis of basic human needs and aspirations, certain universal foundational criteria must exist for a society to be reasonably considered to be a democracy. However, the concept of rights, values, and governance will inevitably reflect the culture, history, and social processes of each society. Accordingly, sovereign statehood is not just a legal construct; it is an expression of community and should be respected on moral grounds. This communitarian thesis is an important counterbalance to globalizing forces and universalist ideas of human rights. The world is not homogeneous, and the democracy debate (as John Keane observes in chapter 14) must embrace cultural relativity. Democracy must stem from, and serve, local conditions; there is no comprehensive universal model. At the same time, cultural relativity should not be a normative barrier behind which states deny democracy or basic human rights. Clearly, a balance must be found that embraces both the communitarian instincts of all societies and cultures to find their own conception of democracy and the cosmopolitan belief that humans everywhere aspire to have some control over their destiny.

Democracy and global forces

At the international level, the changing conception of democracy has a number of implications. According to the Kantian thesis and its modern adherents, republican or liberal democracies are most unlikely to go to war with each other. This provides the normative basis for the spread of democracy and liberal economics, for democracy within states will underpin a more peaceful and stable international society. Bruce Russett's contribution on a democratic, interdependent, and institutionalized order (ch. 10) elaborates upon the democratic peace thesis and argues that there are opportunities to strengthen and promote peaceful interaction between democratic societies on an institutional basis. Clearly, the wider conception of peace and security blurs the distinction between domestic and international peace and security; the existence of stable governance, empirical sovereignty, and human security are all integral to this. Democracy is a vehicle for the fulfilment of the political, economic, and social tenets of human security and therefore underpins the comprehensive and integrated conception of peace and security. Upon this basis, the hope is that democracy supports the idea of a peaceful society of states. However, transition to the market and democracy is inherently fragile within states and, as an extension of this, may introduce an element of uncertainty in the relationships between states. History has demonstrated that new democracies can be aggressive and expansionist. Therefore, democratic safeguards are essential for the society in question *and* for the wider international society – mechanisms that ensure that the adverse social and political consequences of transition do not undermine the processes of democracy and cause repercussions in the international system.

In practical terms, ideas of democracy and "good governance" have been attached to international trade, aid, and diplomatic relations. This emerging conditionality is evident in the United Nations, in international economic institutions such as the World Bank, in regional organizations, and in bilateral relationships. The "most favoured nation" status, international investment, loan approval, and membership of some regional organizations have reflected the concept of conditionality. This practice has generated disharmony in international relations and, again, indicates the extent to which the democracy debate is politicized. There are concerns that external intervention or manipulation through the vehicle of democracy is the hidden agenda of the democracy crusade. Crusades usually involve the imposition of values or institutions. Moreover, the manner in which sanctions are imposed and conditionality is attached in the areas of diplomacy, trade, or aid is clearly inconsistent. A comparison of the cases of Indonesia, Haiti, and Nigeria demonstrates this. This inconsistency serves only to contribute to the worries that these practices reflect an agenda that is not entirely humanitarian. The debate on conditionality and sanctions also highlights an interesting division of opinion and policy towards democracy and international relations. There is the rough distinction between the cosmopolitan and nation-state/communitarian traditions. Adherents of the former – often in the West – advocate norms that transcend state boundaries and are applicable irrespective of cultural, social, and religious factors. This thesis is often accompanied by the belief that democracy within states forms the foundations of domestic and international peace. Accordingly, this approach sees international pressure – conditionality, sanctions, and even intervention – as a legitimate means of promoting domestic reform and democratization in the most recalcitrant cases, although cooperative methods are more ideal. In contrast, communitarian thinking rejects abstract and universal notions of rights and governance in favour of local processes and local solutions. This approach is, therefore, resolutely against ideas of conditionality, sanctions, and intervention, rejecting these as arrogant and hypocritical. This debate has been clearly reflected in a number of high-profile cases, and it is at the heart of the changing nature of democracy.

There is also often a tension between idealism and *realpolitik* in state decision-making, where statesmen and politicians employ the language of good governance and democratization when it suits but whose policy is determined by the effects that imposing conditionality and sanctions would have upon the balance-of-trade accounts. The Western countries cannot forego the market opportunities of undemocratic countries and usually defend this stance on the basis that if they did not deal with regressive or undemocratic states – on the basis of "constructive engagement" – then a competitor would. Moreover, there is a common argument that isolating undemocratic states is not the most effective way to encourage change. There is often a difference between words and deeds on the part of governments. It is important, therefore, to encourage even-handedness in the multilateral context in promoting democracy within states and not to allow democracy to be an instrument of external manipulation. The acknowledgement of different models of democracy according to

11

different social contexts is the first step in the process; the second step is imbuing a sense of responsibility and accountability in leading states and in international organizations and avoiding a manipulation of the democracy debate.

International organizations have played an important role in promoting and supporting democracy and pluralism, especially in transitional societies. The practical assistance of the UN system and regional organizations – often in conjunction with non-governmental organizations (NGOs) – has taken a wide variety of forms. For the United Nations, assistance in establishing democratic institutions and a culture of democracy is conceived of in the context of the organization's comprehensive approach to peace-building and to social and economic development. Accordingly, the United Nations subscribes to a wide conception of peace and human security within which democracy is an integral component. The range of its activities in transitional societies includes assistance in monitoring and supervising peace settlements; establishing civil and legal institutions, human rights and humanitarian issues; and assistance with (re)building infrastructure. Organizing, supervising, monitoring, and validating elections are crucial activities in assisting the practicalities of – and giving confidence to – a fragile process. Historically, the United Nations' assistance in domestic transition to democracy may transpire to be comparable in importance to its role in decolonization, although it would be premature to pronounce all cases successful. The United Nations can assist in the establishment of the institutions and procedures of democracy and in giving a degree of confidence to democratic transition, but it cannot determine the content or substance. In addition, long-term commitment on the part of multilateral organizations is necessary to support the consolidation of democracy, yet the fatigue which pervades many international organizations is not conducive to this.

The impulse in the UN Security Council, for example, is to withdraw as soon as possible – to save money and to avoid complicated political entanglements. The message from many recent examples is that this is a false economy: democratization in post-conflict societies is not irreversible, and pulling out early can result in a loss of the effort expended. Unless the international community is satisfied with establishing merely cosmetic democracy, it must stick the course; this was one lesson learned in Central America. There is a paradox here: multilateral organizations are embracing a wider conception of peace and security which embraces democracy and human security and are less preoccupied with the distinction between the domestic and international realms; yet multilateral fatigue and a shortage of money are imposing severe constraints upon what organizations can do on the ground.

A further issue relating to the increasing prominence of international organizations is the question of accountability and democracy *within* these organizations. Traditionally, the concept of democracy did not extend beyond the domestic arena, and a different set of norms governed international relationships. According to some observers, this tradition has evolved into a democratic deficit in many organizations. Even in the case of those that can wield enormous leverage upon the domestic policies of some states and exert a significant impact upon the lives of many millions of people, there is little transparency or public input into the policy of such organizations. Why should international organizations be exempt from democratic accountability and public participation? Daniele Archibugi (ch. 15) thus highlights the hypocrisy inherent in the structure of the United Nations and argues for an extension of democratic principles and procedures into the organization. There are pressures for change within and outside many international organizations, including the United Nations, where the reform agenda embraces various ideas to increase representation and participation. The Commission for Global Governance likewise encouraged proposals to reverse the democratic deficit.

The traditional conception of a dichotomy between domestic and international politics, where international politics is the realm of diplomats and statesmen, has created a vacuum of public involvement: the private citizen was seen as having no right or opportunity to be involved in international politics. This vacuum is being filled gradually by the proliferation of NGOs in a wide spectrum of activities, which represents a transnational – sometimes even global – mobilization of non-governmental opinion. This network of organizations exerts leverage upon governments and governmental organizations in agenda setting, in providing advice and information, and in administering policy, and it provides a forum for public discussion. The respective fate/logic of governmental organizations and NGOs has become closely intertwined, and the functional expertise of NGOs is now relied upon in many issue areas, such as the environment, human rights and humanitarian assistance, social and economic development, de-mining and disarmament, and refugee issues. The UN system has developed various mechanisms which embrace this expertise, although NGOs are not formally enfranchised; the United Nations is state centric and this is still its organizing principle. NGOs are not necessarily democratic but, if one sees them as social initiatives that encourage participatory public politics, then this may lead to the idea of an emerging international civil society that imparts values which transcend the traditional agenda of state-centric international politics.

The implications of this for a democratic ethos at the international level and in encouraging the norm of democracy within state borders are interesting, because NGO networks embrace a wide spectrum of public involvement and, arguably, reflect an emerging cosmopolitan spirit or global ethos. Drawing upon the Kantian ethic of international peace and security, NGOs may serve to promote international cultural, economic, and political exchange and, therefore, affinities across borders. It has long been accepted that NGOs have a bearing upon the unit of analysis debate in international relations, but it appears that they are moving towards the mainstream of the international agenda. There is certainly room for research into the future role of NGOs in the matrix of international networks. Of course, the proliferation of NGOs has not been entirely positive: the motives and practices of some of these organizations have been questionable, and many suffer from a democratic deficit at least as severe as that of governmental organizations. Nevertheless, in tandem with the UN system, NGOs have the potential to be a major force for social and economic development and democratic pluralism.

Democracy and the social framework

Gender is a relatively recent focus to the study of democracy and a part of the new agenda. The application of gender to political theory has encouraged the re-examination of established notions of social structures and the distinction between the public and private spheres. Democracy is inextricably linked with the concept of equality, but political equality – in the sense of enfranchisement – has not reversed the underrepresentation of women in public political life, despite their prominent and vital role in private life and in the economy of most countries. In established countries there have long been efforts to redress this imbalance through various corrective measures, including anti-discriminatory legislation and positive discrimination. However, progress has been slow, although attitudinal changes are occurring towards an equal citizenship between the sexes. The role of gender in post-conflict and transitional societies is interesting. In a number of cases, women played a major role in liberation struggles – including the adoption of traditionally "male"-oriented tasks – and, with the return of normality, the issue is whether women should maintain momentum for public political leverage or revert to the traditional private spheres of activity.

Transitional societies may well be among those that have to contend with the development of democracy in the context of social fractures and different identities. Ethnicity, religion, and nationalism are examples of subgroups or identities that have a bearing upon the consolidation of a democratic culture and democratic institutions. Whilst these forces are integral to the state-building process in many circumstances, they can harbour an ideology of exclusion and "otherness" towards minorities which obstructs the development of a healthy culture of democratic equality among citizens. The phenomenon of fragmentation and identity politics inevitably finds expression in the democratic process; arguably, democracy and democratization even encourage fragmentation and identity politics. They can also lead to expressions of majoritarianism and resentment. If religious, ethnic, or national minorities do not feel that they are represented in the political process, there can be conflict. In particular, in situations of ethnic cleavages and irredentist pressures, the democratic process can be threatened by the resurgence of identity politics. In giving expression to, and encouraging, identity politics and majoritarianism, the democratic process can itself promote disharmony in multinational and fractious states. The "common good" is elusive. Again, democratic safeguards are necessary.

Amongst the myriad forms of identity politics, religion is often singled out as having a bearing upon the theory and practice of democracy. Religion is inherently exclusionary in the sense that it distinguishes between believers and non-believers. Religion, therefore, has a bearing upon the relationship amongst people and between citizens and the state. Religion clearly imparts a particular conception of the rights and duties of citizenship, and, in societies which embrace a number of religions, this has an impact upon public dialogue and democratic processes. When religion and public policy occupy the same space, questions can be asked regarding governance and democracy; if multiple religions share the same space, the outcome can be more delicate. The typical liberal or secularist conception of democracy has seen a separation of church and state. However, religion, along with all other identities and associations, is not inherently antithetical to democracy when the democratic process and the public sphere of the society are able to accommodate different – and even competing – conceptions of citizenship. It is only when incommensurable ideas and practices clash that democracy is threatened. Incommensurable ideas can occupy the same space, if the democratic process allows the expression of all views and if there is a culture of tolerance from the bottom up. In particular, some commentators have questioned if Islam – especially in its Islamist interpretation – is compatible with democracy, owing to its world view, its prescriptions regarding gender relationships, and its exclusivist tendencies. If a religion does not accept equality and inviolable rights to all, can it be truly democratic? However, in the West there is the danger of generalizing from a few Islamic states and groups to the Islamic world as a whole. Indeed, some of the "most" democratic countries in the world have Islamic majorities and enjoy representative legislatures and governments, including the representation of women at the highest office. Saad Eddin Ibrahim's chapter (ch. 13) explores the area of Islam, civil society, and democracy and argues that Islamic societies are experiencing a sociopolitical transition that can put religion at odds with democracy. Nevertheless, in its truest interpretation, Islam is the epitome of tolerance and can coexist with other faiths in a democratic context. And there are contexts, such as Turkey, where the revival of Islam may have democratic effects.

In post-conflict societies, the transition to democracy and reconstruction can be particularly fragile. The continuation of fear, suspicion, and hostility; the need for justice; and the presence of groups that do not support the peace process, can undermine the transition and reignite violence. The balance between reconciliation and justice is fragile: justice is necessary for reconciliation and reconstruction, but the search for justice can hamper reconciliation. The holding of free and fair elections is essential in giving confidence and reflecting desires, but elections themselves may not bring democracy other than in a cosmetic sense. Elections do not create a culture of democracy if there is no general will for reconciliation or for an emerging civic competence which transcends past enmities. The situation in Bosnia–Herzegovina is one such example, where the election process may merely reflect the social and nationalist discord that still remains. The role of party-political leadership is crucial to the post-conflict peace-building process in supporting and encouraging an inclusive democratic process and cohesive social reconstruction. A revisionist leadership can undermine fledgling democracy and processes of reconstruction by manipulating latent enmities and causing panic. An impartial and independent judiciary, armed forces, and police force are similarly critical factors in the establishment and consolidation of democracy.

The media have a major, if unpredictable, role in established democracies. An informed citizenship is the basis of a healthy democracy, and the media serve the function of communication of ideas, cultivating civic awareness and public discourse. Moreover, the media form the most significant arena of public debate for the majority and one of the most direct forms of interface of communication between the people and the government. Thus, the media can help to create and sustain political democracy and serve civil society. Yet the relationship between the media and the democratic process is an ambivalent one: the media inevitably filter information and represent their own political agenda; they can be an instrument of control or of instability and subversion, especially in a conflict or post-conflict situation.

The new agenda: Invigorating democratic ideas and institutions

It is not easy to establish a framework for analysis for the study of democracy and democratization. Democracy involves tangible characteristics, such as free and fair elections, legislatures, the rule of law, and an independent judiciary. It also involves less tangible factors regarding culture and participation. How does one measure democracy and attitudes towards participation and democratic processes, as distinct from personalities and parties? Is it possible to construct a methodology through which it may be possible to investigate these issues?

This volume embraces a plethora of ideas which reflect the breadth of the democratic debate. A number of issue areas form the agenda for a re-examination of democracy in the context of a number of changes and pressures: globalizing pressures and global issues; the expansion of the sphere of activity which is considered to be legitimately conditioned by democracy; the resurgence of identity politics and fragmentation; the proliferation of market economic systems; developments in thinking relating to peace and security and, in particular, the emphasis on human security; changes in leadership style and expectations; and the blurring of the distinction between public and private, and domestic and international, are some such issues. To make democracies perform, social scientists and policy makers need to examine the causes of democratic decay and explore the means of revitalizing democratic political processes. The challenge for transitional societies and the consolidation of democracy is to achieve safeguards against the worst rigours of economic change and to foster a sense of public empowerment in the changes. In turn, confidence in public-life changes helps to achieve support for democratic norms and institutions and to avert support for anti-democratic and regressive movements. The role of the state will, in time, reach an equilibrium, and the participatory culture of democracy will determine the balance between top-down governmental structures and bottom-up movements. It is within this context that the development of civil society weaves together a matrix of governmental and non-governmental activity.

In an era of democracy, academic communities must devise a widely applicable analytical framework for increasingly diverse democracies and establish criteria to compare various types of democratic societies. In this regard, the importance of synthesizing the results of previous empirical studies on both old and new democracies cannot be overemphasized. Furthermore, we must critically examine the changing environment for democracy in this information age and study its implications for democratic politics. Democracy may be an obsolete idea, an atavistic instinct, and an outdated institution. Nevertheless, it seems to be the only feasible institutional arrangement to promote civil and political freedoms, social and economic rights, human dignity, and international harmony. Perhaps, we still cannot rebut Winston Churchill's dictum that democracy is an inefficient system, but it is better than any other alternative. The main areas of concern and interest that arise from the contributions to this project pose a number of questions and issues:

- How have the oldest democracies evolved in terms of content and procedure; is there disillusionment towards established party structures, institutions, or even the democratic system itself? Is disillusionment a natural phase of mature democracies or can it be reversed? Can democracy be revitalized?
- How can transitional societies safeguard against the most adverse effects of political and economic change? How does the market shape the democratization process and the consolidation of democracy? Where is the balance between development and prosperity, and social support? How can such societies safeguard against the alienation of sections of society brought about by the transition process? As the transition to democracy and market economics

accelerates the divisions between rural and urban life, how can the adverse effects of this process be cushioned?

- What is the role of civil society in transitional societies, and are voluntary associations and movements fulfilling a different function here than in mature democracies?
- What is the role for external actors – and particularly international organizations – in assisting the transition to democracy and in militating against the problems and tensions of this process?
- Are there universal foundations of democracy? How are religion, culture, and social contexts reflected in different models of democracy? Where is the balance between universal cosmopolitan and communitarian conceptions of democracy and citizenship? Is there a global ethic of democracy?
- Are democratic systems and fledgling democracies successfully accommodating the challenges posed by fractious states?
- Is gender a viable focus for the study of democracy? Has the renaissance of democracy fulfilled its pretensions of equality?
- How can the opportunities of the communications revolution be harnessed for increased levels of participation? Are globalizing forces de-territorializing democracy?
- How can the pressures for democracy and accountability beyond the state be utilized? Do NGOs reflect and embrace an emergent international civil society? How can accountability and transparency in international organizations be improved?
- As democracy evolves, has its sphere of applicability enlarged? What areas of life are, or should be, conditioned by democratic processes? Are there attitudinal changes regarding this sphere of applicability, and are institutions and procedures responding to such changes? Are conceptions of "public" and "private" evolving?

Notes

1. Boutros Boutros-Ghali, "Democracy: A Newly Recognized Imperative," *Global Governance* Winter 1995; 1(1): 4.

Definitions and criteria

2

Some basic assumptions about the consolidation of democracy

Philippe C. Schmitter

The notion of a "consolidated democracy" seems oxymoronic – a contradiction in terms. Democracies are never supposed to be fully consolidated: unique among regime types, they should contain within themselves the potentiality for continuous evolution and, eventually, self-transformation. By a process of deliberation and collective choice, citizens can both peacefully remove governments from power and, presumably, choose to alter their governments' basic rules and structure. They can even – as happened several times in the history of the Athenian *polis* and Roman republic – democratically decide to become a different form of regime. Indeed, the very concept of dictatorship originated in democratic practice.

This "historico-theoretical" reflection clashes, however, with the everyday experience of well-established democracies. Not only have their patterns and norms become routinized into a highly predictable *de facto* structure, but considerable effort is expended *de jure* to make it quite difficult to change these structures. The formative, so-called "founding," generations wrote constitutions which sought to bind subsequent ones to a specific institutional framework and set of rights and they deliberately made them difficult to amend. They also drafted statutes and codes which rendered certain kinds of political behaviour punishable, created specific constituencies and rewarded particular clientele, and made the entry of new parties into the electoral arena difficult or impossible, and thus conferred monopolistic recognition upon certain associations and élites. Whilst constitutions can be ignored, policies can be reversed, and laws can be changed in response to pressures from the *demos*, one should not exaggerate how easily and frequently this can occur in even the most loosely structured of democracies.

Uncertainty may well be, as Adam Przeworski has argued, a central characteristic of this type of regime, but it is a form of relative uncertainty.[1] For citizens to tolerate the possibility that unexpected persons or groups may occupy governance over them and that these newly empowered authorities may pursue different, possibly damaging, courses of action requires a great deal of mutual trust, backed by a great deal of structural reassurance.

Democratic consolidation can be conceptualized as the process – or processes – that underlies such trust and reassurance and, therefore, makes regular, uncertain, and yet circumscribed competition for office and influence possible. It seeks to institutionalize uncertainty in one subset of political roles and policy arenas, while institutionalizing certainty in others.

Defining the challenge

How does democracy accomplish and legitimize such a delicate task? What is the underlying principle that provides the essential elements of trust and reassurance? The simple answer is "the consent of the people"; the more complex one is that it depends on "the contingent consent of politicians and the eventual assent of citizens – all acting under conditions of bounded uncertainty."[2]

The challenge for democratic consolidators, therefore, is to create and maintain a set of institutions which embody contingent consent among politicians, are capable of invoking the eventual assent of citizens, and can limit the high degree of uncertainty that is characteristic of the transition from autocracy. They do not necessarily have to agree upon a set of goals or substantive policies that command widespread consensus. This "democratic bargain," to use Robert Dahl's felicitous expression,[3] can vary a great deal from one society to another, depending on inequalities and cleavage patterns as well as on such subjective factors as the degree of mutual trust between the government and citizens, the standard of fairness, the willingness to compromise, and the legitimacy of different decision-making rules. It may even be compatible with a great deal of dissent on specific, substantive policy issues.

My self-assigned task in this essay is to try to understand where these generic democratic principles come from and how they become embodied in regular practices and rules without becoming distorted or undermined by the legacies of autocracy or the compromises between competing interests.

Establishing some assumptions

Before turning to a more detailed elaboration of what is involved in the consolidation of democracy,[4] it may be useful to establish some general assumptions:

1. The consolidation of democracy poses distinctive problems to political actors and, hence, to those who seek to understand – usually retrospectively – what they are doing. It is not just a prolongation of the transition from authoritarian rule. To a significant extent, the consolidation of democracy engages different actors, behaviours, processes, and, perhaps, even new values and resources. This is not to say that everything changes when a polity "shifts" towards democracy: many of the people and collectivities will be the same, but they will be facing different problems, making different calculations and, it is hoped, behaving in different ways.

2. This opens up the possibility – but not the inevitability – of contradictions and tensions within the process of regime change. As O'Donnell and I have stressed in previous work,[5] the conditions which encouraged the demise of authoritarian regimes are not always, and not necessarily, those most appropriate for ensuring a smooth and reliable transition to political democracy. Concordantly, those "enabling conditions" most conducive to reducing and managing the uncertainty of this crucial interim period may turn into "confining conditions" that can make the consolidation of what has been accomplished more difficult. Moreover, the shift in problem–space may reduce the significance of actors who previously played a central role and enhance that of others who, by prudence or impotence, were marginal to the demise and transition. Revolutions have a tendency to "eat their own children"; more peaceful and less consequential regime changes seem likely to "disavow their own parents."[6]

3. Even more provocative is the possibility that the study of democratization requires an epistemological shift on the part of the analyst to accompany the behavioural changes that the actors themselves are undergoing. During the transition, an exaggerated form of "voluntaristic political causality" tends to predominate in a situation of rapid change, high risk, shifting interests, and inde-

terminate strategic reactions. Actors believe that they are engaged in a "war of movement," where dramatic options are available and the outcome depends critically on their choices. They find it difficult to specify *ex ante* which classes, sectors, institutions, or groups will support their efforts. Indeed, most of these collectivities are likely to be divided or hesitant about what to do.

Once this heady and dangerous moment has passed, some of the actors begin to "settle into the trenches."[7] They organize their internal structures more predictably, consult bases more reliably, and consider the long-term consequences of their actions more seriously. In so doing, they are compelled to experience the constraints imposed by deeply rooted material deficiencies and normative habits that have not changed with the fall of the *ancien régime.*

For the theorist/analyst, this implies shifting from a raw form of "political causality," characterized by singular and even unprecedented choices taken by unpredictable and often courageous individuals,[8] towards a more settled form of "bounded rationality." This is conditioned by capitalist class relations, long-standing cultural and ethnic cleavages, persistent status conflicts, and international antagonisms and is staffed by increasingly professional politicians filling more predictable and less risky roles. From the heady excitement and underdetermination of the transition from autocracy comes the adjustment to the prosaic routine and over-determination of consolidated democracy.[9]

4. The consolidation of democracy requires explicit treatment as a theoretical subject and as an object of empirical inquiry. One can draw more confidently from previous scholarly work than when trying to make sense of the demise of authoritarian regimes or the initial transition to democratic ones. However, there remains a great deal of difficult and delicate work in explaining to the actors how to become more predictable and prosaic and why so many of them may have to find another way of making a living.

Defining the subject

When a society changes from one political regime to another, it initially passes through a period of considerable uncertainty during which regression to the *status quo ante* remains possible and the destination to which the efforts of the actors are leading remains unclear. The transition period can vary in length, depending in large measure on the manner of regime change that has been adopted, but eventually it must end. The costs – both psychological and material – are simply too great for the actors to endure indefinitely. While there will always be some for whom the exhilaration of participating in a continuous "war of movement" remains an end in itself, most actors look forward to settling into a "war of positions" with known allies, established lines of cleavage, and predictable opponents – or to getting on with other careers or pursuits.

The genus of social processes of which the consolidation of democracy is a subspecies has been given a number of labels. "Structuration" is the currently fashionable one, thanks to the growing influence of the work of Anthony Gidden.[10] Routinization, institutionalization, and stabilization – not to mention reification – were concepts earlier used to refer to this process. The basic idea common to these phenomena is that social relations can become social structures or institutions (the two will be used interchangeably in this text). Patterns of interaction can become so regular in their occurrence, so endowed with meaning, so capable of motivating behaviour, that they become autonomous in their internal functioning and resistant to externally induced change. In ordinary parlance, structures/institutions are collectivities in which "the whole has become greater than the sum of its parts." The strategies and norms of individuals within these collectivities are constrained by the whole. Their actions and goals are not reducible to those of its component parts: structures and institutions cannot be understood purely by aggregating the decisions – least of all, the preferences – of the individuals within them.[11]

These notations are rather elementary and much of the theorizing about them is quite abstract and devoid of clear statements from which one could derive discretely researchable propositions. At best, they can be exploited for a few broad guidelines and orienting hypotheses. For our purposes, this very generic approach has an unfortunate tendency to overlook the specificities of political action in general and democratic processes in particular. A subtle analyst like Gidden may well insist on the relative freedom of choice which actors have even in highly "structurated" contexts, on the ambiguity of the rules that bind them, and the indeterminacy of the resources that they can bring to bear upon collective decisions. Yet this is still a long way from conceptualizing the intrinsic competitiveness and dynamic uncertainty of democratic politics. What we need is a more specific definition and theory of the processes embraced by structuration, institutionalization, stabilization, and routinization that captures these features and explains not only *how* they come to be adopted, but also *why* actors might willingly prefer them.

Focusing on the state

The consolidation of democracy involves the structuration of a particular regime type. Democracies, in turn, come in several different types and they can exist at various levels of aggregation and autonomy. Nevertheless, all democracies presumably share certain characteristics. The ones which interest us here are all regimes of the state in the sense that they are organized at the level of the most comprehensive, "sovereign," unit of authority and collective choice in the present world-system. In our work on transition, O'Donnell and I defined a regime as follows:

The *ensemble* of patterns, explicit or not, that determines the forms and channels of access to principal governmental positions, the characteristics of the actors who are admitted and excluded from such access, and the resources and strategies that they can use to gain access.[12]

Retrospectively, I would add only that a state regime must also have some explicit rules for determining how collective decisions are made. Regime consolidation, then, reflects a transformation of the accidental arrangements, prudential norms, and contingent solutions that have emerged during the uncertain struggles of the transition into institutions, and relationships that are reliably known, regularly practised, and normatively accepted by the participants/citizens/subjects of such institutions.

When actors change from some form of autocracy to democracy, the problem of consolidation takes on special characteristics.[13] The number and variety of persons who are potentially capable of proposing new rules and practices increase greatly. Moreover, these empowered citizens, and the groups they form, have much more autonomy in deciding whether they will accept the rules and practices that are being offered to them. This is not to suggest that modern political democracies are anarchies in which everyone is free to choose his or her own norms and to act without regard for the norms of others. Yet the problem of reducing uncertainty and ensuring the orderly governance of the unit as a whole is likely to be more acute than, for example, in the aftermath of implanting an autocracy.

Democracy does not, however, seek to remove all sources of

uncertainty. A polity in which there was no uncertainty about which candidates would win elections, what policies the winners would adopt, or which groups would be likely to influence those policies could hardly be termed "democratic."[14] But the uncertainty that is embedded in all democracies is *bounded*. There are limitations to which actors can enter the competitive struggle, raise issues, co-operate with others, and expect to hold office or exercise influence. There are limitations to what can be decided by any procedure, even if the procedure reflects the majority and the minority was represented in the making of the decision. What the exercise of democracy begins to do during the transitional period is to reduce "abnormal" uncertainty to "normal" uncertainty, through the generation of formal rules and informal practices. Rules and practices that manage to acquire some autonomy and to reproduce themselves successfully over time become institutions.

As a process, democratic consolidation involves choosing these institutions. Much of this takes place in an open and deliberative fashion and manifests itself in formal public acts – the drafting and ratifying of a constitution, the passing of "framework legislation" by parliament, the issuance of executive decrees and administrative regulations. Some of it, however, emerges more incidentally and unselfconsciously from the ongoing "private" arrangements within and between the organizations of civil society and from the inter-actions between them and various agencies of the state.

Disaggregating the process into partial regimes

Rather than "a single regime," modern democracy should be con-ceptualized as a composite of "partial regimes." As the consolidation of democracy progresses, each of these partial regimes becomes institutionalized in a particular sequence, according to distinctive principles, and around different sites. All, however, concern the representation of social groups and the resolution of their conflicts. Parties, associations, movements, localities, and various clientele compete and coalesce around these different sites in an effort to capture office and influence policy. Their structured activity has the effect of channelling conflicts toward the public arena, thereby diminishing recourse to such private means as settling disputes by violence and imposing one's will by authoritarian fiat. Authorities with different functions and at different levels of aggregation interact with these representatives, base their legitimacy upon their accountability to different citizen interests (and passions), and reproduce that special form of authority that stems from exercising an effective monopoly over the use of violence.

Constitutions are efforts to establish a single, overarching set of "meta-rules" that would render these partial regimes coherent, assign specific tasks to each, and impose some hierarchical relation among them. But such formal documents are rarely successful in delineating and controlling all such relationships. The process of producing an acceptable draft and ratifying it by vote and/or plebiscite undoubtedly represents a significant moment in the consolidation of democracy, but many partial regimes will be left undefined. For it is precisely in the interstices between different types of representatives that constitutional norms are most vague and least prescriptive.[15] Imagine trying to deduce from even the most detailed of constitutions – and they are becoming more detailed – how parties, associations, and movements will interact to influence policies, or trying to discern how capital and labour will bargain over income shares under the new meta-rules.

If political democracy is not a regime but a composite of regimes, then the appropriate strategy for studying its consolidation must be disaggregated. This is both theoretically and empirically desirable. Figure 2.1 attempts to sketch out the property–space that is involved and to suggest some of the specific partial regimes that are likely to emerge. On the vertical axis, the space is defined in terms of the institutional domain of action, ranging from authoritatively defined state agencies to self-constituted units of civil society. Horizontally, the variance concerns the power resources that actors can bring to bear on the emerging political process: numbers in the case of those relying primarily on the counting of individual votes; intensities for those that are based on weighing the contribution of particular groups of citizens.

Competing theories of democracy – liberal–statist, majoritarian–consociational, unitary–federal, presidential–parliamentary – have long argued the merits of the particular locations cited in figure 2.1. In my view, all are potentially democratic, provided that they respect the overarching principles of citizenship and the procedural minimum of civil rights, fair elections, and free associability. Given the growing diversity of tasks performed by public authorities, the number and variety of partial regimes has tended to increase. Most scholars still place the party and electoral systems – the arrangements regulating government formation and executive–legislative relations and the formula for the territorial division of authority – at the core. It has

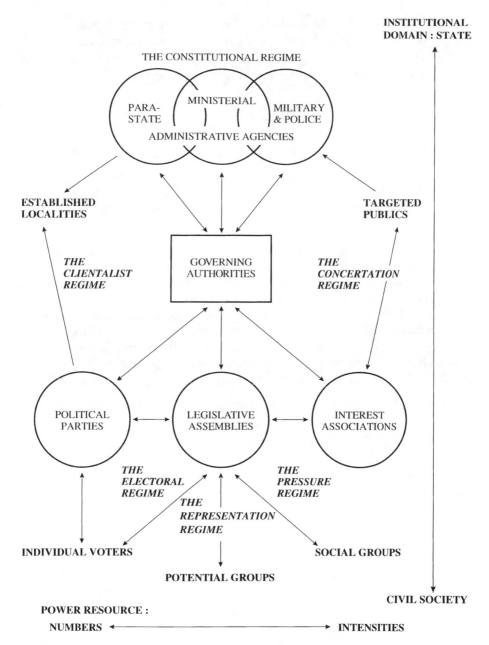

Fig. 2.1 **Property–space involved in the consolidation of whole and partial regimes in modern democracies**

been argued that the system of interest intermediation deserves equivalent attention,[16] and that, given the specific circumstances of most transitions from autocracy, it would seem prudent to include the nature of civil–military relations in that inner circle.[17]

Putting the pieces back together

The consolidation of democracy, then, consists of transforming the ad hoc political relations that have emerged partially into stable structures in such a way that the ensuing channels of access, patterns of inclusion, resources for action, and norms about decision-making conform to an overriding standard:

... that of citizenship. This involves both the right to be treated by fellow human beings as equal with respect to the making of collective choices and the obligation of those implementing such choices to be equally accountable and accessible to all members of the polity. Inversely, this principle imposes the obligation on the ruled to respect the legitimacy of choices made by deliberation among equals (or their representatives), and the right for the rulers to act with authority (and, therefore, to apply coercion when necessary) in order to promote the effectiveness of such choices and to protect the regime from threats to its persistence.[18]

Conformity to the principle of citizenship and its corollary rights and obligations by no means guarantees that regime structuration will result in a particular or unique set of institutions. Lots of different decision-making rules, inclusion formulas, distributions of resources, forms of participation, strategies of influence, and so forth, can claim to embody this generic principle. Across time and space – not to mention culture and class – opinions have differed concerning what institutions and rules are to be considered democratic. The concrete institutions and rules which have been established in different "democratic" countries have similarly differed. Given the positive connotation which the term has acquired, each country tends to claim that the way its institution and rules are structured is the most democratic. The "others," especially one's enemies and competitors, are accused of having some inferior type of democracy or another kind of regime altogether. With the United States of America, this meant that the particular – not to say, peculiar – configuration of its regime was often taken as "the" model of conformity to the citizenship principle. Not so long ago it was Great Britain, the "mother of Parliaments," that was regarded as the model. In the contemporary period, the appeal of both American and British practices has diminished considerably. Neodemocracies are likely to look elsewhere for their institutions – to France, Germany, Sweden, and now Spain.

Coping with the plurality of institutions

The major implication of the preceding discussion is that no single set of institutions and rules – and, above all, no single institution or rule – defines political democracy. Not even such fundamental characteristics as majority rule, territorial representation, competitive elections, parliamentary sovereignty, a popularly elected executive, or a "responsible party system" can be taken as its distinctive hallmark. Needless to say, this is a serious obstacle when it comes to measuring the consolidation of democracy. One cannot simply seize on some key "meta-relation" such as the manner of forming executive power – for example presidentialism versus parliamentarianism – and trace its transformation into a structure, assuming that all the others – such as the party system, the decision-making rules – will fall into line once it has crossed some critical threshold. What must be analysed is an emerging gestalt, a network of relationships involving multiple processes and sites. It may not be difficult to agree on what Robert Dahl has called the "institutional guarantees" and others have called the "procedural minimum" without which no democracy could be said to exist – secret balloting, universal adult suffrage, regular elections, partisan competition, associational freedom, and executive accountability.[19] Yet underlying these accomplishments and flowing from them are much more subtle and complex relations which define both the substance and form of nascent democratic regimes.

Of course it is important that elections be held; that parties compete with varying chances of winning; that voter preferences be secretly recorded and honestly counted; that associations be free to form, recruit members, and exercise influence; that citizens be allowed to contest the policies of their government and hold leaders responsible for their actions. The longer these structures and rules of the "procedural minimum" exist, the greater is the likelihood they will persist. Polities that have had regular elections of uncertain outcome for, say, 40 years are more likely to continue having them in the future than is a polity which has only had them for, say, 10 years. Therefore, it is probably correct, *ceteris paribus*, to assume that Italian democracy is more consolidated than Portuguese or Spanish democracy.

But the sheer longevity of such structures and rules is an inad-

33

equate base upon which to build an understanding of the consolidation of democracy. Indeed, it does not adequately answer why or how they have persisted; it just records the fact *ex post*. A more serious accusation is that such an approach tends to privilege one set of democratic institutions – usually political parties and elections – and reifies (not to say, fetishizes) their presence at the expense of others. It could even lead to adopting a historically or culturally peculiar outcome as the standard against which to measure the progress of contemporary new democracies. The obvious danger is to consider the popular election of the chief executive and competition between two centrist "catch-all" parties as the norm for institutions, and rotation in exclusive responsibility for governance as the hallmark of success: that is, to apply the US model to evaluate what is happening in Europe, Latin America, Asia, and Africa. Whatever metric one applies, it must be capacious enough to embrace the emergence of a wide range of possible types of democracy.

Notes

1. For this emphasis on uncertainty as "the" characteristic of democracy, see Adam Przeworski, "Some Problems in the Study of the Transition to Democracy," in Guillermo O'Donnell and Philippe C. Schmitter (eds) *Transitions from Authoritarian Rule: Prospects for Democracy*, Vol. III (Baltimore: Johns Hopkins University Press, 1986), pp. 57–61.
2. See Philippe C. Schmitter and Terry Lynn Karl, "What Democracy is … and is not," *Journal of Democracy* Summer 1991; 3(3): 75–88.
3. Robert Dahl, *After the Revolution: Authority in a Good Society* (New Haven: Yale University Press, 1970).
4. Throughout this essay I refer to "the consolidation of democracy" and never to "democratic consolidation" because I am convinced that much that is done to consolidate this particular type of state regime is not itself democratic. In other words, it may be occasionally necessary to use undemocratic means to accomplish democratic ends. For an early statement of this conundrum, see my "Patti e transizioni: Mezzi non-democratici a fini democratici?," *Rivista Italiana di Scienza Politica* December 1984; 14(3): 363–382.
5. G. O'Donnell and P. C. Schmitter, op. cit.
6. One might refer to the "Suarez Factor" and its presumed inhibiting effect upon possible candidates to lead the transition. Named for its first "victim," Spain's Adolfo Suarez, it implies that the politician who is initially appointed or elected and who accepts public responsibility for governing during the highly uncertain period of transition to democracy will be subsequently and massively rejected by the electorate. The reason is simple: this political entrepreneur will have to bear the concentrated costs of disturbing established practices, while the eventual benefits will come later and be dispersed over a wider public.

   In the case of Suarez, despite having led a relatively successful regime change, he suffered the greatest electoral defeat in Spanish history (a decline in 29.3 percentage points between 1979 and 1982), from which his UCD party never recovered. Presumably, if the Suarez factor were well known and reliable, all ambitious politicians would prefer to have someone else form the first government so that he or she could benefit from the inevitable backlash and even manage to win several successive elections, as has Suarez' successor, Felipe Gonzalez.

Although the Suarez Factor has worked in Portugal, Brazil, Argentina, Peru, Bolivia, Ecuador, Uruguay, Bulgaria, Romania, and Lithuania, where the incumbent president or prime minister was unable to pass on the succession to someone of his own party, there are recent signs that it might be waning: the Chilean Christian Democrats were able to pass on the mantle to one of their own in 1994; no one seems to have doubted that Carlos Salinas would be succeeded by a PRI candidate of his choosing; Corazon Aquino handed over to someone in her own government – admittedly, under ambiguous circumstances. South Korea and Taiwan seem to be headed for even greater executive continuity. Singapore has seen so much of it that it is questionable to classify this polity as democratic, given the fact that the margin for the victorious governing party has been so consistent and large.

7. Antonio Gramsci, *Selections from the Prison Notebooks*, trans. by Q. Hoare and G. N. Smith (New York: International Publishers, 1971), pp. 105–120, 229–239.

8. A book that brilliantly captures this situation is J.G.A. Pocock, *The Machiavellian Moment* (Princeton: Princeton University Press, 1975). Put in Machiavelli's language, the transition places a high premium on the "crafting" skills of individual politicians. Once consolidation has set in, such individual initiatives become less frequent and less consequential; routines and rituals take over.

9. Once challenged at a conference to stop spinning elaborate webs around the concept of "consolidation of democracy" and to produce a simple definition that everyone would understand, I reflected a moment and answered: "You know that a democracy has consolidated itself when its politics has become boring." De Tocqueville once made a distinction between two kinds of politics: one based on "the will of certain men"; the other based on "the never-ending action of institutions." The consolidation of democracy involves the movement from the former to the latter.

10. Anthony Gidden, *The Constitution of Society. Outline of a Theory of Structuration* (Cambridge: Polity Press, 1984).

11. Another way of expressing this difference has been explored by James March and Johan P. Olsen in their distinction between "normal" institutionalized politics rooted in a predictable and internalized "logic of appropriateness" and a less well-structured type of politics based on a more contingent and opportunistic "logic of choice." *Rediscovering Institutions: The Organizational Basis of Politics* (New York: The Free Press, 1989).

12. Guillermo O'Donnell and Philippe C. Schmitter, *Tentative Conclusions about Uncertain Democracies*, p. 73, note 1. Note that the subject is regime, not order, which means that it is confined to certain mechanisms of political choice and authoritative coercion. What accounts for the ensemble of social, economic, and cultural institutions and how they relate to each other in a given society to produce "order" is quite a different matter. Confined in this fashion, the existence of a democratic regime at the national level is no guarantee that families, firms, religions, schools, tribes, clubs, associations, parties, trade unions, villages, and even competent political units will all be governed democratically. Following de Tocqueville, it seems reasonable to hypothesize that equality tends to be contagious, i.e that once the citizenship principle is firmly entrenched in national political institutions, it will place pressure on other institutions to conform to it. Nevertheless, the time since he wrote his monumental *De La Démocratie en Amerique* has clearly shown the functional limits and the successful resistance by privileged groups to further equality.

13. For the purpose of this essay, democracy will be defined as "a regime or system of governance in which rulers are held accountable for their actions in the public realm by citizens, acting indirectly through the competition and cooperation of their representatives." For further explication, see Philippe C. Schmitter and Terry Lynn Karl, "What Democracy is … and is not", op. cit.

14. Hence, the reluctance of most observers to classify Singapore as a democracy, despite its holding regular elections and respecting – most – procedural niceties.

15. For a fascinating argument that it is often the "silences" and "abeyances" of constitutions – their unwritten components – that are most significant, see Michael Foley, *The Silence of*

Constitutions. Gaps, 'Abeyances' and Political Temperament in the Maintenance of Government (London: Routledge, 1989).

16. See Peter Lange and Hudson Meadwell, "Typologies of Democratic Systems: From Political Inputs to Political Economy," in Howard Wiarda (ed.), *New Directions in Comparative Politics* (Boulder: Westview Press, 1985), pp. 80–111.

17. For the best general comparative treatment, see Filipe Agüero, "Democratic Consolidation and the Military in Southern Europe and Latin America," in R. Gunther, P. N. Diamandouros, and H.-J. Puhle (eds), *The Politics of Democratic Consolidation. Southern Europe in Comparative Perspective* (Baltimore: Johns Hopkins University Press, 1995), pp. 124–165.

18. Ibid., pp. 7–8.

19. Robert Dahl, *Polyarchy* (New Haven: Yale University Press, 1971), pp. 2–4.

3

Fifty years after the "Great Transformation": Reflections on social order and political agency

Claus Offe

Neo-liberal orthodoxy has targeted the "strong" state and "big government" as the chief culprits responsible for social malaise and economic malperformance, and as a consequence of democratic overload. However, it is not evident what is meant by "big" government. The question of size can be considered in two ways – structural and functional – and both hold implications for citizenship and the relationship between democracy and the market. Both seem to be orthogonally related – that is, at least potentially unrelated.

The structural concept of big government concerns indicators such as the number of intervention points, the size of the state apparatus (in terms of personnel), and the size of the budget. The functional measurement involves an analysis of the number of people being affected by state policies, as well as the intensity of the impact of such interventions.

Using these two rough measures, we see interesting plus/minus combinations. One such effect could be an inflated state apparatus with little regulatory and governance capacity. The other would be the result of a policy of deregulation, withdrawal, neglect, and inaction – such as the set of policies often associated with "Thatcherism" – which has, and is intended to have, a major and often devastating impact upon the life chances of great numbers of people. After all, privatization and marketization are "policy" interventions, not a return to an allegedly innocent and natural state of "undistorted" social order. The market is here used as a political weapon targeted, for reasons that may be deemed legitimate or illegitimate, against particular categories of people for particular purposes. It is exactly the function and purpose of neo-liberal orthodoxy to conceal this discretionary use of market forces that is employed by political authorities for strategic purposes not self-evidently natural or legitimate. One might well argue that, at the time before economic regulation and social policy redistribution were ever experimented with or even conceived of, the tool kit of public policy was so limited that nobody could even think of policy choices of a more interventionist sort. At that time, the market was actually "outside of" and "prior to" policy choices, although historians of ideas (such as Hirschman) have forcefully argued that the rule of market-mediated interests was itself the outcome of a powerful moral, political, and ideological campaign by the eighteenth century bourgeoisie and intellectual protagonists. After these allegedly "innocent times" were over and the Keynesian welfare state became an ideological and practical reality, marketization has been turned into a policy as much as any of its alternatives.

If marketization is seen as one policy instrument among many others, what combination of structural and functional indicators is most rational, beneficial, and desirable? The answer is not one that can be given in the form of a compelling economic or philosophical argument, but only in the course, and as the outcome, of democratic deliberation. The answer is a matter of "voice," rather than "proof." As a consequence, almost any assertion or model of the proper role and size of macro-social organizing principles will be controversial and contested. If the market – and its extensions – is thus a matter of public policy, the relative size, scope, and intensity of the market versus the government versus the community must correspondingly be a matter and a consequence of democratic politics. It is this syllogism to which the neo-liberal orthodoxy is radically and consistently opposed. Rather than providing an input into the conduct of democratic debate, thereby raising the level of discourse and improving the quality of "voice," the proponents of such orthodoxy silence or emasculate this process by claiming superior insight. Hence, the epistemological principle of Thatcherism: "There is no alternative."

The (anti-)politics of neo-liberal orthodoxy is to disenfranchise citizens and to pre-empt potential issues of public debate in the name of truth and scientific insight. It closes the agenda by imposing non-decisions. As Lindblom observed, it uses the market as a prison. If, however, the state is reduced to a contract-enforcing agency sub-servient to market forces, democracy becomes either pointless or distorted. This distortion I have in mind is the displacement of issues of public debate. Issues of justice, prosperity, and the distribution of life chances – the core issues of what Lipset refers to as "the demo-cratic class struggle" – are silenced, and what flourishes instead is the politics of morality, religion, identity, and (ultimately) personalistic populism. Under the intellectual and political regime of neo-liberal orthodoxy, elections turn into shallow – though sometimes passionate – moral beauty contests over issues that have nothing to do with the core question of how to organize the political economy. A con-comitant phenomenon is the vanishing of the institutional and actual role assigned to collective intermediary actors of all sorts, from trade unions to city councils, from business associations to universities. This in turn makes the orderly reconciliation of conflict more difficult, the institutional vacuum of interest intermediation giving rise to symp-toms of social disorganization.

Polanyi's concern in *The Great Transformation* – which first appeared in 1944 – was to demonstrate that "the institutional arrangements of market societies cause them to be inherently unsta-ble."[1] This is the famous "satanic mill" argument. It derives in turn from the "fictitious commodities" argument that labour,[2] land, and money are commodities that differ from all other commodities in that they do not come into being *as* commodities, that is, as the outcome of an acquisitive production process aimed at the sale of its results for profit.[3] The market cannot create "social order" because some of the key ingredients of social order cannot be the result of market inter-action. The market is, both genetically and structurally, the creation of non-market actors.

On the basis of the "satanic mill" argument, we can draw the inverse conclusion. If a market economy actually develops into a sustainable social order, this must be due not to its quality of *kosmos* – spontaneous order due to the operation of the invisible hand – but of *taxis* – consciously arranged, instituted, and controlled order – to employ an important distinction introduced by Hayek.[4] The question then becomes one of who creates and manages the *taxis*, and of how the social institutions in which the market is embedded come into being.

Polanyi argued that it is the state which is the guardian of integra-tion, coherence, and solidarity. How does the state come to perform that function? There is a strong functionalist argument in *The Great*

Transformation: "objective reasons of a stringent nature forced the hands of the legislators." But legislators as social actors must be conscious of those objective reasons, and they must also be able and willing to comply with what these reasons mandate. The necessary protective devices on which a market society depends for its integration and sustainability do not become operative automatically, nor are they self-evident and determinate. No outside observer can tell what measures of what scale and scope must be adopted in order to make a market economy a viable social order. Any practical answer to this question must be willed, and the ultimate source of this will is a theory of social justice that guides political action within society. The protective institutional devices must be instituted and enacted in accordance with such a theory .

Polanyi has shown, in his analysis of Speenhamland and its repeal in 1832–1834, that market capitalism is not something that comes into being by the force of evolutionary superiority alone; rather, it originates from conscious efforts and strategic interests on the part of the holders of state power to create institutional and administrative arrangements that are best suited to it, and, most importantly, the marketization of labour. Capitalism, and the commodification of labour as its core prerequisite, is thus a political construction.

The protective regulatory framework that eventually emerged is also a political construction, based upon the experience that market society, if left wholly unregulated, does not result in a stable social order. This is the "powerful counter-movement"[5] by which political actors within market society react to its instabilities. If, as Polanyi insists time and again, "the market has been the outcome of a conscious and often violent intervention on the part of government which imposed the market organization on society for non-economic ends," why should the same not be true for the reverse process in which markets are contained and regulated? There is an inconsistency here: while Polanyi is very specific as to the agents that brought about marketization, he lapses into the anonymity of functionalist logic in explaining the reverse process: "ultimately what made things happen were the interests of society as a whole." He maintains that it was not class interests which gave rise to protective regulation and self-preservation, but that "such measures simply responded to the needs of industrial civilization with which market methods were unable to cope." Again, the question is who understood those needs, acted upon them, and eventually succeeded in addressing them?

Contrary to the simplistic reading of Marxism of which Polanyi was utterly critical, this self-correcting tendency within market society cannot be attributed to class actors alone. Yet it must be attributed to specific actors, the means and opportunities available to them, and the ideas that guided them. Let me briefly turn to a review of the principal actors which played a role in the creation of the various kinds of protective economic and social policy regimes in Europe as it emerged from the horrors of the Second World War. These are the centres of agency which have shared – or at any rate partially over-lapping – projects of social order. I shall then turn to the question of whether the order imposed by these social and political forces is likely to be a permanent one, or whether (and, if so, for what reasons) we are now in the midst of a second Polanyi cycle of disorganization with the need for reorganization still unanswered.

The post-war settlement of the problem of social order in West European countries was helped by a number of favourable factors, all of which have now virtually disappeared. The first of these factors was the unique historical condition of sustained economic growth supported by a social order in which the experience and expectation of a lasting positive-sum game imposed relative, not absolute, sacrifices. Second, a consolidated system of nation-states provided the opportunity for building economic and social policy regimes within each country, without reason to fear adverse transnational repercussions in terms of diminished competitiveness. Third, the memories of the horrors of the war and the Nazi regime, as well as the anti-totalitarian consensus that emerged from the Cold War, all helped to solidify the alliance of political forces which, with only minor variations, endorsed patterns of regulatory state intervention and a qualified collectivism involving corporate groups.

Within these conditions, an inter-class alliance of Liberal, Christian, and Socialist normative traditions emerged, embodying, respectively, the justice intuitions of desert, needs, and rights. Taken together, these three intuitions make up the model of what in the German terminology is called "social market economy," which has parallels in most other advanced capitalist economies and their respective "welfare state regimes."[6]

Today, we see the atrophy of this alliance, due to the disintegration of the normative theories on which society can rely in order to protect itself from the destructive impact of the market. There are three regulatory paradigms of a just social order, which have their respective political proponents. In order to simplify, one can employ the conceptual triplets of liberalism and the concomitant ethos of desert and the market, socialism and positive rights in the context of the state, and Christian politics associated with community-based needs.

Liberalism honours desert as measured by, and rewarded through, the market. In the original theories of political liberalism, what people deserve includes not only the uninhibited use of property rights and the fruits of such use, but also equal and universalistic admission to opportunities and market access, such as schools and health services. In the absence of these universalistic premises – as well as others, such as conditions of reasonably full employment – liberty may well exist to some extent, but is rendered worthless to all those who are not in a position to make choices as to their place in society. Today's liberals have largely turned libertarian, shedding off the egalitarian component of "equal liberty" which embraces equal opportunity and entitlement to compensation. Market libertarians have also discarded traditionalist admixtures of social conservatism; the fate of the British "one-nation Tories" under Thatcher illustrates this. Or they have turned from cosmopolitan liberalism to chauvinism (as in Austria), promising the protection of national citizens through the exclusion of those who do not belong to that community. Ironically, the stronger that inclusive and egalitarian liberalism has become as a sophisticated moral and political theory, the more deficient it has become in practice.

Socialists originally had a vision of how distribution should be organized on the basis not only of positive rights but also of production, both through the use of state power. Apart from some "green" caveats concerning how production should *not* be organized, the theme of production and how best to organize it has virtually vanished from the socialist or social democratic agenda.[7] As socialist distributive projects are today widely seen as being parasitic upon growth and production – and so cannot promote growth in any distinctive socialist ways – these distributive projects become dubious and easily discredited. As the inherited corporatist rights of workers often stand in the way of economic performance, Social Democrats, exposed to the pressures of fiscal crisis, find themselves in the embarrassing situation of having to tolerate the sacrifice of status and distributive rights for competitiveness and performance. In southern Europe – Spain, Italy, also France – Socialists even seem determined to outcompete Market Liberals in their emphasis upon deregulation. Indeed, it is hardly possible to recognize a specifically "socialist" concept of industrial organization, modernization, and the promotion of industrial prosperity from any of its competitors. The concepts of intelligently regulating production in ways that guarantee workers' rights at the point of production, together with full employment, are similarly difficult to come by in today's open economies. For instance, the core concept of post-war social democratic economic policy-making, the concept of full employment, was conspicuously absent from the rhetoric of the Social Democrats during the German 1994 election campaign, only to be replaced with the more modest and realistic call for creating more jobs.

Finally, Christian politics in general, and Roman Catholic-inspired politics in particular, are based upon the protection of the needs of individuals and communities, preferably not directly through the state but in indirect ways that help the community to help itself in the context of subsidiarity. In particular, a form of protection from the market is envisaged upon the family and the natural law entitlements that supposedly are to govern the relations between the sexes, generations, and social classes. Many of the doctrines invoked in support of this kind of protection from the market are so grotesquely out of touch with demographic conditions, actual gender, and intergenerational relations that they hardly qualify as a plausible rationale for an effective control of the "satanic mill" of the market.

The post-Second World War period came to a definitive end with the year 1989, if not even earlier with the oil price shocks of the mid-seventies. Its end has marked the end of a broad consensus concerning the regulatory regimes underpinning social order and the mode in which disruptive market forces should be contained. While grand coalitions reflecting a broad conservative–social democratic consensus on the basics of social order have become rare, the failure of each of the three ideological "camps" to provide for, and implement, a coherent concept of order is also manifest. Thatcher's infamous claim that there is no British "society," just British individuals and families, actually denies the very object of any effort to establish a "social order." This denial is complemented by her refusal to acknowledge the existence of a society as a subject of the creation of such order as public policy. According to her – and to many of her libertarian followers – public policy cannot be guided by democratic representation and collective choice, but by some meta-social logic.

No potentially hegemonic vision of a just social order is at hand, other than that presumably brought about through the unfettered operation of market forces within and between irrevocably open economies. This applies to the West as well as to the East. The breakdown of state socialism has rendered obsolete a model of statist authoritarian protection, leaving behind, according to Vaclav Klaus, a craving for a "market economy without an adjective" in many of the post-socialist societies. Many of the post-communist élites in Eastern Europe follow the belief that problems of social order and social protection can be postponed until after an adjective-less market economy is firmly installed. In the meantime, they stare in disbelief upon the electoral resurgence of the advocates of paternalistic social protectionism.

The great virtue and attraction of market forces and private property consist not in their being the medium of private profit maximization but in their capacity for collective loss minimization. Markets eliminate in a smooth, continuous, and inconspicuous way all those factors of production that fail to perform according to current standards of efficiency. These failing factors are thus forced to adapt and to find alternative and more productive uses. The power that drives this continuous search is more potent than any political authority or planning agency, be it authoritarian or democratic. This is so because the market is an anonymous power that we cannot talk to: it is not to be irritated by election results or any other kind of "voice." The potency of market forces derives from their anonymity and non-intentionality: if factors of production fail in a particular allocation, nobody can be blamed for having caused this event. The market inflicts damage upon inefficient producers that even the most totalitarian system of governance would not dare to impose. Hence, as "no one else" can be blamed for negative market outcomes, the market invites self-attribution of individual failures. The market is a powerful socializing agent. It constantly brings to mind the maxim proclaimed by Abraham Lincoln: "If you need a helping hand, look at the lower end of your right arm!" Adaptation, however, does not come automatically: it depends on adaptivity-enhancing infrastructure, assistance, and incentives.

The market invites victim-blaming. As we know, anonymous efficiency-enhancing pressure is just one side of the market. The other side is the tendency of the market to spread to every aspect of social life: the market cannot easily be contained or kept in its "proper place" while respecting the autonomy of the "life world" of culture, socialization, and the shape of human biographies. Moreover, the market, far from being the favourite arrangement of producers, is, wherever possible, undermined by cartelization and monopolies, or distorted by clientelistic favours extracted from the holders of political power. Finally, and perhaps most importantly, what speaks against the market as a generator of social order is its blindness: it fails to register and to translate into price signals both present and future externalities, including the external effects which result in the permanent exclusion of people and entire regions. It is these three classes of market deficiencies and market failures which must be addressed in any attempt to integrate market societies and impose upon them a viable social order.

To turn to the central question, how do we explain the apparent disarticulation of the political camps and forces that have shaped political processes? A traditional – and highly optimistic – view of the competitive democratic process – the "political market-place" – has been that it brings to power those forces that are best capable of contributing to the integration and thus to the long-term sustainability of industrial societies. Electoral competition is a mechanism in which the best problem solver wins and the loser will consequently have to learn from the winner and eventually try to outbid him on the next election day. Today, a more realistic picture is that of a downward spiral of fatalistic routines, in which each party relies on the fact that its competitor does not have any promising ideas either, which renders unnecessary efforts to develop those of its own. The side-effects of this spiral are mass political cynicism, low electoral turnout, the decline of stable political support, the denunciation of the "political class" as corrupt and self-serving, and an increasing structural premium on the populist politics of resentment.

The explanation for the atrophy of not just socialist doctrines but also of competing doctrines must be addressed on the levels of both the micro-motives and the macro-context of politics and public policy. Within Western civil societies – centres of political agency – collective action based upon recognized similarities of status, interest, culture, and the potential for solidarity have largely eroded. If anything, communities based on consumption and lifestyle are more likely to arise than those based on similarities within the sphere of production and division of labour. The image that emerges from the vast sociological literature on "post-modern" social structures – as well as from the communitarian critique of liberal individualism – is that of rapid fluctuations of loyalties, allegiances, and commitments between individuals and diachronically across generations and along the life

course of individuals. Again, structural disembeddedness and atom-
ization are prevailing features of both West and post-communist East
European societies. The threat of marginalization through unemployment dominates these societies, and the resulting insecurities and
anxieties generate a rational preference for social advancement and
social security through individual rather than collective means. These
feelings and perceptions in turn inculcate a lifeboat logic into social
life that reckons with the absence or unreliability of communal or
state-provided safety nets.

The macro-context of economic, technical, and cultural globalization is mediated, respectively, by the "three non-verbal Ms" of money,
mathematics, and music, to which we might add the fourth M of
migration. This context discourages any effort to invest in, or develop
commitments toward, social order, for it is feared that such efforts
and commitments will precipitate adverse transnational repercussions. It is increasingly uncertain to what extent a tight domestic regulatory regime is actually helping international competitiveness, for
example through the reliable protection of social peace and infra-
structural advantages. Beyond which, such a regime offers opportunities for dumping to *tertii gaudentes*, or otherwise becomes vulnerable to exploitation by others. As borders are increasingly unable
to provide a bulwark against the outward flow of capital and the
inward flow of labour, the sense of a loss of sovereignty undermines
the tightly confined nation-state, within which the social democratic
welfare state must be seen to be parasitic. Moreover, this loss of
domestic sovereignty is essentially not compensated through effective
mechanisms of territorial and functional representation at the level of
transnational regimes.

What results from both the micro- and macro-contexts that I have
briefly sketched is the apparent impotence of state power, as well as
the political forces and ideas that are willing and capable of using it in
the continuous process of creation and fine-tuning social order.
Again, this applies to East and West alike. Needless to say, the cures
of these ills are as well known as they are hard to administer: they
involve the cultivation of the associative life of civil society and its
legal premises on the one hand, and the development of democratically accessible and responsive transnational regimes on the other.
In the meantime, it remains a case of misplaced concreteness to ask
the time-honoured question of what is to be done: the real – and
logically prior – question is whether there is anybody who can do
anything.

Notes

1. Michael Hechter, "Karl Polanyi's Social Theory: A Critique," *Politics and Society* 1981; 10(4): 405; Karl Polanyi, *The Great Transformation* (Boston: Beacon Press, 1971).
2. Some consequences of the fictitiousness of the commodity form for the socio-economics of labour markets are explored in Claus Offe and Karl Hinrichs, "The Political Economy of the Labour Market," in Claus Offe, *Disorganized Capitalism* (Oxford: Polity, 1995).
3. That is to say, human beings as the bearers of labour power are not manufactured, but born as children. Land and the resources it contains are provided by geological and other processes; these resources are limited and cannot be augmented. Money (as well as taxes, tariffs, and exchange rates) is legislated into being and administered by central banks and other authorities.
4. Friedrich A. Hayek, *Law, Legislation, and Liberty*, Vol. 2 (Chicago: University of Chicago Press, 1976), chapter 2.
5. Fred Block and Margaret R. Somers, "Beyond the Economistic Fallacy: The Holistic Social Science of Karl Polanyi", in Theda Skocpol (ed.) *Vision and Method in Historical Sociology* (Cambridge: Cambridge University Press, 1984), p. 57.
6. The details and diverse configurations of these regimes have been analysed by Gösta Esping-Anderson in *The Three Worlds of Welfare Capitalism* (Princeton: Princeton UP, 1990).
7. See the apt warning of Joel Rogers and Wolfgang Streeck: "Leaving efficiency to capital and limiting Left intervention to distributive justice not only surrenders the Left's claim for power, but results in less than optimal efficiency and thus hurts society as a whole." In "Productive Solidarities: Economic Strategy and Left Politics," in David Miliband (ed.) *Reinventing the Left* (Oxford: Polity, 1994), p. 143.

4

Toward consolidated democracies

Juan J. Linz and Alfred Stepan

Three minimal conditions must obtain before there can be any possibility of speaking of democratic consolidation. First, in a modern polity, free and authoritative elections cannot be held, winners cannot exercise the monopoly of legitimate force, and citizens cannot effectively have their rights protected by a rule of law unless a state exists. In some parts of the world, conflicts about the authority and domain of the *polis* and the identities and loyalties of the *demos* are so intense that no state exists. No state, no democracy.

Second, democracy cannot be thought of as consolidated until a democratic transition has been brought to completion. A necessary (but by no means sufficient) condition for the completion of a democratic transition is the holding of free and contested elections (on the basis of broadly inclusive voter eligibility) that meet the seven institutional requirements for elections in a polyarchy that Robert A. Dahl has set forth.[1] Such elections are not sufficient, however, to complete a democratic transition. In many cases – in Chile as of 1996, for example – in which free and contested elections have been held, the government resulting from elections like these lacks the *de jure* as well as *de facto* power to determine policy in many significant areas because the executive, legislative, and judicial powers are still decisively constrained by an interlocking set of "reserve domains," military "prerogatives," or "authoritarian enclaves."[2]

Third, no regime should be called a democracy unless its rulers govern democratically. If freely elected executives (no matter what

This chapter is reprinted, with changes, by permission of the authors and the Johns Hopkins University Press, from the *Journal of Democracy* April 1996; 7(2): 14–32.

the magnitude of their majority) infringe the constitution, violate the rights of individuals and minorities, impinge upon the legitimate functions of the legislature, and thus fail to rule within the bounds of a state of law, their regimes are not democracies.

In sum, when we talk about the consolidation of democracy, we are not dealing with liberalized non-democratic regimes, or with pseudo-democracies, or with hybrid democracies where some democratic institutions coexist with non-democratic institutions outside the control of the democratic state. Only democracies can become consolidated democracies.

Let us now turn to examining how, and when, new political systems that meet the three minimal conditions of "stateness," a completed democratic transition, and a government that rules democratically can be considered consolidated democracies.[3]

In most cases, after a democratic transition is completed there are still many tasks that need to be accomplished, conditions that must be established, and attitudes and habits that must be cultivated before democracy can be regarded as consolidated. What, then, are the characteristics of a consolidated democracy? Many scholars, in advancing definitions of consolidated democracy, enumerate all the regime characteristics that would improve the overall quality of democracy. We favour, instead, a narrower definition of democratic consolidation, but one that none the less combines behavioural, attitudinal, and constitutional dimensions. Essentially, by a "consolidated democracy" we mean a political regime in which democracy – as a complex system of institutions, rules, and patterned incentives and disincentives – has become, in a phrase, "the only game in town."[4]

Behaviourally, democracy becomes the only game in town when no significant political group seriously attempts to overthrow the democratic regime or to promote domestic or international violence in order to secede from the state. When this situation obtains, the behaviour of the newly elected government that has emerged from the democratic transition is no longer dominated by the problem of how to avoid democratic breakdown. (Exceptionally, the democratic process can be used to achieve secession, creating separate states that can be democracies.) Attitudinally, democracy becomes the only game in town when, even in the face of severe political and economic crises, the overwhelming majority of the people believe that any further political change must emerge from within the parameters of democratic procedures. Constitutionally, democracy becomes the only game in town when all of the actors in the polity become habituated to the fact that political conflict within the state will be resolved according to established norms, and that violations of these norms are likely to be both ineffective and costly. In short, with consolidation, democracy becomes routinized and deeply internalized in social, institutional, and even psychological life, as well as in political calculations for achieving success.

Our working definition of a consolidated democracy is then as follows. *Behaviourally*, a democratic regime in a territory is consolidated when no significant national, social, economic, political, or institutional actors spend significant resources attempting to achieve their objectives by creating a non-democratic regime or by seceding from the state. *Attitudinally*, a democratic regime is consolidated when a strong majority of public opinion, even in the midst of major economic problems and deep dissatisfaction with incumbents, holds the belief that democratic procedures and institutions are the most appropriate way to govern collective life, and when support for anti-system alternatives is quite small or more-or-less isolated from pro-democratic forces. *Constitutionally*, a democratic regime is consolidated when governmental and non-governmental forces alike become subject to, and habituated to, the resolution of conflict within the bounds of the specific laws, procedures, and institutions sanctioned by the new democratic process.

We must add two important caveats. First, when we say that a regime is a consolidated democracy, we do not preclude the possibility that at some future time it could break down. Such a breakdown, however, would be related not to weaknesses or problems specific to the historic process of democratic consolidation but to a new dynamic in which the democratic regime cannot solve a set of problems, a non-democratic alternative gains significant supporters, and former democratic-regime loyalists begin to behave in a constitutionally disloyal or semiloyal manner.[5]

Our second caveat is that we do not want to imply that there is only one type of consolidated democracy. An exciting new area of research is concerned with precisely this issue – the varieties of consolidated democracies. We also do not want to imply that consolidated democracies could not continue to improve their quality by raising the minimal economic plateau upon which all citizens stand, and by deepening popular participation in the political and social life of the country. Within the category of consolidated democracies there is a continuum from low-quality to high-quality democracies. Improving the quality of consolidated democracies is an urgent political and intellectual task, but our goal in this essay, though related, is a different one. As we are living in a period in which an unprecedented number of countries have completed democratic transitions and are attempting to consolidate democracies, it is politically and conceptually important that we understand the specific tasks of "crafting" democratic consolidation. Unfortunately, too much of the discussion of the current "wave" of democratization focuses almost solely on elections or on the presumed democratizing potential of market mechanisms. Democratic consolidation, however, requires much more than elections and markets.

Crafting and conditions

In addition to a functioning state, five other interconnected and mutually reinforcing conditions must be present, or be crafted, in order for a democracy to be consolidated. First, the conditions must exist for the development of a free and lively *civil society*. Second, there must be a relatively autonomous *political society*. Third, throughout the territory of the state, all major political actors, especially the government and the state apparatus, must be effectively subjected to the *rule of law* that protects individual freedoms and associational life. Fourth, there must be a *state bureaucracy* that is usable by the new democratic government. Fifth, there must be an institutionalized *economic society*. Let us explain what is involved in crafting this interrelated set of conditions.

By "civil society," we refer to that arena of the polity where self-organizing and relatively autonomous groups, movements, and individuals attempt to articulate values, to create associations and solidarities, and to advance their interests. Civil society can include manifold social movements – women's groups, neighbourhood associations, religious groupings, and intellectual organizations – as well as associations from all social strata, such as trade unions, entrepreneurial groups, and professional associations.

By "political society," we mean that arena in which political actors compete for the legitimate right to exercise control over public power and the state apparatus. Civil society by itself can destroy a non-democratic regime, but democratic consolidation (or even a full democratic transition) must involve political society. Democratic consolidation requires that citizens develop an appreciation for the core institutions of a democratic political society – political parties, legislatures, elections, electoral rules, political leadership, and inter-party alliances.

It is important to stress not only the difference between civil society and political society but also their complementarity, which is not always recognized. One of these two arenas is frequently neglected in favour of the other. Worse, within the democratic community, champions of either civil society or political society all too often adopt a discourse and a set of practices that are implicitly inimical to the normal development of the other.

In the recent struggles against the non-democratic regimes of Eastern Europe and Latin America, a discourse was constructed that emphasized "civil society versus state" – a dichotomy that has a long philosophical genealogy. More importantly for our purposes, it was also politically useful to those democratic movements emerging in states where explicitly political organizations were forbidden or extremely weak. In many countries, civil society was rightly considered to be the hero of democratic resistance and transition.

The problem arises at the moment of democratic transition. Democratic leaders of political society quite often argue that civil society, having played its historic role, should be demobilized to allow for the development of normal democratic politics. Such an argument is not only bad democratic theory, it is also bad democratic politics. A robust civil society, with the capacity to generate political alternatives and to monitor government and state, can help start transitions, help resist reversals, and deepen democracy. At all stages of the democratization process, therefore, a lively and independent civil society is invaluable.

But we should also consider how to recognize (and thus help overcome) the false opposition sometimes drawn between civil society and political society. The danger posed for the development of political society by civil society is that normative preferences and styles of organization perfectly appropriate to civil society might be taken to be the desirable – or, indeed, the only legitimate – style of organization for political society. For example, many civil-society leaders view "internal conflict" and "division" within the democratic forces with moral antipathy. "Institutional routinization," "intermediaries," and "compromise" within politics are often spoken of pejoratively. But each of the above terms refers to an indispensable practice of political society in a consolidated democracy. Democratic consolidation requires political parties, one of whose primary tasks is precisely to aggregate and represent differences between democrats. Consolidation requires that habituation to the norms and procedures of democratic conflict-regulation be developed. A high degree of institutional routinization is a key part of such a process. Inter-mediation between the state and civil society, and the structuring of compromise, are likewise legitimate and necessary tasks of political society. In short, political society – informed, pressured, and periodi-cally renewed by civil society – must somehow achieve a workable agreement on the myriad ways in which democratic power will be crafted and exercised.

The need for a *Rechtsstaat*

To achieve a consolidated democracy, the necessary degree of auto-nomy of civil and political society must be embedded in, and sup-ported by, our third arena, the rule of law. All significant actors – especially the democratic government and the state apparatus – must be held accountable to, and become habituated to, the rule of law. For the types of civil society and political society we have just described, a rule of law animated by a spirit of constitutionalism is an indispensable condition. Constitutionalism, which should not be confused with majoritarianism, entails a relatively strong consensus regarding the constitution, and especially a commitment to "self-binding" procedures of governance that can be altered only by excep-tional majorities. It also requires a clear hierarchy of laws, inter-preted by an independent judicial system and supported by a strong legal culture in civil society.[6]

The emergence of *Rechtsstaat* – a state of law, or perhaps more accurately a state subject to law – was one of the major accom-plishments of nineteenth-century liberalism (long before full democ-ratization) in continental Europe and to some extent in Japan. A *Rechtsstaat* meant that the government and the state apparatus would be subject to the law, that areas of discretionary power would be defined and increasingly limited, and that citizens could turn to courts to defend themselves against the state and its officials. The modern *Rechtsstaat* is fundamental in making democratization possible, since without it citizens would not be able to exercise their political rights with full freedom and independence.

A state of law is particularly crucial for the consolidation of democracy. It is the most important continuous and routine way in which the elected government and the state administration are subjected to a network of laws, courts, semi-autonomous review and control agencies, and civil-society norms that not only check the state's illegal tendencies but also embed it in an interconnecting web of mechanisms requiring transparency and accountability. Freely elected governments can, but do not necessarily, create such a law-bound, constraint-embedded state. Indeed, the more that all the institutions of the state function according to the principle of the state of law, the higher the quality of democracy and the better the society.

Constitutionalism and the rule of law must determine the offices to be filled by election, the procedures to elect those office-holders, and the definition of (and limits to) their power in order for people to be willing to participate in – and to accept the outcomes of – the democratic game. This may pose a problem if the rules, even if enacted by a majority, are so unfair or poorly crafted and so difficult to change democratically that they are unacceptable to a large number of citizens. For example, an electoral law that gives 80 per cent of the seats in parliament to a party that wins less than 50 per cent of the vote, or an ideologically loaded constitution that is extremely difficult to amend, is not likely to be conducive to democratic consolidation.

Finally, a democracy in which a single leader enjoys, or thinks he or she enjoys, a "democratic" legitimacy that allows him or her to ignore, dismiss, or alter other institutions – the legislature, the courts, the constitutional limits of power – does not fit our conception of the rule of law in a democratic regime. The formal or informal institutionalization of such a system is not likely to result in a consolidated democracy unless such discretion is checked.

Some presidential democracies – with their tendency toward populist, plebiscitarian, "delegative" characteristics, together with a fixed term of office and a "no re-election" rule that excludes accountability before the electorate – encourage unconstitutional or anti-constitutional behaviour that threatens the rule of law, often democracy itself, and certainly democratic consolidation. A prime minister who develops similar tendencies toward the abuse of power is more likely than a president to be checked by other institutions – votes of no confidence by the opposition, or the loss of support by members of his own party. Early elections are a legal vehicle available in parliamentarianism – but unavailable in presidentialism – to help solve crises generated by such abusive leadership.

A usable bureaucracy

These three conditions – a lively and independent civil society, a political society with sufficient autonomy and a working consensus about procedures of governance, and constitutionalism and a rule of law – are virtually definitional prerequisites of a consolidated democracy. However, these conditions are much more likely to be satisfied where there are also a bureaucracy usable by democratic leaders and an institutionalized economic society.

Democracy is a form of governance in which the rights of citizens are guaranteed and protected. To protect the rights of its citizens and to deliver other basic services that citizens demand, a democratic government needs to be able to exercise effectively its claim to a monopoly of the legitimate use of force in its territory. Even if the state had no other functions than these, it would have to tax compulsorily in order to pay for police officers, judges, and basic services. A modern democracy, therefore, needs the effective capacity to command, to regulate, and to extract tax revenues. For this, it needs a functioning state with a bureaucracy considered usable by the new democratic government.

In many territories of the world today – especially in parts of the former Soviet Union – no adequately functioning state exists. Insufficient taxing capacity on the part of the state, or a weak normative and bureaucratic "presence" in much of its territory, such that citizens cannot effectively demand that their rights be respected or receive any basic entitlements, is also a great problem in many countries in Latin America, including Brazil. The question of the usability of the state bureaucracy by the new democratic regime also emerges in countries such as Chile, where the outgoing non-democratic regime was able to give tenure to many key members of the state bureaucracy in politically sensitive areas such as justice and education. Important questions about the usability of the state bureaucracy by new democrats inevitably emerge in cases where the distinction between the Communist Party and the state had been virtually obliterated (as in much of post-communist Europe), and the party is now out of power.

Economic society

The final supportive condition for a consolidated democracy concerns the economy, an arena that we believe should be called "economic society." We use this phrase to call attention to two claims that we believe are theoretically and empirically sound. First, there has never been, and there cannot be, a consolidated democracy that has a command economy (except perhaps in wartime). Second, there has never been, and almost certainly will never be, a modern consolidated democracy with a pure market economy. Modern consolidated democracies require a set of sociopolitically crafted and accepted norms, institutions, and regulations – what we call "economic society" – that mediate between the state and the market.

No empirical evidence has ever been adduced to indicate that a polity meeting our definition of a consolidated democracy has ever existed with a command economy. Is there a theoretical reason to explain such a universal empirical outcome? We think so. On theoretical grounds, our assumption is that at least a non-trivial degree of market autonomy and of ownership diversity in the economy is necessary to produce the independence and liveliness of civil society that allow it to make its contribution to a democracy. Similarly, if all property is in the hands of the state – along with all decisions about pricing, labour, supply, and distribution – the relative autonomy of political society required for a consolidated democracy could not exist.[7]

But why are completely free markets unable to coexist with modern consolidated democracies? Empirically, serious studies of modern polities repeatedly verify the existence of significant degrees of market intervention and state ownership in all consolidated democracies.[8] Theoretically, there are at least three reasons why this should be so. First, notwithstanding certain ideologically extreme – but surprisingly prevalent – neo-liberal claims about the self-sufficiency of the market, pure market economies could neither come into being nor be maintained without a degree of state regulation. Markets require legally enforced contracts, the issuance of money, regulated standards for weights and measures, and the protection of property, both public and private. These requirements dictate a role for the state in the economy. Second, even the best of markets experience "market failures" that must be corrected if the market is to function well.[9] No less an advocate of the "invisible hand" of the market than Adam Smith acknowledged that the state is necessary to perform certain functions. In a crucial but neglected passage in *The Wealth of Nations*, Adam Smith identified three important tasks of the state:

First, the duty of protecting the society from the violence and invasion of other independent societies; secondly, the duty of protecting, as far as possible, every member of the society from the injustice or oppression of every other member of it, or the duty of establishing an exact administration of justice; and, thirdly, the duty of erecting and maintaining certain public works and certain public institutions which it can never be for the interest of any individual, or small number of individuals, to erect and maintain; because the profit could never repay the expense to any individual or small number of individuals, though it may frequently do much more than repay it to a great society.[10]

Finally, and most importantly, democracy entails free public contestation concerning governmental priorities and policies. If a democracy never produced policies that generated government-mandated public goods in the areas of education, health, and transportation, and never provided some economic safety net for its citizens and some alleviation of gross economic inequality, democracy would not be sustainable. Theoretically, of course, it would be anti-democratic to take such public policies off the agenda of legitimate public contestation. Thus, even in the extremely hypothetical case of a democracy that began with a pure market economy, the very working of a modern democracy (and a modern advanced capitalist economy) would lead to the transformation of that pure market economy into a mixed economy – or that set of norms, regulations, policies, and institutions which we call "economic society."[11]

Any way we analyse the problem, democratic consolidation requires the institutionalization of a politically regulated market. This requires an economic society, which in turn requires an effective state. Even a goal such as narrowing the scope of public ownership – through privatization – in an orderly and legal way is almost certainly carried out more effectively by a stronger state than by a weaker one. Economic deterioration due to the state's inability to carry out needed regulatory functions greatly compounds the problems of economic reform and democratization.[12]

In summary, a modern consolidated democracy can be conceived of as comprising five major interrelated arenas, each of which, to function properly, must have its own primary organizing principle. Rightly understood, democracy is more than a regime: it is an interacting system. No single arena in such a system can function properly without some support from another arena, or often from all of the remaining arenas. For example, civil society in a democracy needs the support of a rule of law that guarantees to people their right of association, and needs the support of a state apparatus that will effectively impose legal sanctions on those who would illegally attempt to deny others that right. Furthermore, each arena in the democratic system has an impact on other arenas. For example, political society manages the governmental bureaucracy and produces the overall regulatory framework that guides and contains economic society. In a consolidated democracy, therefore, there are constant mediations among the five principal arenas, each of which is influenced by the others.

Two surmountable obstacles

Two of the most widely cited obstacles to democratic consolidation are the dangers posed by ethnic conflict in multinational states and by disappointed popular hopes for economic improvement in states undergoing simultaneous political and economic reform. These are real problems. Democratic theorists and crafters alike must recognize that there is often more than one "awakened nation" present in the state, and that there can be prolonged economic reversals after democratic transition begins. None the less, we are convinced, on both theoretical and empirical grounds, that democracy can still make significant strides toward consolidation under such conditions. We are, furthermore, convinced that if democratic theorists conceptualize what such obstacles mean and do not mean, this may lessen the dangers of democratic disenchantment and help to identify obstacle-reducing paths. That is our task in the rest of this essay.

Under what empirical conditions do "nation-states" and "democratization" form complementary logics? Under what conditions do they form conflicting logics? If they form conflicting logics, what types of practices and institutions will make democratic consolidation most, or least, likely?

Many political thinkers and activists assume that Weberian states, nation-states, and democracy cohere as part of the very grammar of modern polities. In a world where France, Germany, Portugal, Greece, and Japan are all Weberian states, nation-states, and democracies, such an assumption may seem justified. Yet in many countries that are not yet consolidated democracies, a nation-state policy often has a logic differing from that of a democratic policy. By a nation-state policy we mean one in which the leaders of the state pursue what Roger Brubaker calls "nationalizing state policies" aimed at increasing cultural homogeneity. Consciously or unconsciously, the leaders send messages that the state should be "of and for" the nation.[13] In the constitutions they write and in the politics they practise, the dominant nation's language becomes the only official language and occasionally the only acceptable language for state business and for education; the religion of the nation is privileged (even if it is not necessarily made the official religion); and the culture of the dominant nation is privileged in state symbols (such as the flag, national anthem, and even eligibility for some types of military service) and in state-controlled means of socialization (such as radio, television, and textbooks). By contrast, democratic policies in the state-making process are those that emphasize a broad and inclusive citizenship that accords equal individual rights to all.

Under what empirical conditions are the logics of state policies aimed at nation building congruent with those aimed at crafting democracy? Empirically, conflicts between these different policies are reduced when almost all of the residents of a state identify with one subjective idea of the nation, and when that nation is virtually co-extensive with the state. These conditions are met only if there is no significant irredenta outside the state's boundaries, if there is only one nation existing (or awakened) in the state, and if there is little cultural diversity within the state. In these circumstances – and, we will argue, virtually *only* in these circumstances – leaders of the government can simultaneously pursue democratization policies and nation-state policies. This congruence between the *polis* and the *demos* facilitates the creation of a democratic nation-state; it also virtually eliminates all problems of "stateness" and should thus be considered a supportive condition for democratic consolidation. Under modern circumstances, however, very few states will begin a possible democratic transition with a high degree of national homogeneity. This lack of homogeneity tends to exacerbate problems of "stateness."

Democracy is characterized not by subjects but by citizens; thus, a democratic transition often puts the question of the relation between *polis* and *demos* at the centre of politics. From all that has been said thus far, three assertions can be made. First, the greater the extent to which the population of a state is composed of a plurality of national, linguistic, religious, or cultural societies, the more complex politics becomes, since an agreement on the fundamentals of a democracy will be more difficult. Second, while this does not mean that con-solidating democracy in multinational or multicultural states is impossible, it does mean that especially careful political crafting of democratic norms, practices, and institutions is required. Third, some methods of dealing with the problems of "stateness" are inherently incompatible with democracy.

Clear thinking on this subject demands that we call into question some facile assumptions. One of the most dangerous ideas for democracy is that "every state should strive to become a nation-state and every nation should become a state." In fact, it is probably impossible for half of the territories in the world that are not now democratic ever to become both "nation-states" and "consolidated democracies," as we have defined these terms. One of the reasons for this is that many existing non-democratic states are multinational, multilingual, and multicultural. To make them "nation-states" by democratic means would be extremely difficult. In structurally embedded multicultural settings, virtually the only democratic way to create a homogeneous nation-state is through voluntary cultural assimilation, voluntary exit, or peaceful creation and voluntary acceptance of new territorial boundaries. These are empirically and democratically difficult measures and hence are exceedingly rare.

The other possibilities for creating a homogeneous nation-state in such settings involve subtle (or not-so-subtle) sanctions against those not speaking the language, wearing the attire, or practising the religion of the titular nation. Under modern circumstances – where all significant groups have writers and intellectuals who disseminate national cultures, where communication systems have greatly increased the possibility for migrants to remain continuously connected to their home cultures, and where modern democratic norms accept a degree of multiculturalism – such sanctions, even if not formally anti-democratic, would probably not be conducive to democratic crafting.[14] If the titular nation actually wants a truly homogeneous nation-state, a variant of "ethnic cleansing" is too often a temptation.

Another difficulty in building nation-states that are also democracies derives from the manner in which humanity is spatially distributed across the globe. One building block for nations is language. But, as Ernest Gellner observed, there are possibly as many as 8,000 languages (not counting important dialects) currently spoken in the world.[15] Even if we assume that only 1 out of every 10 languages is a base for a "reasonably effective" nationalism, there could be as many as 800 viable national communities.[16] But cultural, linguistic, and religious groups are not neatly segmented into 8,000 or 800 nationalities, each occupying reasonably well-defined territories; on the contrary, these groups are profoundly intermixed and overlapping.

We are not arguing against democratically crafted "velvet divorces." We should note, however, that relatively clear cultural boundaries facilitate such territorial separations. Latvia would like to be a nation-state, but in none of its seven most-populous cities is Latvian spoken by a majority of the residents. In Tallinn, the capital of Estonia, barely half the people of this aspiring nation-state speak Estonian. For these and many other countries, no simple territorial division or "velvet divorce" is available.[17]

Democracy and multinational states

Some analysts were happy when the separate nationalities of the USSR became 15 republics, all based on "titular nationalities," on the assumption that democratic nation-states might emerge. In fact, many political leaders in these republics sounded-out extreme nationalist – rather than democratic – themes in the first elections. One possible formula for diminishing conflict between titular nationalities and "migrants" is what David Laitin calls the "competitive-assimilation game." That is, it becomes in the best interests of some working-class migrants to assimilate in order to enhance the life chances of their children in the new environment. This may happen to Spanish working-class migrants in culturally and economically vibrant Catalonia, but is it likely to occur among Russians in Central Asia? In 1989 in Almaty, the capital of Kazakhstan, Russians constituted 59 per cent of the population, and the Kazakhs, the titular nationality, only 22.5 per cent. Less than 1 per cent of the Russians spoke the titular language. In Bishkek, the capital of Kyrgyzstan, the comparable percentages were virtually identical. In such contexts, shaped by settler colonialism, it is utterly implausible that a nation-state would emerge voluntarily through a process of competitive assimilation.[18]

So how can democracy possibly be achieved in multinational states? We have a strong hypothesis about how *not* to consolidate democracy in multinational settings: the greater the percentage of people in a given state who either were born there or arrived without perceiving themselves as foreign citizens, and who are subsequently denied citizenship in the state (when their life chances would be hurt by such denial), the more unlikely it is that this state will consolidate democracy. Phrased more positively, our hypothesis is that in a multinational, multicultural setting, the chances of consolidating democracy are increased by state policies that grant inclusive and equal citizenship and give all citizens a common "roof" of state-mandated and state-enforced individual rights.

Such multinational states also have an even greater need than other polities to explore a variety of non-majoritarian, non-plebiscitarian formulas. For example, if there are strong geographic concentrations of different groups within the state, federalism might be an option worth exploring. The state and the society might also allow a variety of publicly supported communal institutions – such as media and schools in different languages, symbolic recognition of cultural diversity, a variety of legally accepted marriage codes, legal and political tolerance for parties representing different communities, and a whole array of political procedures and devices that Arend Lijphart has described as "consociational democracy."[19] Typically, proportional representation, rather than large single-member districts with first-past-the-post elections, can facilitate representation of geographically dispersed minorities. Some strict adherents to the tradition of political liberalism, with its focus on universalism and individual rights, oppose any form of collective rights. But we believe that in a multinational, multicultural society and state, combining collective rights for nationalities or minorities with individual rights fully protected by the state is the least-conflictual solution.[20]

Where transitions occur in the context of a non-democratic, multinational federal system, the crafting of democratic federalism should probably begin with elections at the federal level, to generate a legitimate framework for later deliberations on how to decentralize the polity democratically. If the first competitive elections are regional, the elections will tend to favour regional nationalists, and ethnocracies rather than democracies may well emerge.[21] However, the specific ways of structuring political life in multinational settings need to be contextualized in each country. Along these lines, we believe that it is time to re-evaluate some past experiments with non-territorial autonomy, such as the kinds of partially self-governing ethnic or religious communities exemplified by the Jewish Kabal of the Polish–Lithuanian Commonwealth, the millets of the Ottoman Empire, or the "national curias" of the late Hapsburg Empire. These mechanisms will not eliminate conflict in multinational states, but they may moderate conflict and help make both the state and democracy more viable.

We also believe that some conceptual, political, and normative attention should be given to the possibility of "state-nations." We call "state-nations" those multicultural or even multinational states that none the less still manage to engender strong identification and loyalty from their diverse citizens. The United States is such a multicultural and increasingly multilingual country; Switzerland is another.

Neither is strictly speaking a "nation-state," but we believe both could now be called "state-nations." Under Jawaharlal Nehru, India made significant gains in managing multinational tensions by the skilful and consensual use of numerous consociational practices. Through this process India became, in the 1950s and early 1960s, a democratic "state-nation'; but if Hindu nationalists win power in the 1990s and attempt to turn India (with its 115 million Muslims) into a Hindu nation-state, communal violence would almost certainly increase and Indian democracy would be gravely threatened.

Multiple identities

Let us conclude with a word about "political identities." Many writings on nationalism have focused on "primordial" identities and the need for people to choose between mutually exclusive identities. Our research into political identities, however, has shown two things. First, political identities are not fixed or "primordial" in the *Oxford English Dictionary*'s sense of "existing at (or from) the very beginning"; rather, they are highly changeable and socially constructed. Second, if nationalist politicians (or social scientists and census-takers with crude dichotomous categories) do not force polarization, many people may prefer to define themselves as having multiple and complementary identities.[22] In fact, along with a common political "roof" of state-protected rights for inclusive and equal citizenship, the human capacity for multiple and complementary identities is one of the key factors that makes democracy in multinational states possible. Because political identities are not fixed and permanent, the quality of democratic leadership is particularly important. Multiple and complementary political identities can be nurtured by political leadership, as can polarized and conflictual political identities. Before the conscious use of "ethnic cleansing" as a strategy to construct nation-states in the former Yugoslavia, Sarajevo was a multinational city whose citizens had multiple identities and one of the world's highest interfaith-marriage rates.

Our central proposition is that, if successful democratic consolidation is the goal, would-be crafters of democracy must take into careful consideration the particular mix of nations, cultures, and awakened political identities present in the territory. Some kinds of democracy are possible with one type of *polis*, but virtually impossible if political élites attempt to build another type of *polis*. Political élites in a multinational territory could initiate "nationalizing policies" that might not violate human rights or the Council of Europe's norms for democracy, but would have the effect, in each of the five arenas of polity, of greatly diminishing the chances of democratic consolidation.

An example of such "nationalizing policies" in each of five arenas would be the following. In the arena of civil society, schooling and mass media could be restricted to the official language. In the arena of political society, nationalizing citizenship laws could lead to a significant overrepresentation of the dominant nationality in elected offices. In the arena of the rule of law, the legal system could subtly privilege a whole range of nationalizing customs, practices, and institutions. In the arena of the state bureaucracy, a rapid changeover to one official language could decrease other nationalities' participation in, and access to, state services. Finally, in the arena of economic society, the titular nationality, as the presumed "owners" of the nation-state, could be given special or even exclusive rights to land redistribution (or voucher distribution, if there was privatization). In contrast, if the real goal is democratic consolidation, a democratizing strategy would require less majoritarian and more consensual policies in each of the above arenas.

A final point to stress concerns timing. Potentially difficult democratic outcomes may be achievable only if some pre-emptive policies and decisions are argued for, negotiated, and implemented by political leaders. If the opportunity for such ameliorative policies is lost, the range of available space for manoeuvre will be narrowed, and a dynamic of societal conflict will be likely to intensify until democratic consolidation becomes increasingly difficult, and eventually impossible.

Democracy and the quality of life

While we believe that it is a good thing for democracies to be consolidated, we should make it clear that consolidation does not necessarily entail either a high-quality democracy or a high-quality society. Democratic institutions – however important – are only one set of public institutions affecting citizens' lives. The courts, the central bank, the police, the armed forces, certain independent regulatory agencies, public-service agencies, and public hospitals are not governed democratically, and their officials are not elected by the citizens. Even in established democracies, not all of these institutions are controlled by elected officials, although many are overseen by them.

These institutions operate, however, in a legal framework created by elected bodies and thereby derive their authority from them.

In view of all this, the quality of public life is in great measure a reflection not simply of the democratic or non-democratic character of the regime but of the quality of those other institutions. Policy decisions by democratic governments and legislators certainly affect the quality of life, particularly in the long run, but no democracy can ensure the presence of reputable bankers, entrepreneurs with initiative, physicians devoted to their patients, competent professors, creative scholars and artists, or even honest judges. The overall quality of a society is only in small part a function of democracy (or, for that matter, a function of non-democratic regimes). Yet all those dimensions of society affect the satisfaction of its citizens, including their satisfaction with the government and even with democracy itself. The feeling that democracy is to blame for all sorts of other problems is likely to be particularly acute in societies in which the distinctive contributions of democracy to the quality of life are not well understood and perhaps not highly valued. The more that democrats suggest that the achievement of democratic politics will bring the attainment of all those other goods, the greater will be the eventual disenchantment.

There are problems specific to the functioning of the state, and particularly to democratic institutions and political processes, that allow us to speak of the quality of democracy separately from the quality of society. Our assumption is that the quality of democracy can contribute positively or negatively to the quality of society, but that the two should not be confused. We, as scholars, should, in our research, explore both dimensions of the overall quality of life.

Notes

1. See Robert A. Dahl, *Polyarchy: Participation and Opposition* (New Haven: Yale University Press, 1971), p. 3.
2. For military prerogatives, see Alfred Stepan, *Rethinking Military Politics: Brazil and the Southern Cone* (Princeton: Princeton University Press, 1988), pp. 68–127. For the electoralist fallacy in Central America, see Terry Lynn Karl, "The Hybrid Regimes of Central America," *Journal of Democracy* July 1995; 6: 72–86. Dahl, in his *Polyarchy*, has an eighth institutional guarantee, which does not address elections as such, but rather the requirement that "[Institutions] for making government policies [should] depend on votes and other expressions of preference," (p. 3). This addresses our concerns about reserve domains.
3. Some readers have accused our work – and other studies of democratic transition and consolidation – of being teleological. If this means advocating a single end-state democracy, we decidedly do not share such a view. If, however, teleological means (as the *Oxford English*

Dictionary says) "a view that developments are due to the purpose or design that is served by them," our analysis is in part teleological, for we do not believe that structural factors *per se* lead to democracy and its consolidation. Social actors (and, in some measure, particular leaders) must also act purposefully to achieve a change of regime leading to some form of governing that can be considered democratic. The design of democracy that these actors pursue may differ from the one resulting from their actions but, without action whose intent is to create "a" democracy (rather than the particular institutionalized form that results), a transition to – and consolidation of – democracy are difficult to conceive. The processes that we are studying do, therefore, involve a "teleological" element that does not exclude important structural factors (or many unpredictable events). In addition, there is not a single motive but a variety of motives for pursuing democracy, as we define it, as a goal.

4. For further discussions about the concept of democratic consolidation, see Scott Mainwaring, Guillermo O'Donnell, and J. Samuel Valenzuela (eds) *Issues in Democratic Consolidation: The New South American Democracies in Comparative Perspective* (Notre Dame: University of Notre Dame Press, 1992).

5. In essence, this means that the literature on democratic breakdown, such as that found in Juan J. Linz and Alfred Stepan (eds) *The Breakdown of Democratic Regimes* (Baltimore: Johns Hopkins University Press, 1978), would be much more directly relevant to analysing such a phenomenon than this essay or related books on democratic transition and consolidation. This is not a criticism of the transition literature; rather, our point is that the democratic-transition and democratic-breakdown literature needs to be integrated into the overall literature on modern democratic theory. From the perspective of such an integrated theory, the "breakdown of a consolidated democracy" is not an oxymoron.

6. On the relationships between constitutionalism, democracy, legal culture, and "self-bindingness," see Jon Elster and Rune Slagstad (eds) *Constitutionalism and Democracy* (Cambridge: Cambridge University Press, 1988), pp. 1–18.

7. Robert A. Dahl, in a similar argument, talks about two arrows of causation that produce this result; see his "Why All Democratic Countries Have Mixed Economies," in John Chapman and Ian Shapiro (eds) *Democratic Community, Nomos XXXV* (New York: New York University Press, 1993), pp. 259–282.

8. See, for example, John R. Freeman, *Democracies and Market: The Politics of Mixed Economies* (Ithaca, N.Y.: Cornell University Press, 1989).

9. For an excellent analysis of inevitable market failures, see Peter Murrell, "Can Neoclassical Economics Underpin the Reform of Centrally Planned Economies?" *Journal of Economic Perspectives* 1991; 5: 59–76.

10. Adam Smith, *The Wealth of Nations* (London: J.M. Dent and Sons, Everyman's Library, 1910), Vol. 2, pp. 180–181.

11. Robert A. Dahl's line of reasoning follows a similar development. See his "Why All Democratic Countries Have Mixed Economies," op. cit. pp. 259–282.

12. In post-communist Europe, the Czech Republic and Hungary are well on the way to becoming institutionalized economic societies. In sharp contrast, in Ukraine and Russia the writ of the state does not extend far enough for us to speak of an economic society. The consequences of the lack of an economic society are manifest everywhere. For example, Russia, with a population 15 times larger than that of Hungary and with vastly more raw materials, received only 3.6×10^9 US\$ of direct foreign investment in 1992–93, whereas Hungary received 9×10^9 US\$ of direct foreign investment in the same two years.

13. See Roger Brubaker's "National Minorities, Nationalizing States, and External National Homelands in the New Europe," *Daedalus* Spring 1995: 124: 107–132.

14. See, for example, the outstanding monograph by Eugen Weber, *Peasants into Frenchmen: The Modernization of Rural France, 1870–1914* (Stanford: Stanford University Press, 1976), which analyses in extensive detail the wide repertoire of nation-state mandated policies in the schools, the civil service, and the military that were systematically designed to repress

and eliminate multilingualism and multiculturalism and to create a nation-state. From today's perspective, similar endeavours of modern states appear far from admirable and represent a cost that many of us would not like to pay. However, it is not just a question of how we evaluate such efforts of state-based nation-building, but of how feasible these efforts are in the contemporary context.

15. See Ernest Gellner, *Nations and Nationalism* (Ithaca, N.Y.: Cornell University Press, 1983), p. 44.

16. This conjecture is developed by Gellner in *Nations and Nationalism*, op. cit, pp. 44–45.

17. See the excellent, and sobering, book by Anatol Lieven, *The Baltic Revolution: Estonia, Latvia, Lithuania and the Path to Independence* (New Haven: Yale University Press, 1993), p. 434.

18. For David Laitin's analysis of what he calls a "migrant competitive-assimilation game" in Catalonia and his analysis of a possible "colonial-settler game" in the Central Asian republics of the former Soviet Union, see his "The Four Nationality Games and Soviet Politics," *Journal of Soviet Nationalities* Spring 1991; 2: 1–37.

19. See Arend Liphart's seminal article "Consociational Democracy," *World Politics* January 1969; 21: 207–225.

20. For the argument that some notion of group rights is, in fact, necessary to the very definition of individual rights and necessary to the advancement of universal norms in rights, see the work by the Oxford philosopher Joseph Raz, *The Morality of Freedom* (Oxford: Oxford University Press, 1986), pp. 165–217. Also see Will Kymlicka, *Multicultural Citizenship: A Liberal Theory of Minority Rights* (Oxford: Oxford University Press, 1995), pp. 107–130.

21. We develop this point in greater detail in our "Political Identities and Electoral Sequences: Spain, the Soviet Union and Yugoslavia," *Daedalus* Spring 1992; 121: 123–139; and in our *Problems of Democratic Transition and Consolidation* in the chapters on Spain, on "stateness" in the USSR, and on Russian speakers' changing identities in Estonia and Latvia.

22. In our *Problems of Democratic Transition and Consolidation*, we show how in Catalonia in 1982, when respondents were given the opportunity to self-locate their identities on a questionnaire offering the following five possibilities – "Spanish," "more Spanish than Catalan," "equally Spanish and Catalan," "more Catalan than Spanish," or "Catalan" – the most-chosen category, among respondents with both parents born in Catalonia, as well as among respondents with neither parent born in Catalonia, was the multiple and complementary category "equally Spanish and Catalan." We also show how identities in Catalonia were becoming more polarized and conflict ridden before democratic devolution.

Democracy and
social framework

5

Democracy and constitutionalism

Jean Blondel

The question of the relationship between democracy and constitutionalism has raised many controversies – indeed, almost as many as the parallel problem of the relationship between equality and liberty. The two sets of concepts seem to belong to a common family: they are both concerned with attempts to give answers to the question of the relationship between the bottom and the top, between the ruled and the rulers. On democracy and constitutionalism, viewpoints have varied between two extremes: on the one hand, noted constitutional lawyers such as Ely and Holmes have claimed that the two concepts were close to each other and perhaps indissolubly linked. Ely stated, to quote S. Holmes, that "constitutional restraints, far from being systematically anti-democratic, can be democracy reinforcing."[1] Meanwhile, S. Holmes, having examined the views of Hayek and Shapiro, says that democrats and constitutionalists should be regarded as mutually supportive. Others, on the contrary (including many of the "classics" such as Rousseau, Paine, or Jefferson), have felt that the two concepts were fundamentally opposed. They believed that they were incompatible because they regarded constitutionalism as a means for the dead to control the living. S. Holmes notes, for instance, that Jefferson stressed that "the earth belongs to the living and not to the dead." The conclusion which is drawn is therefore that constitutionalism is undemocratic.

The marked difference between constitutionalism and democracy is epitomized historically by the manner in which, during a large part of the nineteenth century, most members of the "better classes" tended to consider democracy as "mob rule" that rendered "civilized" government impossible, while, on the contrary, constitutionalism was deemed to achieve orderly and just government. Democracy had a negative connotation, rather like anarchy: it conjured up visions of uneducated masses storming the fashionable houses of the enlightened middle classes. This view continued to be widely held throughout Europe up to the latter part of the nineteenth century; even in the United States, similar views had been broadly held, at least at the time the constitution was drafted.

One does not need to go as far back, however: in the post-Second World War period, constitutionalism was often attacked by leaders of the third world as being an obstacle on the road to democracy. These, as well as Communist rulers, may have had occasionally to pay lip service to constitutionalism but they reduced and, in some cases, wholly undermined such constitutional bodies as legislatures and courts, on the alleged ground that these had the effect of perpetuating the privileges of the ruling classes of the past. As a result, in large parts of the third world, constitutionalism was in disrepute and was labelled as a mere Western "invention" designed to maintain imperialism. In the West, on the contrary, the prevailing sentiment was that the two concepts reinforced each other. For decades after the Second World War, both sides remained on these positions, with little scope for the development of a common understanding.

A middle course was occasionally proposed, which was embodied in the expression "constitutional democracy." This meant that in some cases democracy might be "constitutional" while in others it might not be: there could be democracy without constitutionalism; there could also be constitutionalism without democracy, as had manifestly been the case in some countries of Western Europe in the first half of the nineteenth century. Such a view was held by Friedrich, who gave the title of *Constitutional Government and Democracy* to the second edition of his comparative government text published in 1942.[2] In that conception, there is merely an area of intersection between the two concepts; no less, but also no more. Such a suggestion does not go to the heart of the problem, however: the question of the nature of the link between the two concepts continues to arise. Not surprisingly, those firmly committed to there being a close link were not likely to be satisfied.

Suddenly, after decades of difficulties, the controversy seems to be over: with the fall of the Berlin Wall and the end of communism in Europe (in turn following the collapse of dictatorships in Southern Europe in the 1970s and, in the 1980s, the end of military rule and other forms of authoritarianism in most of Latin America, in parts of Black Africa, and in some Asian states), constitutionalism and democracy appear to go hand in hand. The end of communism in Europe played a central role in this process, as communist leaders had been among those who had led the attack against the "bourgeois" values which were held to be embodied by the constitutionalism of the West. Given that military regimes and socialism had come to be very widely regarded as tragic mistakes and that, in general, authoritarian regimes seemed to have little to commend themselves, constitutionalism, however "old-fashioned" and "bourgeois," began to be viewed as an improvement. Its benefits came to be recognized as universal and not limited to some types of societies. Constitutionalism may have produced Western "bourgeois" democracy, but the balance sheet of "bourgeois" democracy appeared rather positive in comparison with that of other regimes. Indeed, the notion that Western democracy had to be qualified as "bourgeois" ceased to prevail as a result of the demise of "proletarian" or "popular" democracy. It seemed more reasonable to conclude that constitutionalism helped to bring about – or perhaps even to characterize – democracy *tout court*.

When regimes tumble in the context of the collapse of an entire idcology, the pendulum often swings sharply – indeed, too sharply. The difficulties under which the victorious regimes operate are, for a time, forgotten; in such a context, these regimes cease to be assessed realistically. This is, to an extent, what occurred in the 1990s. Such enthusiasm is a welcome breath of fresh air, but it must not be allowed to dominate thinking and to obscure the fact that the problems which existed in the past continue to exist. Since democracy and constitutionalism have been viewed as distinct, as antagonistic, perhaps as incompatible, well before communism appeared on the scene, the reasons for this antagonism need to be explored. The problems which are posed by the opposition between the two concepts do not depend on whether "real socialism," communism, or military regimes are in existence or not.

The distinction between constitutionalism and democracy cannot be given here the full treatment it deserves, but we can at least consider the three planes on which this distinction arises and must be analysed. The first plane is that of the fundamental difference about "human nature in politics" between supporters of constitutionalism and democrats, the first holding a pessimistic and the second an optimistic standpoint about social relations. The second plane is that of the goals to which priority is to be given: is the major emphasis to be placed on establishing and maintaining rules or are the key questions who holds and who should hold power? Finally, the third plane relates to the nature of the bond which is felt to exist between the members of the society: is society exclusively composed of individuals living side by side or is there also a "communitarian" element which goes beyond – and occasionally against – what the members of the society may desire as individuals?

Human nature in politics

Perhaps the most obvious way in which democracy and constitutionalism differ from each other stems from a sharp contrast between the manifest pessimism about human nature of constitutionalists and the equally basic optimism of the supporters of democracy. Such a contrast was particularly marked in the past but it continues to constitute a major source of distinction. It was, indeed, pessimism about human nature in politics which accounted for the fact that constitutionalism was used to attempt to stop the spread of democracy. Indeed, in the United States, the arrangements devised in the 1787 constitution were in part designed as a means to control the masses, especially the ignorant masses. Although the American polity was founded on the basis of a broadly optimistic standpoint, this optimism was not sufficiently widespread to lead to a fully democratic order at the outset. Many held the views expressed in the Federalist papers, which clearly stated that government had to be limited to avoid the dangers which might otherwise result from majority rule. The indirect election of the president and of the senate were part of this plan; the separation of powers was to ensure that the tyranny of the few would become impossible, but it also provided a barrier against the possible tyranny of the many. Constitutionalism was thus elaborated and implemented in order to limit the power of both monarchs and people, not to bring about democracy and broadly based participation.

Democracy, on the contrary, is based on an optimistic view. It makes no sense to support democracy unless one feels that all human beings – at least, those above a certain age – are able to make intelligent use of political power. The eventual result of popular involvement, balanced against any possible negative consequences, is in benefiting the polity. For "true" democrats, society has to be opened up, as social problems result from the state of subservience in which most human beings find themselves. Once liberated from this subservience, individuals will work for the common good. Thus, to return to the contemporary scene, it is not sufficient to accept democracy because it is no longer practically possible to avoid universal suffrage and a degree of popular participation. Such a view still constitutes a pessimistic standpoint, as it amounts to stating that, a dose of democracy being inevitable, it is better to cut one's losses and try to prevent the worst which might occur. "True" democrats hold the different and markedly more positive view that the participation of all will enhance the quality of life in the polity and render citizens both better and happier.

Thus, constitutionalism and democracy correspond to profoundly distinct approaches. They are not distinct merely because the former started in the oligarchical context of late eighteenth century Europe and North America; they are distinct because they are rooted in differing views of humankind. Contrary to the somewhat restricted ideal of limited government propounded by constitutionalists, supporters of democracy propound the more expansive ideal of a participatory polity whose members share a common destiny.

This has a natural corollary. To achieve limited government, constitutionalism has to focus on protection. The "vital elements" of political and social life might be in jeopardy if full democracy is installed, as everything would become subject to challenge. Mechanisms must therefore be devised to ensure that these "vital elements" are as close to being untouchable as possible and are protected for ever. The way in which this protection is achieved is by entrenching the "vital elements" in the constitutional document and thus ensuring that change cannot take place without going through complex procedures. Other instruments, such as laws and regulations, also play a part in the defence of what has been set up. This protection of the "vital elements" of social and political life means that constitutionalism is mainly turned towards the past, especially towards those glorious moments during which the constitution was drafted. The past has, therefore, a hold on the present. "Pre-commitment" is inevitable: it is the very essence of constitutionalism.

While constitutionalism turns towards the past to regulate the present, democracy, on the contrary, is concerned with *promotion* and looks at the future as an open book in which improvements are gradually made. In theory, at least, the past must not be allowed to commit the present. Moreover, if there is to be improvement, this is because there can be progress; and, if there is to be progress, it is based on the belief that democracy will unfold gradually. Democracy cannot be established instantly; indeed, it is not likely to be quickly, or even easily, established. There may be strong opposition on the part of those who monopolize power or as a result of the low material and educational attainments of many citizens – largely, in turn, because the society has kept them in a state of ignorance. Such a situation has to be redressed and it can be redressed if consistent efforts are made in the right direction.

The belief that the polity is in a continuous process of development constitutes a further major difference between the basic tenets of democracy and the basic tenets of constitutionalism. Because the concept of constitutionalism links the present to the past, it tends to be "declarative" and static: the people saw the light at one very special moment; the constitution was drawn and, as the "Tables of the Law," it must be followed for ever. On the contrary, because democracy is to be promoted and therefore inevitably looks to the future and at the conditions under which it will operate in the future, change and progress are central to the democratic ideal; in truth, democracy is based on a dynamic vision. Constitutionalism and democracy thus represent radically contrasting approaches to politics and society.

This is not the whole story, however, at present in particular. In the course of the twentieth century, an interaction began to take place between constitutionalism and democracy. This occurred because the very idea of democracy came to be attacked or, more insidiously, profoundly undermined from inside by rulers who claimed that they wished to install popular participation but found ways of stealing this power for themselves. In such a context, democracy came to need protection; constitutionalism could offer such protection. Meanwhile, with the passing of time, constitutionalists came to accept a number of democratic principles – especially the idea of universal suffrage – and their opposition to democracy declined. They realized, first, that democracy could be "tamed," so to speak, and did not necessarily mean "mob rule" after all. They then began to see that democracy could be an important – even an essential – part of the justification of constitutionalism. In an age ·in which the virtues of the "common man" (and woman) were extolled, it was becoming clear that constitutionalism was relevant only if it, too, endorsed democratic principles; indeed, constitutionalism could discover a new mission for itself by protecting democracy against those who tried to subvert it. To an extent, therefore, constitutionalism has had to incorporate democratic elements in order to remain acceptable, while democracy, too, has needed constitutionalism to "survive." A compromise has been struck and a *modus vivendi* has been found. This does not mean fusion between the two concepts, however; only an alliance has been forged.

Process versus substance

There is clearly a profound unease – perhaps even suspicion – in the relationship between constitutionalism and democracy, because of diametrically opposed views about human nature in politics: this unease is prolonged at a more practical level as well. Constitutionalism is primarily a juridical concept; democracy is a social and political concept. Since it is essentially juridical in character, constitutionalism is principally concerned with rules, with procedures, and with process; since it is fundamentally a social and political concept, democracy's concern is with the distribution of power, and, first and foremost, with the distribution of political power in society.

As constitutionalism is mainly directed towards protecting, it is essentially interested in an overall endeavour to ensure that decisions are taken and implemented on the basis of regular arrangements. These arrangements, naturally, must be decided in advance of their introduction; hence, the fact that two of the main tenets of constitutionalism are the rule of law and the existence of a hierarchy of rules. There cannot be protection unless "inferior" rules are drafted in conformity with "superior" ones, the whole edifice being ultimately based on the constitution. On the other hand, the content of these rules is not primarily of concern to constitutionalists; what is crucial to them is the manner in which they are elaborated. Constitutionalism has, therefore, been able to support – or even propound – rules which are constitutionally valid but are undemocratic in content. In nineteenth century Europe, most constitutions sharply restricted the right to vote while constitutional rules which Friedrich described as "monarchical" also gave major powers – of veto, for instance – to monarchs who were not democratically elected. Several Latin American constitutions have markedly restricted the right to vote in a perfectly "constitutional" manner up to the last decades of the twentieth century. Most restrictive of all, the harsh rules under which apartheid was organized in South Africa did not necessarily violate constitutionalist principles; if they may be regarded as being close to having done so, this is more because they were arbitrary in much of their implementation rather than because they limited the citizenry to a minority.

In a general manner, the philosophy behind constitutionalism can be described as being associated with the concept of "good government": it is a government which abides by the rules on the basis of which it has been organized. At the limit, constitutional rule can merely be government *for* the people and not government *by* the people, a government which is regarded as "civilized" because it is based on the rule of law and on "rational," Weberian, principles. While some of the forms which such rule might take may well be regarded as being constitutional in name rather than in spirit, they can be praised by some constitutionalists as helping the social and economic development of the country concerned and even, perhaps, its political development. These views stretch the concept of constitutionalism to its most undemocratic limit, to be sure, but they do not abandon it altogether.

It is valuable to stress the "rational" directions in which constitutionalism may go in order to contrast more sharply these directions with those of democratic government. Democratic government is not primarily concerned with rules, even at the limit with legalism, let alone with efficiency of administration: it is concerned with the distribution of political power and with achieving a more equal distribution of that power. The goal is to ensure that "the people" be brought "back in." This means changing the substance of the political process in two ways, one being more formal than the other. In the first instance, there must be formal political equality, the most obvious step being universal suffrage, but there must also be a degree of social and even economic equality. While one can, and should, distinguish political democracy from social and economic democracy, the socio-economic conditions in which the population lives must be such that it is possible for that population to exercise political rights meaningfully in a democracy; hence, the importance given to education as a key underpinning.

Political democracy also involves a substantial amount of participation on the part of the population. It cannot be limited exclusively to the introduction of universal suffrage and to the right to vote at elections. This right must be accompanied by others and by concrete facilities designed to give the people the opportunity to be involved in discussing, criticizing, and opposing the government. There can be – and there have been – many disagreements among supporters of democracy as to what should be the limits and levels of participation, but there can be no doubt about its importance if a society is to be democratic.

Given such contrasts over the fundamental goals and over the practices, what brings constitutionalism and democracy closer to each other in the life of many contemporary governments? Such a *rapprochement* results from the realization, on both sides, that practical necessities make it currently very difficult, if not impossible, to achieve one of the goals without adopting at least some elements of the other.

There are two principal reasons why supporters of democracy have had to recognize the positive part which constitutionalism can play. First, experience – often, bitter experience – has made democrats realize that democracy has to be protected and, furthermore, that it is probably not possible to build democracy in the context of a political system which is not constitutional. Democracy does not merely need protection, it needs established institutions; as a result, it also needs rules. The idea that democracy does not entail any kind of "precommitment" is not only unrealistic, it is wrong. As S. Holmes states: "A collectivity cannot have coherent practices apart from all decision-making procedures."[3] Building democracy outside a constitutional framework is, at the limit, impossible, as S. Holmes also observes that "It is meaningless to speak about popular government apart from some sort of legal framework which enables the electorate to have a coherent will ... Formulated somewhat facetiously: without tying their own hands, the people will have no hands."[4]

Second, perhaps even more importantly from a substantive standpoint, constitutionalism has a more positive value for democracy, as it enables citizens to acquire a sense of "autonomy." Only constitutionalism can do so, because, while limiting the powers of government, it is the one form of political system that gives human rights real importance. The limitations on government are introduced in order to enable human beings to fulfil their destiny. Democracy needs autonomous citizens. In his analysis, *Constitutional Domains*, R.C. Post states: "We could not plausibly characterise as democratic a society in which 'the people' were given the power to determine the nature of their government, but in which the individuals who made up 'the people' did not experience themselves as free to choose their own political fate."[5] He adds: "The essential problematic of democracy thus lies in the reconciliation of individual and collective autonomy."[6]

Democracy cannot truly exist if relationships are heteronomous. This is, indeed, why we are, rightly, quick to denounce as a sham a regime in which the relationships between the political "class" and the bulk of the population are essentially clientelistic. That clientelism cannot ever be wholly eradicated is highly probable; that there is a substantial dose of clientelism in "advanced democracies" is also very likely. Yet clientelism has also been declining in these democracies and this decline has meant that the autonomy of citizens has increased. Half a century ago, Piaget noted the uniqueness of democracy in this respect: "The essence of democracy resides in its attitude towards law as a product of collective will and not as something emanating from a transcendent will or from the authority established by divine right."[7]

To ensure that the autonomy of citizens is maintained, democracy needs to be buttressed. Typically, this must be done by somewhat artificial means, as the autonomy of citizens does not exist naturally in a polity, especially if it is large and complex. This is achieved by introducing safeguards aimed at combating the tendency of the few to establish their authority over the many, whether these few are the central government or local landlords, whether they are a technocratic élite or a local party establishment. Constitutionalism is the mechanism by which these attempts at "controlling" the people can be overcome. The experience of much of the third world since independence has shown that, indeed, the autonomy of citizens does not develop spontaneously and that it is repressed in a context in which there is little respect for constitutionalism. Thus, democracy typically needs constitutionalism to be established and maintained, as it needs constitutionalism to establish the autonomy of citizens. In this way, constitutionalism becomes part of the fabric of democracy. A Latin American scholar, J. Faundez, rejoices in noting that there is currently a "timely revival of constitutionalism."[8] Democracy may need a socio-economic base which constitutionalism cannot give, but it also needs a political base that only constitutionalism seems able to provide.

On the other hand, constitutionalism has come to need democracy and to recognize this need. The point has been seen particularly in the United States, as Post noted: "American constitutional law is exceptional in the intensity of its commitment to the social order of democracy."[9] Yet, while American constitutionalism is more intensely democratic than constitutionalism elsewhere, constitutionalism elsewhere recognizes – or has come to recognize – that it does need democracy.

By doing so, constitutionalism has gradually modified its basic premise: instead of being exclusively concerned with process, it has begun to be involved to an extent with substance. Thus A. A. Boron can state that we are now witnessing the existence of a "mixed constitutionalist corpus."[10] According to this, constitutionalism comes to be committed to "the social order of democracy"; this means taking on board at least part of the substance of the laws and of the rights which constitutionalism defends, and defending the substance together with the process according to which these laws are elaborated. In a sense, it could be argued that this has always been the case, merely because "pure process" does not exist and one always has to look at the substance when one judges whether a rule or regulation conforms to constitutional principles. There are no principles which are so "disembodied" that they bear no relationship at all with the concrete reality.

There have been attacks from both sides. The "traditionalists" wish constitutionalism to be pure and to remain on the plane of form and process; the "critical legal theorists" are opposed to these moves on the ground that rights achieve little on their own. Thus, the ground for an "understanding" between constitutionalists and supporters of democracy remains shaky. The common "domain" remains somewhat limited and it is continuously subjected to contention. This uneasy relationship is inevitable, given the basic contrast which still remains valid – namely, that constitutionalism is ultimately based on legal instruments while democracy has to be concerned primarily with the organization of political power.

Is society merely a collection of individuals?

The greatest problem posed by the relationship between constitutionalism and democracy is probably on the third plane: it results from profound differences with respect to the nature of society. Constitutionalism is connected to an individualistic conception of society: constitutions protect and defend individuals against encroachments; this is, indeed, why they can foster individual autonomy. The democratic ideal is not as clearly and as exclusively related to individualism as it also has a communitarian dimension. There is, admittedly, ambiguity and, perhaps, conflict among democrats on this subject. Occasionally, the communitarian aspect is given great stress; occasionally, on the contrary, the main stress is placed on an individual. The collective conception suffered a major setback with the fall of the Soviet Union and the end of communism in Europe, which appeared to be a facade for dictatorship. Yet the collective conception has not been eliminated altogether, not merely because it is part of a long tradition, starting from Rousseau at least, but also because it is the expression of the point that democracy in a group must result in the coming together of the views – and, indeed, the minds – of the members of the group.

There has at least to be a dialogue between the individualistic and collective conceptions of democracy; constitutionalism has great difficulty in entering this dialogue, however. Post distinguishes community from democracy. He states:

Three forms of social order are especially relevant to understanding our constitutional laws. I call these community, management, and democracy. To put the matter briefly and aphoristically, one might say that law creates community when it seeks authoritatively to interpret and enforce shared mores and norms; it is managerial when it organises social life instrumentally to achieve specific objectives; and it fosters democracy by establishing social arrangements that carry for us the meaning of collective self-determination.[9]

He thus suggests that what he calls "community" is an alternative to democracy, not part of it. Community is a domain of the law and, presumably, of constitutions, but a domain that is concerned with enforcement. This suggests that Post does not accept that democracy could manifest itself through shared mores and norms, perhaps because this would be an example of "heteremony" – an outside set of values would be imposed on the citizen from above.

Yet this conception of shared values and norms is one-sided: "community" and "communitarianism" are not imposed from above only; mores and norms can be voluntarily adhered to in a society in which citizens are concerned with the "general will." It might be argued that such a view of the general will at best is a utopia and at worst is more likely to be in the realm of propaganda than in that of the reality of modern societies. However, two points need to be noted. The first is that many wish to see democratic order established on the basis of these principles: they may be "unrealistic" about the probability that such principles will prevail, but the fact that this conception of democracy exists in the minds of many citizens makes it relevant. What needs to be understood is why there is such a yearning among many democrats for a communitarian ideal and that the desire to implement the communitarian ideal is real, although it is probably more real in some societies than in others. Secondly, while a fully communitarian conception of democracy may be a "brave new world" or may indeed be "totalitarian," to use Talmon's expression, there are in practice partial versions of this formula in the reality of democratic life. Indeed, one might even claim that every society which is democratic embraces at least some fragments of the communitarian version in common goals and commonly held values.

This means that, in reality, the two conceptions – individualistic and collective – are not antinomic: they are not two opposed views which exclude each other. The collectivist communitarian and the wholly individualistic pole do not correspond to any existing polity; societies are located in intermediate positions in which trade-offs occur between these extreme standpoints. The reason why the extreme individualistic position is not adopted is that, while a wholly collective position may be totalitarian, a wholly individualistic position would result in a wholly atomized society with nothing to cement citizens together. At best, such a form of democracy would be purely negative: those who would benefit from the arrangements would be those who would, for a variety of reasons, best understand and best "play the system." More deeply, moreover, a purely individualistic position also depends on a commonly held standpoint. Yet there will always be those who will not accept fully the individualistic standpoint, and it has then to be imposed on these citizens. Others will have to accept the standpoint as a result of their socialization; this means that there will be rules which did not emerge autonomously. An individualistic conception of society is thus based on an ideology: it cannot be said to stem "naturally" from the experience of most citizens; the experience which these have had is more likely to have been communitarian, be it in the family, club, or workplace.

The fact that the individualistic conception of democracy is based on an ideology explains why this conception has been attacked as being "Western" rather than universal. It explains in particular why it has been criticized as being part of an attempt by the West to impose its values upon the rest of the world. Such an interpretation is almost certainly incorrect and at least highly exaggerated. The individualistic conception of society may prevail more in the West than elsewhere, but it is also "imposed" to an extent in the West as well. On the other hand, both Westerners and non-Westerners might have differing views concerning what democracy should be and, in particular, as to whether it should be more individualistic or more communitarian than it is. What is probably true is merely that individualistic views of democracy are more common in the West, where they originated, and communitarian views of democracy are more common elsewhere, as what is felt to be at stake is the defence of cultures that are also felt to be threatened. The 1990s are probably not a typical period to assess the relative strength of individualistic and communitarian values of democracy, since in the post-Cold War context the individualistic conception has been regarded as paramount. Meanwhile, some leaders of non-Western nations have continued to emphasize a communitarian approach. Yet it is not always clear how genuine the claims made by some rulers are, for instance those made in favour of an Asian form of democracy by a number of South-East Asian leaders or those that have been made along similar lines in sub-Saharan Africa. It is not at all clear that these leaders are followed in their claims by the bulk of the populations whom they rule, although this is not to say that these standpoints are not valuable or important.

Support for the collective conception of democracy may have been somewhat toned down in the 1990s, yet it simmers under the surface. It will surely re-emerge with force in the future, because it is part of the human tradition. It may lead to excesses. If communitarianism dominates, society may indeed be totalitarian: there is no longer autonomy of the citizens, but complete heteronomy. However, there is a great difference between recognizing the dangers inherent in a dominant communitarian conception of democracy and stating that the communitarian conception should be wholly rejected.

The constitutionalist approach to democracy forms an essential ingredient in this debate, although it is only an ingredient. It is an essential ingredient because it provides the individualistic view with intellectual support as well as with legal protection: again, protection is the key contribution which constitutionalism makes to democracy. As democracy entails having at least a dose of individualism, constitutionalism is crucial because it defends this individualism and gives teeth to the defence which it puts forward.

One can go somewhat further and suggest that constitutionalism does not need to be wholly individualistic. This is true even if constitutions and laws are easier to implement when they are used to protect individuals while their vagueness makes them difficult to implement when they are concerned with communities. Some constitutionalists have begun to recognize and to incorporate the view that an individualistic approach to democracy cannot fully encompass all the facets of democracy. Groups exist: in particular, there are ethnic and other minorities which are in need of protection as groups and not merely as collections of individuals. One should not deny that groups have elements in common over and above the sum of the desires of the individuals which compose them at a given moment. To do so would also be to ignore an important part of what constitutes the "quality of life" for large sections of the human race, with possibly serious consequences for the stability and welfare of communities.

Constitutionalism and democracy need each other, but they are profoundly distinct concepts. Their basic aims have been, and remain, different in many respects. The relationship between constitutionalism and democracy has therefore to be viewed as having, first and foremost, a pragmatic character. On the one hand, without constitutionalism, democracy is likely to be impotent because it needs the protection of the law; on the other, constitutionalism without democracy lacks one of its main justifications in the contemporary world at least. Without democracy, support for what constitutionalism represents would vanish. The relationship between the two concepts will therefore continue to be both strong and ambiguous.

Although they are currently mostly silent, those among the supporters of democracy who used to discredit constitutionalism still have grounds for stressing the distinction between the two concepts; they will no doubt persist in attempting to drive a wedge between them. Meanwhile, those who prefer constitutionalism (whether with, or at the limit without, democracy) can find a seemingly valid antidote by stressing the need for rationality – a rationality which has to be based entirely on individuals if it is to exist.

For the two concepts to be harnessed together for the common good, supporters of democracy must recognize that constitutionalism has to be continuously part of their agenda because it brings about protection and meaningfulness; it must not be rejected or reduced in scope on the grounds that it is exclusively procedural and that it is therefore only a technique. At the same time, supporters of constitutionalism must have the modesty to recognize that democracy is a great adventure – indeed, that it is *the* great adventure of humankind. They must therefore recognize that democracy transcends constitutions and rules, however sophisticated these may be. Only if both sides are accommodating in this manner can there be some hope that constitutionalism and democracy will continue to act in tandem in the future as they have begun to do in most parts of the world.

Notes

1. J. H. Ely, *Democracy and Distrust* (Cambridge, Mass.: Harvard University Press, 1980), p. 197.
2. C. Friedrich, *Constitutional Government and Democracy* (Boston: Little, Brown, 1941).
3. S. Holmes, "Precommitment and the paradox of democracy," in J. Elster and R. Slagstad (eds) *Constitutionalism and Democracy* (Cambridge: Cambridge University Press, 1988), p. 230.

4. Ibid., p. 231.
5. R.C. Post, *Constitutional Domains* (Cambridge: Mass.: Harvard University Press, 1995).
6. Ibid.
7. J. Piaget, *The Moral Judgment of the Child* (1948), Marjorie Gabain translation, p. 188. Republished, Free Press, 1985.
8. D. Greenberg and Stanley N. Katz (eds) *Constitutionalism and Democracy* (Oxford: Oxford University Press, 1993), pp. 354–360.
9. R.C. Post, op. cit., p. 2.
10. A. A. Boron, in D. Greenberg and Stanley N. Katz (eds) op. cit., p. 349.

Further reading

Bellamy, R., ed. 1996. *Constitutionalism, Democracy and Sovereignty*. Aldershot, Hants: Avebury.

Buchanan, J. M., and G. Tullock. 1962. *The Calculus of Consent*. Ann Arbor, Mich.: University of Michigan Press.

———, and R. E. Wagner, eds. 1978. *Fiscal Responsibility in Constitutional Democracy*. Boston, Mass.: Nijhoff.

Halowell, J. H., ed. 1976. *Prospects for Constitutional Democracy*. Durham, N.C.: Duke University Press.

Preuss, U.K. 1993. *Constitutional Aspects of the Making of Democracy in the Post-communist Societies of Eastern Europe*. WP Bremen.

Schumpeter, J. 1961. *Capitalism, Socialism and Democracy*. London: Allen and Unwin.

6

Mass media and participatory democracy

Elihu Katz

There is an old joke about a wife who reported, with pleasure, that she and her husband had an ideal relationship based on a good division of labour. "My husband," she said, "makes the big decisions, and I make the small ones. He decides things like whether China should be admitted to the United Nations, while I decide such things as where we should live and what schools the children should attend." The story means to imply that the husband is ineffective, delusional, maybe lonely, and compliant. Yet, he is obviously interested in politics and some empirical research might code him politically engaged.

The problem of citizen participation in large-scale democracies is inadequately conceptualized. The agora and the town meeting are metaphors of direct democracy, yet are of little use when applied to modern, complex, large-scale societies. Habermas' conception of the public sphere has had a great vogue but it, too, is little more than an idealized reminder that we have an unsolved problem on our hands. Even in the golden age of the bourgeois public sphere, it is questionable whether newly empowered citizens actually put self-interest aside in order to engage in rational, critical debate over the common weal. We know that such gatherings were exclusionist, but we know very little about the extent of participation, or whether the interaction that did take place was as disinterested, ascetic, or egalitarian as prescribed. Nor do we know enough about the spaces in which these interactions took place, what functions the newspaper fulfilled, how public opinion was formed, how it was aggregated over the myriad discussions, in what form it was conveyed to the powers that be, and what kind of attention it received.

These problems are still with us in the version of the modern representational public sphere which we are said to inhabit, where intrusive government, big business, and the technologies of communication and public opinion all intervene between the citizen and the policy maker. It is facile to speak of electronic town meetings in today's world or to say that public broadcasting is the modern equivalent of bourgeois public space. Indeed, it is downright offensive to hear talk of these possibilities while we are so busy segmenting and privatizing the channels of public communication, and seeing to it that commercial television drives the news out of prime time. In fact, it is appropriate to state at the outset that television, as the locus of nationally shared experience of politics and culture, is dead or dying in most of the Western democracies. Moreover, the number of newspaper readers is on the decline in the West,[1] and so is the number who join or strongly identify with political parties.[2] Increased cynicism is thought to prevail. Robert Entman's *Democracy Without Citizens* provides a good title for the enigma of an allegedly participatory democracy whose members are regularly out of touch with their political institutions.[3]

Approach to media functions and dysfunctions: Introducing G. Tarde

There are a number of ways to approach the functions and effects of mass media in relation to democracy. The least profitable of these approaches, I submit, is the one that concentrates on mass persuasion, on how the media tell us what to think in the short term – who to vote for, for example. More interesting is to look at the ways in which the media tell us what to think in the long term, how they inculcate values, and influence what we take for granted. This is the so-called hegemonic approach, which is thought, intentionally or not, to induce false consciousness in the masses in the interests of the ruling class. A third approach, the liberal or functional one, views the media as a public utility, serving not only individuals but the institutions of the society. A fourth approach is called technological: this looks at how the unique properties of the dominant media – newspaper, radio, television – affect our social and political arrangements.

What follows will combine the latter two of these approaches, the functional and technological, to discuss the media as social organizations that interact with, and serve, the other institutions of democratic politics and as technologies that, I fear, are undermining the very institutions they are serving. This follows the lead of Gabriel de Tarde, French social psychologist and jurist, who proposed a theory of the public sphere long before Habermas and, in my opinion, more realistically. Tarde's essay of 1898, *La Conversation*, written in the throes of the Dreyfus Affair, sought to understand the links among the elements of a participatory democracy, which include a body politic or polity, government, parliament, voluntary associations, media, places of conversation, public opinion, and social action.[4] One hundred years later, scholars are examining Tarde's model of public opinion and mass communication to see if we know any different, or are better informed than he was. There are other political philosophers who were no less wise in their observations than Tarde, but his particular emphasis on the media and public opinion is especially attractive. By reference to Tarde, I will illustrate media functions and dysfunctions.

How media serve democratic institutions

Tarde's functional model concentrates on the nexus among press, conversation, opinion, and action. He argues that the press provides a menu for the myriad everyday conversations that take place in the cafés, coffee-houses, and salons;[5] this is what we have come to call the agenda-setting function of the press, reflecting also the concerns of government and parliament. Tarde proposes that conversation in this sense is a modern phenomenon. Based on norms of open process and equality, conversation is itself a cultivator of equality and, thanks to the press, its subject matter is both uniform throughout the polity and rapidly changing.

Unlike austere Habermassian speech, the rhetoric of Tarde's conversations provides its own pleasures, and slips in and out of politics much more casually. Indeed, for Tarde, political conversation is a less noble form, and a less elegant concern, than conversation about the arts, for example. The political function of conversation, according to Tarde, is to percolate opinion – that is, to refine individual opinion so that it becomes more "considered" and, in ways unspecified, to generate one or two national opinions on a particular subject. Such considered opinion then finds itself once again represented in the pages of the newspaper and constitutes a basis for individual action, which for Tarde – reverting to the role of social psychologist – is essentially the making of political and economic choices, such as choosing a leader or choosing a product.

Thus, Tarde's model not only links press, conversation, opinion, and action systematically, but also points to the ways in which each element propels the next in linear order. It also connects this nexus with government, emphasizing the social control implicit in independent press coverage of an issue and in delivering feedback from public opinion. Tarde implies that everybody talks about politics. He is casual about the problems of opinion aggregation and consensus formation, but that is something we, ourselves, know very little about, except in so far as we allow survey technology to define public opinion. Stated otherwise, if public opinion is the process by which men and women outside government consider that they have the right to communicate with each other about public affairs and the right to express their thoughts to the authorities, then Tarde has dealt in detail with the dynamics of horizontal expression in small groups, less with the dynamics that lead to consensus in the larger society, and least with the vertical process of feedback to government. But that is better than most; indeed, in this sense, Tarde is the forefather of Lazarsfeld's two-step flow of communication that is still holding its own after these 50 years.

Tarde's analysis of the functions of the press altogether fails to address the problematic relationship between journalists and politicians, as Blumer and Gurevitch keep reminding us,[6] although he does assume the independence of the press as a prerequisite to participatory democracy. Important questions about the professional status of journalism arise in this connection. Are journalists professionals, in the classic sense of being specially trained in basic theory and clinical practice that is then applied altruistically to identifying social troubles and addressing them, or are they simply part of a business, or ideology, or a populist art form?

Tarde does not deal at all with current concerns over balance, fairness, and objectivity, for example, which occupies so much of communications research and which, in one way or another, occupies philosophy and all of the sciences as well. Is objectivity possible, it is being asked, and how can minorities be given a voice? Another way of stating the question is: "Who has the right to tell my story?" The performance of the press in representing the distribution of opinion[7] and, indeed, of images of them and us – whether of internal dissent or external enemies – is being called into question.[8] The effects of the presence of the news cameras or the press on social and political action is a related issue. The press is of special importance in the representation of political gesture and political ceremony, such as the moon landings, for example, or the Watergate hearings.[9] Indeed, one of the best functions of a democratic press is to make political process transparent,[10] as well as to teach political norms: that the constitution has made provision for the impeachment of a president, or for succession in case of assassination. Even in the East European revolutions of 1989, the difference between a democratic and a totalitarian heritage could be seen in the behaviour of television in Wenceslas Square – where the tradition of democratic debate and newly re-liberated media was in evidence – and the parallel scenes in Romania, where one junta simply replaced and executed its predecessor on television.

One wonders why journalists have such a poor record in anticipating events – in the Black suburbs of Los Angeles, for example, or in the outbreak of Arab violence in the territories occupied by Israel, or in Eastern Europe in 1989, or in Rwanda. Tarde might have pondered this, although it is certainly not explicit. But social scientists do not have a very proud record in this respect, either. Nor could Tarde have anticipated the changing structure of the communications industry. He did not foresee the monopolizing trends in the newspaper business; or the widespread diffusion of radio, then of television; or of computer-mediated communications, though he did find interest in the telephone. Nor was he sensitive to the genres that are characteristic of the several media and the messages implicit in these narrative and technological forms. One suspects that he would not be surprised, however, by the modern tendency to blur the boundaries between news and entertainment, for the very reason that he saw the press by analogy to conversation – in some ways a continuation of conversation itself – and he posted no such boundaries for conversation.

How the media undermine democratic institutions

Technological considerations in the press and broadcasting have implications for politics and especially for political integration. As a technological theorist, Tarde saw the newspaper as the medium that defined the body politic. Others have similarly remarked that the printed vernacular of the press, together with its portability, create the common linguistic and discursive denominators around which incipient nations can rally in spite of local and regional accents.[11] The press thereby defined the polity, focused all eyes on the centre,[12] and made citizens of the inhabitants. It made them privy to the goings-on in the nation. In this sense, the press is the major operational force in the imagined community which is the nation.[13]

In this process (says Tarde), full of technological determinism, the press overthrew the king. Tarde's king is not Habermas' king, bloated by representational pomp and ceremony. For Tarde, the king's power is based on knowledge of exactly what village A and village B were thinking and doing without them being aware of each other. The king's mind, not only his regalia, defined the state. The press, says Tarde, usurped the king of this function; now village A and village B could see themselves, and each other, in the pages of the newspaper.

In this bold mode, Tarde argues further that the press was no less influential in shaping parliament. Prior to the press, says Tarde, the parliament consisted of representatives of regional and sectoral interests, who did not acknowledge that they had much in common. This segmentation is reflected in the voting pattern whereby each representative had veto power. Majority rule came only as a result of the perception of a common national denominator, says Tarde, which in turn is the result of the sense of nationhood engendered by the press. In other words, the legislature perceived the organic basis of its interdependence and the legitimacy of its corporate decision-making.

Inspired by this technological aspect of Tarde, let us consider the influence on politics of the broadcast media that followed television. We have an equally strong picture of the integrative power of radio. Alluding to John Reith's great social invention, a public medium supported by a quasi-tax but independent both of government and business, scholars describe how early BBC radio "called in" sounds and voices from each of the British regions so that the national holidays could be celebrated *in pluribus unum*.[14] They tell of the annual Christmas message of the King, whose presence at every dining table united the country in common tradition and shared citizenship. These were live broadcasts based on the new technology of *simultaneity*. This is the same simultaneity that allowed American listeners to hear Edward R. Murrow broadcasting the war from London and to panic at the imminent invasion from Mars.

This is also the era of Roosevelt and Hitler. Roosevelt invented the fireside chat, in which he coaxed Americans via radio to accept his New Deal and, later, to agree to enter the war on the side of the Allies. He succeeded in this partly by talking to the people over the heads of Congress, which did not always share his views.[15] This, of course, is also what Hitler did in his strident summons to the German people, having dismissed their parliament and other intermediaries.[16] In the spirit of Tarde, then, we are impelled to ask whether radio – the medium of electronic simultaneity – overthrew parliament in the way that the newspaper overthrew the king. Is this the beginning of the imperial presidency which backfired on Nixon? Is this the beginning of an era of the disintermediation of parliaments by charismatic leaders appealing directly to the people?

There is another aspect to simultaneity that deserves mention in the context of a discussion of the functions of radio: a function, or rather dysfunction, which will be strongly exacerbated by television. This is the illusion of being there, or altogether of being "in" – so much so that one confuses the in-ness and up-to-the-minuteness with actual participation. Thus, in their famous 1948 essay – the classic statement of the modern sociology of mass communication – Lazarsfeld and Merton warn against the "narcotizing dysfunction" of radio news, which certainly may create involvement and a sense of belonging but by no means equals political participation.[17]

Television inherited the task of unifying the polity from its predecessors. Border-to-border broadcasting of soap operas and situation comedies cemented cultural solidarity. New genres, such as the presidential debates on the eve of elections, gave the nation a better look at the candidates.[18] Indeed, the live broadcasting of "historic" events – such as the Coronation of 1952, the Kennedy assassination and funeral, the Olympic Games, the Pope's first visit to Poland – restored a new sense of national belonging, even if they raised the spectre of fascist political spectacle (which they are not) and of the narcotizing dysfunction. These events display television's surprising power to declare a holiday – a time out – in which a whole nation is expected to interrupt its daily routine, turn on the TV set, and commune with some central value, aware that everybody else is performing the same ritual at the same time, just like a holiday.

Television has moved politics – or the illusion of politics – inside. Briggs points out that the early days of television in Britain (1950–1954) saw a 50 per cent drop in attendance at political party meetings.[19] By now, the personality of the leader was ubiquitous, and, often enough, the choice between candidates is simply personal. That personality has superseded ideology, and that grass-roots politics has all but disappeared,[20] suggest that television may have something to do with the undermining of party organization.[21] Party political conventions have lost much of the interest they had in the early days of television, and a desperate effort is being made to salvage them as coronations, even if they have lost their function as nominating contests. Electioneering is done through paid political advertising of a highly personal kind, and mostly on television. In the irreverent spirit of our earlier generalizations – that the newspaper beheaded the king, and that radio disintermediated the parliament – we now propose that television has undermined the political party.[22]

Voluntary associations such as trade unions and political parties are key elements in participatory democracies, as de Tocqueville suggested even before Tarde. Recently, political scientist Robert Putnam has blamed television for the decline that he says he observes in organizational membership in general and, consequently, in the civic trust and social support they engender.

Putnam is just the latest in a long line of academics and publicists who make their living decrying the destructive effects of television. Another of the famous names on this list is Neil Postman: his technological thesis is that television is incapable of, or at least inhospitable to, sustained rational argument. Thus, the elementary requisite of the Habermassian public sphere is undone, according to Postman, who mourns the TV viewers who are "amusing themselves to death."

It is likely that both Putnam and Postman are wrong in their single-mindedness[23] and that, in fact, television both contributes and discontributes to democracy. Nevertheless, research suggests in their favour that television has shortened political statements,[24] has accelerated journalistic coverage of campaign strategies rather than issues,[25] has disconnected parties from candidates,[26] has liberated candidates from party platforms, and has blurred the issue differences between the candidates themselves, as in presidential debates. Targeting everyone and the "undecideds" has a homogenizing effect.

But television is not standing still, either: as with its predecessors, its integrating functions are waning. In part, this is due to the temptation to multiply channels and to privatize them, encouraged by big business and big government – especially Conservative governments, who might have been expected to weigh patriotism and cultural pride against economics. In larger part, it is due to the technology of satellites, cable, and computer communications, which make multiple channels so easy. Indeed, the new media technology is tending in two directions. Individuation or segmentation is one, whereby programming will be so individually tailored that no two people will see the same film at the same time; the other is globalization, whereby the whole world will see the same international blockbusters and the occasional global event. Three implications seem to follow: the first is that television as we knew it – the shared national experience – is well on its way out; the second is that, unlike newspapers and radio, no new medium of national integration is waiting in the wings; the third is that, from the point of view of technological determinism, the nation is walking the plank. Stated otherwise, the teleology of the new media – especially satellite and computer – and the multinational channels that result, point to globalization and individuation, neither of which has much to say about the state. Whether the Internet will define new international polities – or, indeed, diasporas – will not be explored here, but, technically speaking, the lack of fit between media and the body politic is sounding the death knell of the state.

Opposition to the king, the parliament, the political party, and now the state, seems like enough damage for a single chapter on the relationship between mass media and democracy. There remains only one thing to do, and that is to consider a case study of these processes at work.

A case study of the media and Israeli democracy

Radio broadcasting moved out of the Israeli Prime Minister's office in 1965, and became a BBC-like broadcasting authority, with certain unfortunate deviations from the original. Even before 1965, however, a vigorous debate was being conducted in Israel's animated public sphere over the likely merits and demerits of television. The opponents insisted that television would undermine the effort to rebuild a national culture rooted in the Hebrew language, would displace party politics with personality politics, and would encourage materialism; advocates said television would promote national integration and indigenous cultural creativity; of course, both sides were right *and* wrong. As in other countries, imported television soon provided most of the entertainment, but national political integration was certainly enhanced by the 9 p.m. news.[27] Each night, religiously, some two-thirds of the population switched off the telephone, hushed the children, and joined the guests to view and debate the agenda of civic issues proposed by the well-crafted televised newsmagazine. It was also highly credible: Israeli Arabs found it almost as acceptable as Israeli Jews, and it offered a common agenda to hawks and doves for discussion and newspaper commentary the next morning. In short, it came close to the dream of a national town meeting.

But the critics and American experts asked how a democracy could allow itself only one television channel and one "government owned" TV news programme. And then there were two: a second channel and a second news programme, and only stylistic differences between

95

the two. But now, instead of assembling 70 per cent of the population, each channel manages to gather some 18 per cent, for a total of about 35 per cent – about half the number that used to view the news when there was only one channel. The best explanation for the drop seems to be that, if there is a choice of news programmes, one can choose either – or neither – without feeling the civic obligation one previously felt or the need to "prepare" for the next morning's political discussion.

In the meantime there were the 1991 elections, which provide a lot of insight into the role of the media in democracies. The media played a powerful role in determining the outcome of this election, without directly changing anybody's vote. In other words, media influence has more to do with their technologies and the rules of their deployment than with their persuasive power. The rules hark back to the British inheritance, whereby candidates may not appear on the screen for three weeks before the election, that party political broadcasts are the sole form of political advertising on radio and TV (divided in proportion to party strength in the outgoing parliament), and that broadcast journalists are largely neutralized during this period. Of course, these rules interact with the election system which, for the first time in 1996, included party primaries and a two-tier voting pattern – one for the Prime Minister (Peres versus Netanyahu) and a second vote for political parties.

The new election system required that left and right sides of the political spectrum unite around their most promising candidate. In the case of the right, the choice fell to their only obviously televisual candidate. Thus, the two-tier system, plus television, played a large role in the Netanyahu candidacy. Secondly, because of these combined conditions – the direct election for Prime Minister and television – what was expected to be the most ideological elections in Israeli history rapidly became a personality campaign, with both candidates (advised by the usual American experts) looking and sounding more centrist than either ever dreamed to be. In the party political broadcasts and in personal appearances, Netanyahu was a near-dove and Peres a near-hawk, thus confirming the worst fears of those who foresaw that the introduction of television would de-ideologize politics.

Thirdly, television legitimated the candidacy of the hardly known opposition leader. Although he originated from a strong ideological background, Netanyahu himself leap-frogged his way into politics without climbing the party ladder – much as recent American presidents have done in the weakened party climate. The ritual debate (in which Peres had the ostensible advantage) legitimated the Netanyahu candidacy even further, not only by applauding the underdog but by making the two men equal – as television contests are supposed to do – in spite of their unequal credentials.

Fourth, the persistent forecast of a Labour victory by a small margin led the ethnic and religious Arab parties to embark upon last-minute campaigns to mobilize their most remote members. There seems little doubt that the high visibility of the predictions of the most responsible polls in the most widely diffused media, broadcasting and press, made a difference in the turnout of the radical and religious right (as well as the Arab left).

Finally, the media played a role in augmenting the fear appeal of the right. The bus bombings in several cities just weeks before the election more than offset the memory of the Rabin assassination and the hopes of the televised peace ceremonies. By fuelling and refuelling the fear of terror – the major theme of the Netanyahu campaign – television helped defeat the candidate of peace.

It is difficult to avoid taking sides in this matter. The media influence that most researchers are seeking is not where they think it is – in the political advertising, the rhetoric of the candidates, or the jingles. It lurks elsewhere: in the very presence of the media themselves, in the rules which govern them, and in the role assigned them in the design of election campaigns in democratic societies – which leave very much to be desired. Ironically, the first announcement of the new Prime Minister's Government was that it will privatize television, thus to complete the de-politicization – and, perhaps, the internationalization – of the Israeli polity and economy.

Summary: Unanticipated consequences

Alluding to Gabriel Tarde, this chapter has sought to accomplish two things. The nostalgic first part re-examines a theory of the functional contributions of the media to a classical model of participatory democracy: the media survey the goings-on at the centre and the periphery, bringing an agenda of issues to the coffee-house table and stimulating political talk, and thereby generate considered opinion. By reflecting the distribution of opinion, the media exercise influence and control on the establishment in the name of the citizenry. This implies that participatory democracy at the very least requires not only an informed citizenry but an interactive one and, in the Tarde and Speier models, a citizenry that communicates its opinion upwards, directly and indirectly. It also considers various aspects of contemporary relations between media and government that Tarde did not (or could not) anticipate.

The second part of the chapter considers media effects on democratic institutions from the technological point of view. Alluding to Tarde once more, it shows how the newspaper strengthened the national self-consciousness, undermined the power of the king, and caused parliament to consider itself the national decision maker. Applying this approach to the media that succeeded the newspaper, it appears that the technology of radio ultimately weakened the parliament while favouring the national leaders, that television weakened the political party system and grass-roots participation, and that new media – cable, satellite, and computer-mediation – are presently undermining the solidarity of the nation from both within and without.

Thus, by juxtaposing the liberal function approach and technological approach, I am raising the question of whether the mass media have, themselves, contributed to the undermining of their own functions – or, more precisely, whether in the course of fulfilling their functions, they – and their controllers – have subverted the very institutional systems that they were supposed to be serving.

Notes

1. Seymour M. Lipset, "Malaise and Resiliency in America," *Journal of Democracy* July 1995; 6(3).
2. Sidney Verba, Kay Lehman Schlozman, and Henry E. Brady, *Voice and Equality: Civic Voluntarism in American Politics* (Cambridge: Harvard University Press, 1955); Roper Center, *The Public Perspective*, Special Report, 1996.
3. Robert Entman, *Democracy Without Citizens: Media and the Decay of American Politics* (New York: Oxford University Press, 1989).
4. Gabriel Tarde, "Opinion and Conversation," in *L'Opinion et la Foule*, translation by Ruth Morris (Alcan, 1901).
5. Daniel Roche, *The People of Paris* (Berkeley: University of California Press, 1987).
6. Jay G. Blumler and Michael Gurevitch, *The Crisis of Public Communication* (London: Routledge, 1995).
7. Elisabeth Noelle-Neumann, *The Spiral of Silence: Public Opinion, Our Social Skin* (Chicago: University of Chicago Press, 1993).
8. Tamar Liebes and W. Gamson, "Disaster Marathons," in Tamar Liebes, J. Curran, and Elihu Katz (eds) *Media, Ritual, and Identity* (London: Routledge, 1998).
9. Kurt Lang and Gladys Lang, *The Battle for Public Opinion: The President, the Press, and the Polls During Watergate* (New York: Columbia University Press, 1983).
10. Yaron Ezrahi, *The Descent of Icarus: Science and the Transformation of Contemporary Democracy* (Cambridge: Harvard University Press, 1990).
11. Lucien Febvre and Henri-Jean Martin, *The Coming of the Book: The Impact of Printing 1450–1800.* (London: Atlantic Highlands, 1976); Elizabeth Eisenstein, "Some Conjectures

About the Impact of Printing on Western Society and Thought: A Preliminary Report," *Journal of Modern History* 1968; 40(1): Marshall McLuhan, *Understanding Media, the Extension of Man* (New York: McGraw-Hill, 1964).

12. Edward A.Shils, *Center and Periphery: Essays in Macrosociology* (Chicago: University of Chicago Press, 1975).

13. Benedict Anderson, *Imagined Communities: Reflections on the Origin and Spread of Nationalism* (London: Verso, 1983).

14. D. Cardiff and P. Scannel, "Broadcasting and National Unity," in J. Curran, A. Smith and P. Wingate (eds) *Impacts and Influences* (London: Methuen, 1987); Desmond Bell, "Communications, Corporatism, and Dependent Development in Ireland," *Journal of Communication* 1995; 45(4): Also Elihu Katz, "Television Comes to the People of the Book," in Irving Louis Horowitz (ed.) *The Use and Abuse of Social Science* (New Brunswick: Transaction Books, 1971).

15. FDR did this by using radio to "report, review and explain" his New Deal policies; see Edward Chester, *Radio, Television and American Politics* (New York: Sheed and Ward, 1969), p. 33; Elmer Cornwell, *Presidential Leadership of Public Opinion* (Bloomington: Indiana University, 1965), p. 263. These addresses, most of which occurred when Congress was not in session, helped to privilege FDR as the interpreter of the New Deal rather than Congress, and allowed him to build a consensus over time for his programmes that afforded him a measure of political clout when Congress was in session. Perhaps just as important, Roosevelt used radio to go over the heads of Republican newspapers who he felt framed his speeches unfavourably. Indeed, Roosevelt wrote to a friend that he wished "the advent of television could be hastened" to give him more ability to counter adverse press coverage.

16. Although Hitler did not gain control of the radio until becoming Chancellor in January 1933, he used the medium in a single incident that effectively overthrew Parliament. Hitler needed Parliament to approve an Enabling Act granting his cabinet exclusive legislative powers for a four-year period. To do this, he used the ceremony surrounding the opening of the new Reichstag to create a media event heard immediately (on radio) and seen later (in Nazi-controlled press and newsreels). The Potsdam ceremony was rife with Germanic ritual, being held at Bismarck's burial site and in a town that Germans associated with their greatest national triumphs. Hitler made a grand show of genuflecting to Hindenberg, who, flushed with the moment, anointed him with his praise. A week later Parliament granted the Enabling Act and ended the Republic's experiment with democracy; see William Shirer, *The Rise and Fall of the Third Reich* (New York: Simon and Schuster, 1960) and Ian Kershaw, *The Hitler Myth* (Oxford: Clarendon Press, 1987).

17. Paul F. Lazarsfeld and Robert Merton, "Mass Communication, Popular Taste, and Organized Social Action," in Wilbur Schramm (ed.) *Mass Communication* (Urbana: University of Illinois Press, 1948); see also Roderick P. Hart, "Easy Citizenship: Television's Curious Legacy," *The Annals* July 1996; 546.

18. Elihu Katz and Jacob J. Feldman, "The Kennedy–Nixon Debates: A Survey of Surveys," in Sidney Kraus (ed.) *The Great Debates: Background, Perspective, Effects* (Bloomington: Indiana University Press, 1962).

19. Asa Briggs, *The History of Broadcasting in the United Kingdom*, Vols I–IV (Oxford: Oxford University Press, 1979).

20. Mass demonstrations such as abortion rallies in the late 1980s and the Million Man March suggest that, for marginalized groups, television may have actually moved politics *outside*. For example, faced with a mainstream media that refuses to cover them and/or use them as sources, gay and lesbian activists are forced into the streets to garner media attention. If the press will not come to them, they will go to the press. This is the strategy behind demonstrations at the St. Patrick's Day parade in New York City: activists know they can get their message on the air by showing up at an established and routine news event guaranteed to attract cameras.

99

21. Third parties may be an exception. Without television, for example, Ross Perot could never have got onto the public agenda, much less garner 19 per cent of the vote. Of course, he went around the party structure, but on the other hand this would appear to be an example of television performing its liberal democratic function.

22. But note that the post-1969 rules for selecting convention delegates and the post-1968 expansion of the primary system, as well as cynicism-inducing events such as the revelations of the Pentagon Papers and Watergate, may have contributed significantly to the decline in party identification.

23. Roper Center, op. cit.

24. Mary Stuckey, *The President as Interpreter-in-Chief* (Chatham, New Jersey: Chatham House Publishers, 1991); Thomas Patterson, *Out of Order* (New York: Alfred Knopf, 1993).

25. Kathleen Jamieson, *Dirty Politics: Deception, Distraction and Democracy* (New York: Oxford University Press, 1992).

26. Anthony Smith, "Mass Communications," in David Butler, Howard R. Penniman, and Austin Ranney (eds) *Democracy at the Polls* (Washington, D.C.: American Enterprise Institute, 1981).

27. Elihu Katz and George Wedell, *Broadcasting in the Third World: Promise and Performance* (Cambridge: Harvard University Press, 1977).

7

Party representation in the United Kingdom, Australia, and Japan

J.A.A. Stockwin

As a means of organizing and facilitating political representation, political parties are an almost universal feature of contemporary democratic states. Parties exist widely in non-democratic states also, though they tend to be little more than instruments of dictatorial rule or organizations without power retained for propaganda purposes. Parties, however, are a relatively recent historical phenomenon, reflecting the transformation of many societies over the past 200 years or so in the context of industrialization and the dramatic broadening of the political base that this seminal development entailed. Their emergence reflected the fact that it was becoming less possible to organize a state on the basis of narrow court politics or a coalition of local dignitaries, feudal power-holders, or warlords.

In the broadest of terms, political parties are thus an organizational response to the trend of politics to become an affair for everybody. In a modern state – whether democratic or not – virtually everybody is affected by politics, even though not everybody may influence it. Politics even influences the lives of those who profess no interest in it, which is significant since political apathy appears to be increasing in a number of developed countries. Since there are, in principle at least, as many political opinions and political interests as there are people, political parties are a means of aggregating diverse opinions and interests into a coherent programme, which may then form the basis of a bid to attain and exercise power through whatever process of election to office happens to exist in the state concerned. Crudely put, the principle upon which most parties are formed is that there is strength in numbers. The idea whereby parties seek a parliamentary majority in order to put into practice a programme reflecting the interests and opinions of their supporters may, of course, be too rosy a picture. There are many parties where the platform, party membership, and the intention to represent a section of the electorate, are essentially window-dressing; what is important is the interests of the party leaders, or party apparatus, bent on using the electoral process in a bid for power. Nevertheless, if a democratic system of politics and government is working properly, it should be possible for the electorate to see through such naked power-seeking and call politicians to account.

There is, however, one qualification that needs to be made in respect of the argument so far. It tends to assume that the location of political power is to be found essentially within the body to which the representatives of the people have been elected, namely parliament (or whatever it may be called in a particular state). As the business of modern states has become more and more complex, it is widely asserted that effective power has tended to drain away to other locations – including ministries of state, major interest groups, multinational corporations, international financial markets, or even international crime syndicates. It would be idealistic to suggest that parliaments are always supreme arbiters of policy and power.

Parliaments, however, are not themselves interest groups. They are, rather, arenas where contests over policy and power are fought out, typically between (and at times within) the parties of whose members they are constituted. Therefore, the argument that parliaments are losing power is not always as persuasive as it might seem to be at first glance. In so far as legislation, to be valid, has to be endorsed by parliament, and in so far as the law of the land is primarily what matters, then parliaments are likely to remain central. Whether *governments* are losing influence in the face of various kinds of transnational phenomena is another question, but that need not occupy us here.

The states which will be addressed in this chapter are the United Kingdom, Australia, and Japan. In a certain broad sense, all three may be conceived of as belonging to a common democratic tradition. This may appear fairly obvious in the case of the United Kingdom and Australia, where the historical linkages were direct and pervasive, at least in the formative stages of Australian democracy. In the case of Japan, since the cultural and historical background is widely divergent from that of either the United Kingdom or Australia, the similarities are, perhaps, less obvious but none the less significant.

In institutional terms, all three states share the characteristics of what may be termed the "Westminster model." That is to say, governments are formed essentially from the elected members of parliament, organized in rival political parties, with the party or parties enjoying a majority of seats having the automatic right to form a government. The government itself is led by a prime minister who appoints ministers, the large majority of whom are in charge of (or have a position of responsibility in) specific ministries, departments, or agencies of state. None of the three states has an executive president, although all three have "symbolic" heads of state:[1] these are currently Queen Elizabeth II in the case of the United Kingdom; also Queen Elizabeth II in the case of Australia, where she is represented by a governor-general (and by governors in the six constituent states of the federation);[2] and *Kinjô Tennô* (the Current Emperor) in the case of Japan.

The political systems of all three differ fundamentally from that of the United States, where there is a radical separation of power between the president (executive branch) and the congress (legislative branch). Indeed, the political system of the United States may be regarded as highly unusual in a comparative text. The systems also differ institutionally, however, from the French political system, in which – within the Fifth Republic from 1958 – the president is elected by means of an electoral process separate from that used to elect parliament, and the president chooses a prime minister, who may belong to the opposite political persuasion from the president in cases where the president, on the one hand, and the majority in parliament, on the other, are differently composed in a situation of *cohabitation*. It may be useful to draw comparisons between the salient characteristics of party politics in each of the three political systems under discussion.

The United Kingdom

The following characteristics may be noted:
1. There are normally two major political parties competing for power, and, in most circumstances, one of them wins an outright majority of seats in the House of Commons, thus enabling it to form a government in its own right. It has also been normal for there to be one nation-wide party that is much disadvantaged by the electoral system but which can expect to win a small number of seats. In the twentieth century there has been one instance – in the

103

1920s – where a minor party replaced one of the two major parties as a party seriously contending for national office.[3] In addition, there are a number of minor regional parties which have sufficient local following in Scotland, Wales, and Northern Ireland to win a handful of seats but are not contenders for governmental office so long as the United Kingdom remains one state.[4] This pattern is heavily influenced by the system of election to the House of Commons, which is on the basis of single-member constituencies with no vote transferability. To be elected, a candidate must obtain a plurality of votes at the first and only ballot – so large parties are advantaged, swings in votes produce exaggerated swings in seats, and medium-sized parties having geographically dispersed support are hugely disadvantaged. Historically, in the United Kingdom, the system has kept the number of parties small and has produced clear and decisive results from general elections, but at the expense of severely distorting the reflection of public opinion in parliament.

2. The Conservative and Labour parties, the two major parties in recent times, have each represented a distinct subset of electors, though there is a good deal of overlap between them. Most conspicuously, the subsets have been defined along social class lines, with voters in inner-city areas predominately voting Labour and moneyed voters in outer suburban and rural electorates predominately voting Conservative. During the 1980s, however, there was an overlapping regional divide, with the north of the country, particularly Scotland, oriented to Labour and the more populous southern counties leaning principally towards the Conservatives. This in turn overlapped with an old industry (Labour)–new industry (Conservative) divide, but this seems to be breaking down in the 1990s as Labour has moved to the right.

3. Parties have generally presented fairly coherent and recognizable sets of policies (though both policies and salient issues have changed over time), so that one can easily recognize a party by its policies. At the same time, however, there has been a historical dialectic of convergence and divergence between the policies of the parties. For instance, between the 1950s and the 1970s there was a broad consensus between the Conservatives and Labour in support of Keynesian economics and the maintenance of the welfare state; but, as a result of economic crisis in the mid-1970s, the Conservatives came to espouse a radical form of market liberalism, rolling back the public sector and strictly controlling government

spending. Thus the 1980s were essentially a period of policy divergence between the two major parties. In the 1990s, however, Labour under new leadership moved to accept some, though not all, aspects of the Conservative programmes of the 1980s. It should, of course, be noted that a unidimensional "left–right" spectrum of policies is wholly inadequate to convey the differences between party policies.[5]

4. Parties have historically had a relatively committed local membership, with a degree of local autonomy in the selection of candidates. Unlike the situation in the United States, local party organizations in Britain have generally been viable on a continual basis, not merely springing into life from time to time to fight elections. The Labour Party has historically accorded an important role to the trade union movement in votes on policy at annual party conferences, though under the present leadership this role has been reduced.

5. From time to time, each party has experienced a degree of internal factionalism, which tends to be issue based,[6] although strong individuals at times develop a following around their own personality as well as around a set of policies. By comparison with a number of other political systems, including most obviously Japan but also the United States, the incidence at national level of factionalism based on mutual personal obligation and "pork barrel" politics – the use of government funds as a source of political benefit – has been relatively slight, though it has arguably been increasing since the 1980s.

6. Party leaders usually (not always) are able to exercise a great deal of personal power over the party. This is enhanced when the party concerned is in office, because of the bureaucratic support which then becomes available. But where a party is desperate to get into office, a leader is able to exercise a great deal of determining power, simply because none of his subordinates are prepared to bear the opprobrium of "rocking the boat." This has been remarked of the position of the leader of the Labour Party in the mid-1990s.

7. In the United Kingdom, to an extent which is comparatively extreme, the system works on a 'winner-take-all' principle. Generally, one party has commanded on its own a parliamentary majority, and the power of party whips to ensure favourable votes (and thus the maintenance of the government's majority) is notoriously great. The House of Lords – the Upper House of Parliament – has

not, since early in the twentieth century, had the power to block legislation that the government is determined to pass.

8. Parliamentary behaviour – at least in the House of Commons – is characterized by an adversarial style, particularly where sessions are televised, as is the case with Prime Minister's question time. Such an adversarial approach is not, incidentally, popular with the electorate. Despite the adversarial style, however, there is a high level of commitment to the norms of the system as a whole, and the concept of a "loyal opposition" is not entirely dead.

9. Politics has, historically, been based on the existence of a reasonable expectation that government may change at the next election. Even though there have been relatively long periods of dominance by one party (historically, the Conservative Party), including the period from 1979 to 1997, this is not seen as immutable. The result is that elections are generally regarded as a genuine anticipatory check on governments. In the British case it may even be argued that this is practically the only check on government, given the principle of "winner-take-all," and the constitutional inability of the House of Lords to overturn important legislation. Moreover, the deliberate weakening of local authorities which took place from the 1980s, the abolition of big-city authorities such as the Greater London Council, the establishment of large numbers of "quangos",[7] and the civil service tradition of loyally serving the government of the day, have all served to accentuate the power of the government in office and thus to enhance the role of the general election as the one effective democratic check.[8] In addition, the absence of a written constitution and, in particular, the absence of a bill of rights which might enshrine the rights of citizens, may suggest that, in the British case, restraints on arbitrary governmental power have become worryingly fragile.

Australia

Australian politics is similar to that of the United Kingdom in many ways, but there are some important differences. The salient characteristics are listed here, following the same order of topic as devised for the United Kingdom.

1. As in the United Kingdom, there are two principal contending party camps, but with the difference that the conservative side of politics is permanently divided between what, since the Second World War, has been called the Liberal Party (which has a pre-

dominantly urban base) and the National Party (formerly the Country Party), which is heavily supported in the countryside and in small country towns. The dominant party on the other side of politics is the Australian Labor[9] Party (ALP), which has traditionally, like the British Labour Party, enjoyed strong backing from trade unions. Between the late 1950s and early 1970s, however, an anti-Communist and Roman Catholic-influenced party called the Democratic Labor Party (DLP) existed, having broken from the ALP. Although it never won a single seat in the House of Representatives,[10] it is credited with having kept the ALP out of power for some 15 years.

The electoral system of the Australian House of Representatives is like the British system in favouring a "two-camp" system of party contestation but different in permitting divisions (amicable or hostile) within each camp. This may seem paradoxical. The voter at election time is required to place a sequence of numbers indicating degrees of preference against the name of each candidate listed on the voting paper. Those constituencies in which no candidate obtains an absolute majority of first-preference votes have to count and reallocate the second and later preferences of candidates (starting from the weakest) until one candidate obtains an absolute (50+ per cent) majority. This system has made possible the "amicable division" of the conservative camp into the Liberal and National parties (because these two parties in effect "exchange preferences")[11] as well as the "hostile division" that used to exist between the ALP and the now defunct DLP (because the DLP directed its preferences against the ALP).[12]

2. As in the United Kingdom, the two main camps have represented distinct subsets of electors, traditionally based on social class, though there has always been overlap. Similarly, there has been a tendency for these neat divisions to break down in the 1980s and 1990s in Australia, as in Britain, with rapidly changing economic conditions and policies. Australia's federal system, involving relatively strong local identification with the six constituent states (and several territories) of the federation, and the great distances between them, lend a good deal of local variety to patterns of political allegiance, but the patterns also change rather quickly as local political conditions evolve.

3. As in the United Kingdom, in Australia it has normally been easy enough to recognize a party by its policies, even though, with the election of the Hawke Labor Government in 1983, a convergence

107

in favour of deregulation policies became a conspicuous feature of all the major parties.

4. Parties, as in Britain, have active local memberships, but with possibly rather less local autonomy in the selection of candidates in Australia. Unions have been influential in the politics of the ALP.

5. Internal factionalism, on broadly conceived ideological lines, is endemic in the ALP and, to a lesser extent, in the conservative parties. In the ALP, membership of factions, which are generally identified with labels indicating degrees of "leftness" or "rightness," is open and public. Needless to say, strong personalities also tend to attract factional followings.

6. There have been strong leaders as well as weak leaders in all the parties. Robert (later Sir Robert) Menzies came to dominate the Liberal Party, which he himself founded in the middle 1940s, but his three immediate successors – Holt, Gorton, and McMahon – had a far less sure grip over the party. Similarly, Hayden's control of the ALP in the late 1970s and early 1980s was less firm than that of Hawke in the early years of his prime ministership when the ALP won office in 1983, and of Keating who later ousted him.

7. The principle of "winner-take-all" is rather less strong than in the United Kingdom, because the powers of the Senate are greater than those of the House of Lords. In specific circumstances defined by the Constitution, the Senate is able to deny "supply" (that is, budgetary allocations of funding) to a government. Since, in recent times, the Senate has been elected by proportional representation, and the Senate majority not infrequently differs from that in the House of Representatives, the possibility of this happening is real. The constitutional crisis which brought down the Whitlam Labor Government on 11 November 1975 – the most serious political crisis in Australia's recent history – was essentially caused by the fact that the government did not command a majority in the Senate, and the Senate over a period refused supply.[13]

8. Even to a greater extent than in the United Kingdom, in Australia parliamentary debate is adversarial. Paul Keating, whose government was defeated in the general elections of March 1996, was particularly famous for the richness of his vocabulary and for tough and direct debating style, though ultimately this may have contributed to the defeat of his government.

9. As in Britain, there is widespread acceptance of the system and of the principle that it is normal for government and opposition to

exchange places following a general election. The principle became seriously atrophied in the 23 years of conservative dominance of government between 1949 and 1972 but, since the election of the Whitlam Government in December 1972, there have been four changes of party or parties in power at federal level in Australia (1972, 1975, 1983, 1996) as against three in Britain (1974, 1979, 1997). Apart from this there are, in effect, more checks and balances in the Australian political system than in that of the United Kingdom, including those inherent in the federal system and that provided by the powers and composition of the Senate. Taking state as well as federal elections into account, and remembering that voting in Australia is compulsory and that the federal electoral cycle provides for a maximum of three years between elections, it is very arguable that the voter, for good or ill, has more opportunity to influence politics in Australia than in Britain.[14] In some ways, Australia is a very politically oriented state.

Japan

It goes without saying that the cultural and historical background of Japan contrasts greatly with that of the United Kingdom or Australia. For two and a half centuries up until the middle of the nineteenth century, Japan was essentially a closed country whose political institutions were somewhat akin to those of medieval European feudalism. With the forced opening of the country, and a revolutionary change of regime which occurred from 1868, Japan embarked upon a programme of modernization which involved a radical restructuring of political institutions and practices. To simplify a most complex story, a written constitution was introduced in 1889, providing a very limited measure of popular representation to a parliament, only one house of which was elected, on a restricted franchise, and which enjoyed only limited powers. Sovereignty was described as deriving from the Emperor who, however, was for the most part not a personal ruler. Power came to shift from time to time between various élites, among whom the armed forces became predominant, especially from the early 1930s until 1945. The thrust of government policy was modernizing rather than democratizing, nation building rather than concerned with the rights of the citizen, and militarizing rather than seeking international consensus. Japan between 1889 and 1945 was not a democracy but – however imperfectly – experienced government under a written constitution.

In 1946 Japan acquired, under the strong influence of an American army of occupation, an entirely new constitution, embodying democratic principles as understood in Western countries. It is hardly surprising that the practice of this constitution (which remains unrevised) later came to be influenced by previous Japanese experience and cultural norms. This does not mean, however, that Japan simply reverted to the *status quo ante*, since the war, the defeat, the atomic bombing of two major cities, and more than six years of military occupation effected profound changes on attitudes and political culture. Nevertheless, as we shall see, political continuities with the past exist.

Perhaps surprisingly (in view of the fact that it was the Americans who were the principal occupying power between 1945 and 1952), the form of government embodied in the new constitution was, in essence, the "Westminster model." Our comparison between Japan, on the one hand, and the United Kingdom and Australia, on the other, may thus be seen to be based on the significant structural similarity of all three having political institutions deriving – with obvious variations – from a similar set of structural arrangements.

Following the previous format, the salient characteristics of the Japanese system of party politics are as follows.

1. Japan, since the 1950s, has had a "dominant party" system. The Liberal Democratic Party, created from rival conservative groups in the 1950s, formed every government single-handedly (with one hardly significant exception)[15] until August 1993 when, following a split in its ranks and consequent defeat in a general election, it was replaced by a non-LDP coalition of no less than eight parties. In June 1994, however, the LDP returned to power as the largest party in a three-party coalition under a Socialist prime minister and, in January 1996, the prime ministership was once again taken by the leader of the LDP.

   The only significant party of opposition in the late 1950s was the Japan Socialist Party, a party in which far left tendencies were strong in that period. From 1960 onward, however, that party stagnated and much of its vote, particularly in cities, was taken over by a number of smaller parties, most of which (the exception being the Japan Communist Party) were essentially of centrist persuasion.

   Once again, the electoral system for the Lower House (the House of Representatives or *Shûgiin*) has been an important determining factor in the pattern of party representation and interaction. All general elections between 1947 and 1993 were held under a system in which each elector cast a single, non-transferable vote, but each constituency elected several (typically three, four, or five) candidates.[16] Moreover, adequate provisions were lacking for the redrawing of constituency boundaries to reflect the massive shift of population from the countryside to the towns in the period of Japan's rapid economic growth from the 1950s. This latter aspect greatly favoured the LDP interest, and it may plausibly be argued that at least the elections of 1976, 1979, and 1983 were won by the LDP only because of this factor.

The multi-member constituencies also had the effect of helping the dominant party, since it was the only party in a position to run several candidates in most constituencies throughout the country. Given Japanese sociopolitical conditions, this meant that each LDP candidate competed fiercely on the basis of a personal local machine, for a personal vote, almost independently of the party. The intra-party competition was often so fierce that it had the effect of enhancing considerably the overall vote-winning capacity of the party. This system also tended to encourage cohesive leader–follower factionalism within the dominant party and, to a considerable extent, separated off the policy-making function from the power-maximizing and money-distributing functions. The system of election was not a system of proportional representation but, none the less, created some proportionality in its effects, and was relatively permissive to representation from medium-sized parties.

2. It is much more difficult in the case of Japan to argue that the parties represent clearly defined subsets of electors than in the British or Australian cases. In the 1950s and into the 1960s, the Japan Socialist Party vote was fairly distinct (union based, with intellectual support), yet distinctions in the support base of the parties generally have been eroded over the years to the point where easy generalizations are difficult to make. Indeed, the most conspicuous difference in voting behaviour is that between the metropolitan conurbations, which tend to split their vote between a number of parties, and the rest of the country, where the LDP is heavily dominant. To some extent, this pattern may be breaking down with the political party alignments that have been taking place since 1992–1993.

3. One of the complaints often raised about Japanese party politics is that, in policy terms, the parties are virtually indistinguishable from each other. It was not always so: up until the 1970s, the party

system was often castigated for being inordinately confrontational across a range of policy areas. In practice today there are important policy differences in the areas of deregulation, decentralization, constitutional reform, welfare policies, foreign policy, and so on, but these differences are to be found as much within parties as between them.

4. Party membership is problematic in Japan. With the exceptions of one or two minor parties,[17] members tend to be either "ghosts"[18] or party officials. Party politicians are not generally held in high regard, and there is a widespread aversion to belonging to a political party. Moreover, for the individual election, personal machines of individual parliamentary candidates are often more "real" than the parties with which those candidates happen to be affiliated.

5. Political factionalism has been pervasive, particularly in large parties and especially in the LDP, where factional manoeuvring has often determined the distribution both of cabinet and party posts and the distribution of political funding. Factions, in some respects, may be conceptualized as "parties within a party," except that they do not contest elections under their own labels. Here, however, we find a clear contrast with party politics in the United Kingdom and Australia, where factions most typically are based on policy differences. It should be noted that the transformation of the electoral system effected in 1994 appears to have had the effect of weakening intra-LDP factions, suggesting, once again, that the electoral system is an important independent variable in many of the issues we have been discussing.

6. A perennial criticism of Japanese politics is that the system inhibits strong leadership. An examination of this issue would take us beyond the brief of this chapter, because it relates to the role of the government bureaucracy and principal interest groups in the system as a whole. A key factor that serves to distinguish the Japanese political system from most others (including those of the UK and Australia) is that a high proportion of LDP members of parliament (approximately one-quarter) were previously government employees. To a considerable extent, the argument about whether the LDP or the bureaucracy is the more powerful is the wrong question to ask: both work so closely together that it is more realistic to talk of cross-cutting coalitions of interests. However this may be, the scope for exercise of independent prime-ministerial power is reduced by the many checks and balances

built into the system. This area is, in many ways, the most controversial in discussions of Japanese politics at the present time.

7. In Japan there is a tension between a "winner-take-all" principle and a "checks and balances" or "consensus" principle. The sense that governments ought to take into account the views of those outside government is inbuilt, even though exercises in power and coercion may also plainly be observed in the working-out of many political issues. The Japanese political system is, emphatically, not based on equality of power but neither is it based on monopoly of power. The checks and balances that exist, lead (as is often remarked) to immobilism in policy innovation, but policy dynamism is also far from unknown.[19] The upper house of parliament, the House of Councillors, has substantial powers to block legislation coming to it from the lower house, and this was a severe problem for LDP governments between 1989 and 1993, when the LDP lacked a majority in the upper house.

8. Much parliamentary business takes place in committees, and plenary sessions tend to be insubstantial. As in the United Kingdom and Australia, parliamentary debate (particularly when televised) can be adversarial, but there is also an air of formality about it, suggesting that the real infighting has already been done behind closed doors. Today, there is a general commitment to the maintenance of the system (except on the part of fringe groups, particularly on the far right), although in the 1950s and 1960s there was much activity directed against the system from various quarters. One worrying aspect is that political corruption has been on such a massive scale at times that it greatly discredits politics among the electorate as a whole.

9. Until 1992–1993, it could not reasonably be said that politics was based on an expectation that government might change at the next election. The LDP was in power, and most people expected that state of affairs to continue ad infinitum. In the 1990s, the system – and particularly this expectation – has been in a state of flux, although it is much too early to say that a pattern of alternating (or even occasionally alternating) politics has been established. It is even arguable – but also disputable – that whichever party is in power hardly matters, because real power lies in the hands of the bureaucracy. The first general elections held under the new lower house electoral system, in October 1996, failed to establish a viable opposition, and the fragmentation of the party system was gathering momentum at the beginning of 1998.

Conclusion

The focus of this chapter is on party politics and party representation. In any political system this is a part – though an important part – of the whole. Of the three states examined here, Japan is obviously outstanding in the success of its economic policies since the Second World War and has become the second largest economy in the world. The economic successes of Japan and other states of the East and South-East Asia have given rise to the notion of an "Asian Model of Democracy," with the implication that, somehow, the western side of the Pacific has invented a new form of democracy which is an improvement on the old.[20]

The thrust of this chapter is, by implication, to cast doubt on this hypothesis. The doubt stems, not so much from the financial difficulties that became so visible in Japan and elsewhere in the region in 1997, but rather from a belief that democracy is a universal, not a regional, concept. While it is clear that the Japanese system differs more substantially from the British and Australian than they do from each other, it is also obvious that there are many commonalities and that, in the working out of their political destinies, all three are grappling with vexatious issues that confront East and West alike.

Notes

1. In the case of Japan, the 1946 Constitution specifically avoids the term "head of state" in respect of the *Tennô* ("Emperor"), who is given the appellation "symbol of the State and of the unity of the people." The fact that the *Tennô* may not be treated as "head" of state remains a matter of some controversy.
2. The proposal to make Australia a republic is being actively discussed in the 1990s, and, if this eventuates, Australia will presumably have a president as head of state. It seems most unlikely, however, despite evident preference manifested in public opinion polls for an elected president, that the president will have executive powers.
3. The Labour Party in the 1920s replaced the Liberal Party as the main contestant of the Conservatives. An attempt to reverse this in the 1980s failed.
4. Following the election of the Blair Labour Government in May 1997, majorities were secured in referendums in Scotland and Wales for the establishment of regional assemblies in Edinburgh and Cardiff. The Scottish, but not the Welsh, assembly is to have limited powers of taxation.
5. After its election the Blair government showed its determination to adhere to the government spending constraints laid down by its Conservative predecessor. Its "welfare to work" policies, involving some loss of welfare benefit to vulnerable sections of the community, occasioned protest from sections of the Labour Party itself.
6. For instance "socialism" in the Labour Party in the late 1970s and early 1980s, Europe in the Conservative Party in the 1990s.
7. Quasi non-governmental organizations.

8. The maximum term which a government can serve without calling a general election is 5 years.
9. The adoption of the American spelling "Labor" was deliberate and anti-English.
10. The DLP regularly won a small number of seats in the Senate, which is elected by a form of proportional representation.
11. In the House of Representatives elections, party workers wait outside polling stations with advisory "how to vote" cards, giving the order of preferences favoured by a particular party. Thus, a Liberal voter following the advice of the Liberal Party "how to vote" card will in most cases give second preference to the candidate of the National Party, and vice versa. The fact that this advice is followed by the bulk of Liberal and National Party voters is evidence of the strength of the "two-camp" nature of Australian electoral politics.
12. In elections during that period, many ALP candidates obtained a plurality on first preferences, but were defeated when later preferences were distributed because the preferences of DLP first-preference voters were directed heavily against them. It seems most likely that several elections during the period of the existence of the DLP would have been won by the ALP had the DLP not existed or had it not been so successful in directing its preferences against the ALP. In effect, the DLP was a veto group, whose purpose was to keep the ALP out of power, and in this it was supremely successful.
13. On 11 November 1975 the Governor-General, Sir John Kerr, activated hitherto unused powers of the Constitution and dismissed Whitlam as Prime Minister. For an account of the crisis, see Paul Kelly, *November 1975: The Inside Story of Australia's Greatest Political Crisis* (St. Leonards, NSW, Australia, Allen and Unwin, 1995). There is usually some representation of third parties in the Senate, and the oldest of these, the Australian Democrats, founded in the 1970s, has generally held the principled stand of agreeing not to withhold supply from any government enjoying a majority in the House of Representatives.
14. See Dean Jaensch, *An Introduction to Australian Politics* (Sydney: Longman Cheshire, 1988), pp. 56–83.
15. Between 1983 and 1986 the LDP was in coalition with the tiny New Liberal Club, which had itself split from the LDP in 1976 and re-entered the LDP in 1986.
16. This system has now been replaced by a new system under which there are 300 single-member constituencies elected first-past-the-post, and a further 200 constituencies elected by proportional representation in 11 regional constituencies. Anti-corruption laws have also been substantially toughened.
17. Notably the former *Kômeitô* (based on the Buddhist sect *Sôka Gakkai*), and the Japan Communist Party.
18. The LDP has long had a practice of seeking to boost its membership by enrolling names (with a member of parliament paying the required dues) of people who may have no intention of being party members.
19. See J.A.A. Stockwin, Alan Rix, Aurelia George, James Horne, Daiichi Itô, and Martin Collick, *Dynamic and Immobilist Politics in Japan* (London: Macmillan, 1988).
20. See J.A.A. Stockwin, "Is There Such a Thing as the Asian Model of Democracy?," paper delivered at the International Conference on Korea in Transition: Issues and Alternatives, Graduate School of Labour, Korea University, Seoul, 6 July 1996.

Democracy and global forces

8

The democratization process and the market

Mihály Simai

> A country could create a political democracy in six months and a market
> economy in six years, but ... 60 years would be necessary for a true civil
> society to emerge in Eastern Europe.
>
>   – Sir Ralf Dahrendorf in 1990[1]

Democracy: The current debate

The current dialogue on democracy is far wider and more complex
than that of the past: it has many more roots and dimensions. A
number of trends and issues have stimulated the new discourse: the
political and institutional consequences of the collapse of the dictatorial regimes in a number of developing countries; the systemic
changes in Central and Eastern Europe; the re-evaluation of the role
of the state and the market in the industrial world and in developing countries; the attachment of political conditionalities to development assistance programmes; the universalization of human rights;
the implications of the globalization process; and the dialogue generated by the UN Agenda for Development and the anticipated
document on the Agenda for Democracy, are some such issues.

In the context of the changes in Central and Eastern Europe, but
also in a broader perspective, an important dimension of the dialogue
on democracy is related to the failures of communism to fulfil its
promise to create a world "free from need and war" and, as a corollary, the future of capitalism and its liberal democratic regimes. Many
political thinkers view this process as the global victory of constitutional democracy and particularly of its liberal version.

Capitalism is not, of course, a closed or homogeneous ideological system. Different ideologies exist upon its socio-economic foundations and from a broad spectrum, including libertarians, liberals, and right-wing populists. The system has also accommodated some fanatical ideologies such as violent nationalism and fascism, which lamentably are gaining ground again in various parts of the world. Fuelled by growing socio-economic problems and political impasses, these creeds preach such divisive doctrines as racism, ethnic hatred, and religious bigotry. Such ideologies cannot be expected to encourage global solutions to the problems of poverty, environmental degradation, and crime.

Although certain values of liberal internationalism – such as the honouring of human rights and democracy – are enjoying increasing acceptance in many parts of the world, contemporary forms of liberal internationalism may not necessarily be effective in addressing the needs and concerns of the developing world. Pope John Paul II has squarely identified the problem:

The Marxist solution has failed, but the realities of marginalization and exploitation remain in the world, especially in the Third World, as does the reality of human alienation, especially in the more advanced countries ... Indeed, there is a risk that a radical capitalistic ideology could spread which refuses even to consider these problems, in the a priori belief that any attempt to solve them is doomed to failure, and which blindly entrusts their solution to the free development of market forces.[2]

Democracy is not a political ideology like liberalism, communism, socialism, or Nazism. It is not a set of political ideas about the values, instruments, goals, and outcomes of social actions. It describes a particular system of government and the distribution of power within a system. In fact, most of the different political ideologies employ the concept of democracy, with certain qualifications, based on their views and preferences. Liberal democracies constitutionally limit governmental power, safeguard civil liberties, and ensure representation, in political offices through competitive elections.

Democracy, by definition, is rule by the people. Any theory of democracy must specify how the people should rule – whether by direct participation, elected representatives, referendum, or other means. But, prior to this question, one can ask: "who are the people?" The usual answer is, all affected by government and public administration. This implies that the rule by the people should be extended to all those who are influenced by the decisions of power, on different levels. Both as an ideal and as an actual system, democracy has changed over the two millennia since its "invention." Through the long history of human efforts for achieving democracy, it has been interpreted as a interminable process of change toward an ideal political system. Many political thinkers considered democracy to be a goal shaped by subsequent generations. It has also been interpreted as a set of political institutions and processes that are attainable at least with certain limitations. At the end of the twentieth century, democratization is increasingly considered to be an international or global process, closely related to global sociopolitical changes and, particularly, the international and universal character of human rights.

The historical experiences of the Western world and developing countries may offer a few important principles and lessons germane to post-communist countries in transition.

1. Relations between the market system, economic development, and democracy are complex and multidimensional. The pre-Second World War patterns of Central and Eastern Europe demonstrated that market economies coexisted with various forms of political systems – dictatorial or democratic. Historical evidence also suggests that market economies preceded the democratic changes of governance. The progress of democracy was, in most cases, a long historical process. Democratic rights were progressively expanded, often following bitter social and political conflicts. There are, however, no historical examples, where liberal, democratic systems could be established before the emergence of a market economy with clearly defined and transparent property rights, a fairly wide dispersion of economic power, a free entry and exit, and a non-discriminatory system of economic competition.

2. Democracy is not necessarily a prerequisite of the market system, nor is it indispensable for promoting economic development. Empirical evidence supports the fact that authoritarian governments were often less vulnerable against powerful interest groups and popular pressures in implementing important socio-economic policies.[3] They have been more decisive in carrying out painful structural reforms, whilst democratic methods proved to be fragile in troubled times. Non-democratic regimes were often able to create higher savings, through enforced public savings and other measures; the concept of the "developmental dictatorship" has been applied to East Asian countries. A thorough cost–benefit analysis of the non-democratic regimes would, however, be dif-

121

ficult, and political and social costs of the non-democratic regimes were, in many cases, extremely high despite their favourable influence on some economic indicators.

3. A number of important conditions must be fulfilled for the democratic process to succeed itself, without creating situations that result in non-democratic methods of governance. The first condition concerns the necessity of having high-quality people elected to serve in the parliaments and, particularly, national governments.[4] Second, the scope of governance must be relatively limited, which should be a consequence of the mechanisms of democracy. Third, there must be a well-trained, professional, and technically competent bureaucracy which has continuity. The civil service should be committed to pursue professional excellence yet should be subject to democratic control aimed at ensuring administrative responsiveness to popular needs and desires. Fourthly, an open and consultative system of governance facilitates a greater articulation of interests and allows compromises and consensus building. In this context there must be a climate of tolerance, for the expression of different opinions. Fifth, in order to sustain democracy, there must be a degree of justice, participation, and a fair distribution of welfare. Sixth, democracy must not be treated as a process, or an effort, isolated from other social or economic processes.

4. A fundamentally important issue for the development and sustainability of democracy is the progress of the civil society. There are a great number of definitions of this phenomenon, but for these purposes it is "the independent self-organization of the society, the constituent parts of which voluntarily engage in public activity to pursue individual, group or national interests, within the context of a legally defined state–society relationship."[5] The development of civil society cannot be isolated from political, social, and economic changes. The power of the state, for example, has always been a major influence on the manner in which civil society articulates and protects its interests. Civil society implies, by definition, participation. Participation, however, particularly in the literature on development, is considered simultaneously in different contexts – in public life, in the workplace, at home. An important dimension of the development of civil society and participation is related to globalization. An ideologist of globalization, for example John Naisbitt,[6] would suggest that globalization increases the possibilities of small groups, or firms, because they have greater flexibility

than large units. According to him, the essence of the global paradox is that, the more global or universal humankind is becoming, the more "tribal" people are acting. This reduces and changes the traditional role and functions of the state: "Now, with the electronics revolution, both representative democracy and economies of scale are obsolete. Now everyone can have efficient direct democracy."[7] The fragmentation process is, however, a consequence not just of "new tribalism" but also of the fact that it is constantly resulting in marginalization and exclusion due to the highly unequal character of the globalization process. All these indicate that the development of civil society should not be simplified: it must be related to the processes of democratization; the development of institutions and legal codes; and the manner in which social actors seek to find their interests, values, and identity.

The process of transition to the market system in the former socialist countries also added some experiences to the global democratic process. The postulates for implanting democracy from above must not be confined to the formal institutions. It is relatively easy to change the institutional framework of governance by centrally initiated reforms; it is, however, extremely difficult to implant a new behavioural infrastructure from above. The establishment of a legitimate, democratic system is a long and painful process. The introduction of a multi-party system does not itself mean that a country can manage its internal conflicts and social problems more easily, particularly when the governments are restrained by external forces beyond their control, and people do not see a direct relationship between their welfare and the democratic process.

During the Cold War, political sciences and scientists divided the world into democracies and dictatorial regimes, with almost nothing in between the two. As the result of the transition in the former socialist countries, attitudinal changes in developing countries, and varying levels of economic development and national consolidation, the process of democratization has resulted in a greater diversity of democracy. Any effort to measure democracy on the basis of textbook models of Western democracy, which expanded gradually as the result of political struggles and long political experiences, is in error.

The international "demonstration effect" plays a significant, but only a limited, role in creating sustainable democratic systems. Such questions as "does democracy travel?"[8] may be rooted more in wishful thinking than in global realities. Democracy must be based on a civil society, developed from the grass roots. Simultaneously, the sustainability of democracy also requires strong external support and guarantees.

Liberalization democracy and the market

Democratization in Central and Eastern Europe and the successor states of the Soviet Union has been considered as an integral part of their transition to the market system. The liberalization of the former command economies and the opening and the pluralization of the "closed" societies were probably the most important postulates in the changes.

The three types of liberalization – shock therapy, the gradual approach, and partial liberalization – have been "competing" in national policies and in the recommendations of the external experts in the former socialist countries. The definition of the market economy was the classical textbook case: private ownership of the means of production; free competition among economic agents; the right freely to enter and exit any line of production, employment, and trade for all the actors; and the determination of prices and the allocation of resources through the free play of market forces. In fact, few economies conform to this concept in reality.

The ongoing debate on the role of the state and the market has had a major influence in the countries which have been statist regimes.[9] The need to dismantle costly and inefficient bureaucracies; to create democracy, accountability, and transparency; and to end corruption were some of the main slogans. Similarly, integral to the introduction of a liberal market system has been the dismantling of the institutions of central planning. Internationally, liberalization and the introduction of free-market policies have been the most important underpinnings of the new contractual relationships with Bretton Woods institutions. These have included deregulation of the price system, the abolition of subsidies, sweeping reforms in public expenditures, privatization, the encouragement of foreign direct investments, and the liberalization of the foreign trade regimes.

Many of the Western economic advisers of the new regimes have suggested that fast liberalization is the key remedy for curing all the economic ills of transition and developing their export potentials. However, many experts have failed to understand the complex nature of the process, owing to limited information on the given countries, the mechanical copying of the patterns of the developed industrial countries, ideologically motivated approaches, economic expectations based on textbooks, political pressures, and wishful thinking.

A further important source for liberalization has been the need for foreign direct investment and the liberalization of entrepreneurship, capital movements, prices, and exchange rates. There were great expectations attached to the direct and indirect role of the transnational corporations. New governments in the former socialist countries expected a rapid increase of foreign direct investments in the important branches of the economies and, with it, the introduction of new technologies, new products and processes, expertise, skills, and the promotion of exports. Some of the governments, especially those of indebted countries, looked to transnational corporations primarily as sources of new capital. These expectations related to the active and accelerating role of transnational corporations in the systemic transition process. In this context, there have been two important areas receiving particular emphasis – institution building and privatization.

The building of new market institutions, the development of the legal system, and the establishment of the necessary business infrastructure, have been indispensable conditions for the appropriate functioning of private enterprises. Efforts to attract foreign investors resulted in positive steps toward accelerating market institution building and were, in fact, more significant for the acceleration of the institutional changes than the domestic political and economic pressures.

In order to attract foreign direct investment, governments have had to introduce legislation on national and foreign entrepreneurship[10] – such as tax concessions or, in certain cases, direct subsidies – to create a conducive business environment. Close to 60 specific bilateral investment treaties have been concluded between the former socialist countries of Europe to give assurances on this matter.[11] However, in the relationships with the transnational corporations, such elementary issues as the unequal bargaining position and shift from state monopolies have implications for economically weak countries, with fragile new institutions.

A further source of liberalization was basically domestic – the shift in thinking against public ownership, controls, regulations, state monopolies, subsidies. These were the legacy of the communist regimes, and those who tried to resist the measures were considered as relics of the past. The state-owned enterprises – the majority of which had, in the past, strong vested interests in protectionism – lost their bargaining power. Their leaders were, by and large, discredited and, in order to save their positions, they remained silent. The combined force of the pressures for liberalization was historically unprecedented in the speed in which it opened up the countries. The greater the difference between the past and the present, the greater the impact of the measures. In political terms, the introduction of the Western model of liberal democracy was favoured by most domestic forces and foreign actors – governments, international agencies, NGOs, and experts – who helped in promoting the institutional changes.

However, the external and internal constraints on the transitional economies often do not facilitate the building up of a new, more competitive, institutional system. Indeed, transition can undermine their capabilities and reduce their adaptive efficiency. In the transition debates, the former socialist countries are often considered as a homogeneous group, with the same legacy of Cold War totalitarianism. They are considered as a region, basically without democratic traditions, where the democratization process has had to start from zero. Commentators have drawn attention to the "backwardness" of Eastern European political culture, especially compared with the old liberal democracies of the West. Indeed, the middle class, which is arguably the most important social group upon which a political culture is nurtured, still represents only a small group in Central and Eastern Europe. Nevertheless, the region has never been a politically or economically homogeneous part of the world. The differences were quite substantial, both in the progress of the market system and in terms of democratic experience.

First, certain countries had quite important democratic traditions before the German occupation or the introduction of the Soviet-type totalitarian regimes. Some others had no democratic tradition at all. But, even in these countries, the minimal political and legal conditions of a market system existed – transparent property rights, an effective legal system for the enforcement of contracts and legal undertakings, and the legal equality of the economic agents. Moreover, over time, there were also changes across the socialist regimes: some became more liberal and less oppressive – Kadarism in Hungary, the reforms of Gorbachev in the Soviet Union, the liberalization in Poland – whilst others such as the Ceaucescu regime in Romania sustained, or even strengthened, the dictatorial rule.

The achievements and the problems

The achievement of introducing almost unrestricted freedom, as the first step of the democratization process, has been impressive in its speed. It has taken place much faster than in the history of the Western countries but with the result of adverse side-effects and instability, in some instances.

All the European post-communist countries, excluding the states that emerged from the disintegration of Yugoslavia, have been plunged into political freedom. The restrictions imposed by the totalitarian regimes have vanished, with the disintegration of the political institutions of the communist regimes. There are practically no restrictions upon civil society and freedom of association along various lines, including political parties and trade unions. In Hungary, for example, there were about 42,000 organizations or voluntary associations in 1996. In none of the post-communist countries, except the former Yugoslavia, is there widespread political persecution or imprisonment for political reasons. There is also considerable freedom of demonstration and political agitation, including that of an anti-government nature, and complete freedom of movement. In some cases the political freedom of some transitional countries is more liberal than that of many long-established parliamentary democracies.

Democracy is, however, more than just freedom: it is a set of procedures for choosing rulers and exercising control over them; for providing guarantees for minorities; a defined balance between the executive and the legislative power, the rule of law, and the independence of the judiciary. Furthermore, a culture of democracy embraces participation and public discourse. Not all these elements of democracy exist in all the post-communist countries. There are indisputable achievements. Governments in these countries possess democratic credentials and have been democratically elected. New constitutions have been enacted – except in Russia, where it was decreed – or old ones fundamentally amended, such as in Hungary and Poland. Institutions have been established for the protection of democracy, including constitutional courts and ombudsman systems. Throughout the region, independence of the judiciary has been proclaimed and enshrined in legislation. In some countries, local authorities are now elected by democratic process. However, these changes are far from being equally strong everywhere, and such procedural/institutional achievements do not ensure the substance of democracy.

Today, the social structures of Central and Eastern European countries differ greatly from those of pre- and early Cold War days: they are no longer "traditional" peasant societies where authoritarian rule can easily be enforced; they have large professional groups, a broad industrial working class, and a small (but growing) entrepreneurial middle class. Any open or disguised political effort to introduce new dictatorial regimes would be strongly opposed by them. One can, at the same time, notice that most of the countries in Central and Eastern Europe are highly divided internally, along different lines. The first years of transition changed the optimistic expectations which were, in fact, often illusions encouraged from the West and the political forces that comprised the new political élite. In reality, the new regimes often did not understand fully the complex interplay between the domestic and external factors and forces involved; in some countries, they looked more to the pre-Second World War era for policy models and missed the early opportunities for building up large coalitions based on popular consensus. They also failed to establish conditions facilitating a more equitable distribution of costs and benefits.

Many people are disappointed, and some have become attracted to political extremism. Political apathy and disillusionment are also widespread. Why has the path towards liberal democracy experienced problems and been fragile?

The main pillar of the Western concept of democracy is a pluralistic society that displays and articulates the heterogeneity of interests. The political process is based on institutionalized political competition and electoral legitimacy. Power does not stem from "divine will," physical force, or hereditary right; it is a mandate from the population, expressed by free elections. Conflicts of interests appear in the form of differing or contrasting political ideas, goals, and policies represented by parties or other organized groups. Shifts in power are based on free elections, and the possibility of change is inherent in the system. The great majority of the members of society must support this mechanism and the principles of freedom of beliefs, opinion, association, and mobility. There must be a broad consensus on the shifts in power through free elections, on the willingness of the ruling party to step down after political defeat, and on the tolerance of organized opposition by those who are in power. In many transitional societies, these democratic foundations are not fully developed. There is, to begin with, a weakness in the political party structure, which sprang up across the region with the fall of single-party domination. Parties can be broadly divided into three groups – the new parties which emerged from the anti-communist opposition, the "historical" parties which existed before the communist take-over and revived after the changes, and the parties which are a product of changes in the power structure in the communist era and derive chiefly from reformist currents in the old communist parties or their allies. In addition, parties of a "non-political" character have appeared – the greens, the feminists, and eccentric groups attracting every imaginable interest and activity.

Certain patterns can be discerned. No united anti-communist opposition front has proved to be sustainable. When such united political movements existed and held power, they quickly split into numerous factions and found their influence diminishing. The most striking example of this is former East Germany, where the old Democratic Forum has vanished from the political scene, which is now entirely dominated by the parties of the old Federal Republic. But even in Poland, where Solidarity was such a powerful movement, the majority of the parties which spun off from it were unable, in the 1993 elections, to gain the required 5 per cent of the popular vote and ended up with no seats in parliament at all. Most political parties are weak, not only in numbers but in size of constituency. There are few well-organized grass-roots parties: most of them are parliamentary groups, organized for the participation in the elections. After the first well-supported democratic elections, the turnout tends to be approaching the low Western European patterns – in the region of 50 per cent – and a large proportion of parties collect only a fractional percentage of the vote.[12]

Democratic states must be based on the rule of law in order to protect basic human security and human rights and to safeguard personal freedom from arbitrary interventions. Yet general standards of legal culture in most of the transition countries have been relatively low. This applies to both the bureaucracy and society at large, where repercussions of transitional instability are reflected in various social ills. Law and order even appear to be under threat, in some instances, and the social diseases associated with the transition process, together with a decline of human solidarity, do not augur well. Adaptations in the legal system comprise a very difficult task for transitional countries, and there are great differences between them in the degree of progress. In some countries – notably Poland, Hungary, and the Czech Republic – reasonably swift progress has been made in the process of modernizing the legal framework. From the point of view of the functioning of democracy, the rules related to the electoral system are particularly important; in most of the transitional countries, the electoral systems became a highly complicated mixture of the proportional and majority systems. The combination of the two was shaped by the political struggles and by the efforts to avoid fragmentation and "Weimarization" of the new democratic systems. The Ukrainian system, for example, has resulted in a situation which makes the allocation of the seats in parliament impossible until several months after the election. Even in Poland, the electoral system – which was formulated by a democratically elected parliament – has resulted in parties that together collected almost 30 per cent of the popular vote in September 1993 having no parliamentary representation. The new electoral system became an important target of criticism, particularly by the smaller parties which could not get into parliament. The debate on the reform of the electoral system will remain an important legal and political issue.

A further weakness of the legal system, influencing political life and the conduct of government in practically all the former socialist countries, concerns the distribution of power between the supreme authorities of the state and the central government and the local authorities. The legal framework became an important subject of political struggle, and the hastily adopted or amended constitutions reflect more the compromises in those struggles than legal or political rationality. The dispute over the character of governance reflected deep political roots and was not just a case of copying Western patterns, like the American or the French presidential system; it reflected the outcome of domestic political struggles between the autocratic tendencies and the forces of liberal democracy. The advocates of presidential government in the post-communist countries wanted, in most cases, far greater power – especially complete freedom for the selection of government ministers, the right to issue decrees with the force of law (that is, to bypass the legislature), and relatively wide powers of dissolving inconvenient parliaments. Such advocates spring from the traditions of the region, whether recent and communist – particularly in the successor states of the Soviet Union – or more distant and pre-communist (Walesa's idol was Marshal József Piludski, who staged a military *coup d'état* in Poland in 1926 and subsequently exercised a moderate dictatorship). An important factor behind the authoritarian tendencies is, undoubtedly, the difficulties in the transformation process. In a number of Western countries with long democratic traditions, both presidential and cabinet government can function without endangering the democratic system. In the former socialist countries, however, where democratic traditions are limited and political culture and parties are relatively weak, a presidential system can very easily turn in an authoritarian direction, especially if combined with a limitation of the role of parliament. In Poland and in Hungary, presidential government is favoured by populist groups, while democratic parties prefer a cabinet system or a balanced mixture of the two.

The socio-economic difficulties inherent in the transformation process are particularly important sources of problems, given the fragility of the process. Markets are not institutions of welfare or equity: shock therapy and multilateral financial institutions basically ignore the democratic agenda. If the first experiments with democracy result in inflation, unemployment, increasing inequalities, and a declining standard of living for the "silent majority" of the population, the result will be fear, alienation, and distrust. For 40 years, under the "promise of communism," the state sought to convince people of the necessity of sacrificing their present welfare state for some future promise. Many people have seen parallels between this and the vague promises of the new regimes advocating market reforms and democracy. In certain cases, the majority of the population looked at the evolving regimes as "redistributive coalitions" in the interests of a small new minority. The transition process proved that, while the majority of the population support democracy, marketization was not able to bring sufficient or attractive enough goals for the masses, especially if they experienced the adverse consequences of the process and saw the conspicuous gains of the small minority. In those countries, where the "post-socialist" coalitions were voted out of power, people were voting against the increasing poverty, unemployment, the declining standard of living, and other economic and social difficulties. To a certain extent, it was also a protest vote against those political forces that wanted to restore the political and ideological values of the pre-Second World War regimes. People were voting not for the restoration of the communist past but for equal opportunities and greater security. This draws attention to the changing relationships between the state, capital, and labour. The issue of the bargaining power of the workers and their relations to the reforms and the increasing inequalities will, inevitably, occupy a more important role in the future political struggles of the countries. In the future, particularly in the absence of faster economic growth and more equitable income distribution, the pressures toward extremist solutions, based on the interests of certain groups and not on social consensus, may come from the side of labour and also of capital, in different political dressings. This may undermine the functioning of liberal democracies and may result in pressures for some forms of command systems or autocratic regimes.

Ethnic problems in the former socialist countries comprise another source of tension in the democratization process. Recent empirical experiences indicate that no states are completely neutral ethnically; they reflect the ethnic power structure of the given society, which means that – more often than not – they reflect the interests, values, and policies of the ruling ethnic majority. The other side of the coin concerns the extent to which ethnic groups accept the institutions, and whether they are imposed on them by the majority or are a result of a political consensus.

The political and ethnic frontiers established in this region after the First and Second World Wars created sources of latent tension that the dictatorial regimes of the Cold War years were unable and ill-prepared to defuse. While the communist regimes vainly tried to ignore the underlying antagonisms, by emphasizing loyalty to social classes over loyalty to nations, their actions contributed only to the divisions among their nations. The regimes limited the movement of their peoples, provided few guarantees for honouring the rights of national minorities, and in some cases – such as Romania – undertook the forcible assimilation of minorities. By promoting the establishment of autocratic economic regimes that were connected bilaterally with the Soviet economy and had very little interest in real multilateral cooperation, these regimes strengthened the new economic foundations of nationalism.

With the demise of regional Soviet hegemony, not only did old ethnic problems rise to the surface but also a new element – separatism – appeared on the political canvas of multinational states. The dismembering of Yugoslavia and Czechoslovakia were the obvious manifestations of this. The revival of nationalism is not confined to Central and East European countries: according to one expert, there are more than 5,000 ethnic groups in the world that desire national independence.[14] Nationalistic and ethnic violence blights areas as diverse as Western Europe, the Middle East, Africa, India, and China. Nationalism in Central and Eastern Europe, however, is particularly strident and presents great dangers to both regional and international security. Historically, the region has been a buffer zone between the great powers, and its conflicts – often exploited by the great powers – have played catalytic roles in precipitating both world wars.

During the Cold War, the struggle for national identity and self-determination was considered by the West to be a legitimate goal in the fight against Soviet domination. Today, Western encouragement of such goals as separatism and ethnic autonomy is no longer to be heard, but nationalism remains, unconstrained by either dictatorial regimes or an established tradition of democratic tolerance. An important aspect of the management of ethnic issues is related to electoral systems: a number of different systems have implications for ethnic interests and facilitate accommodation. Federalism and regional autonomy is another formula. Early membership in the European Union may ease the problems of ethnicity in the case of the Central and Eastern European countries but, in the absence of appropriate democratic solutions, it may remain an important source of tension in the successor states of the Soviet Union. The ethnic issue, therefore, will remain a dangerous and difficult problem which continues to threaten to undermine the democratization process.

Conclusions

The course of democratization has resulted in a diverse system of governance and opened up new possibilities for hundreds of millions of people to govern their own lives, yet it has opened up political tensions along ethnic, tribal, and socio-economic lines. The key question is whether the democratic regimes better serving the social goals of the development process include the honouring of human rights and, particularly, of economic and social rights.

The former socialist countries in Europe are involved in the global liberalization and democratization process with a number of specific characteristics. The social composition of today's Central and East European countries differs greatly from that of the early Cold War period: no longer traditional peasant societies, where authoritarian rule can easily be enforced, these societies have large professional groups, a broad industrial working class, and a small but growing entrepreneurial middle class. Democracy, participation, and the rule of law are aspirations which are becoming deeply rooted. Any open or disguised political effort to introduce new dictatorial regimes would thus encounter strong internal opposition, not to mention adverse international reaction, which would prove highly damaging to countries so heavily dependent on external economic relations.

The success of democratic changes in Central and Eastern Europe requires wise and honest leadership, good governance, popular support, and also external political encouragement and material support. Favourable social and economic conditions within the countries and in the external environment will assist these factors. Several decades must elapse before we can know whether this region will become a

Europeanized, democratic network of friendly states which will provide an acceptable standard of living for the great majority, or whether the twin paths to democracy and the market will yet be undermined in the midst of poverty, turmoil, and new forms of autocracy. At the end of the 1990s, some of the countries had made important steps toward the establishment of sustainable democratic market economies, whereas, in others, the processes of democratic development and marketization were still weak and uncertain.

Notes

1. Ralf Dahrendorf, *Reflections on the Revolution in Europe* (New York: Times Books, 1990).
2. John Paul II, "On the Hundredth Anniversary of *Rerum Novarum: Centesimus Annus*," *Encyclical Letter*, 1 May 1991 (Publication 436-8) (Washington, D.C.: Office for Publishing and Promotion Services, United States Catholic Conference) p. 82.
3. An important Western political scientist, Richard Lowenthal, suggested in an early stage of the debate that "every measure of freedom is paid for with slowing down economic development," in *Staatsfunktionen und Staatsreform in den Entwicklungsländern*, repr. in F. Nuscheler (ed.) *Politikwissenschaftliche Entwicklungsländerforschung* (Dortmund, 1986), pp. 241–245.
4. Joseph A. Schumpeter, *Capitalism, Socialism and Democracy* (London: George Allen and Unwin, 1947), pp. 289–296.
5. Marcia A. Weigle and Jim Butterfield, "Civil Society in the Reforming Communist Regimes: The Logic of Emergence," *Comparative Politics* 1992; 23(4): 1–23.
6. John Naisbitt, *Global Paradox* (New York: Avon Books, 1995), p. 25.
7. Ibid. p. 47.
8. An American scholar, James Turner Johnson, formulated the question in the following way: "Is liberal democratic self-government, in the form it has taken in the West, capable of being developed also in societies whose traditions and cultures are different from those of the Western democracies?" His answer is: "... even though this achievement is historically and culturally tied to certain particular societies and their intellectual and social histories, such democracy may also 'travel' across historical and cultural lines to become the basis of political life in other societies." See "Does Democracy Travel? Some Thoughts on Democracy and its Cultural Context," *Ethics in International Affairs*, 1992; 6: 41–55.
9. During the past decades, the debates on national institutional change have been influenced by two extreme utopias. One extreme has been the utopia of the Soviet model, which suggested a development process managed by the state, completely subordinated by the collective will, and allegedly expressed by the "visible hand," central government. Here it is interesting to note that Marx never denied the historical role of the market in the development process. In his analysis, the market was the solvent that would break down traditional rigidities of society and allow development. The other extreme has been the liberal utopia, where the master is the "invisible hand" of the market. In these ideas the developmental role of the state was at best limited to ensuring property rights and eliminating obstacles to the emergence of efficient markets. The advocates of this ideology suggested that allocative inefficiency in the developing countries is caused by market failures, a consequence of strong state intervention. Both extremes have been highly ideological, and counterproductive. (There is a third direction, suggesting full decentralization, based on cooperatives, voluntary associations, non-profit structures, and NGOs. This can be called the populist utopia and it has an increasing influence in the debates in many countries.) The historical analysis of the costs and benefits of the visible and invisible hands may be an interesting exercise for future scholars.

10. The new legal and regulatory framework had to ease or liberalize the entry procedures, the rights of establishment, the repatriation of profits, and capital investments. It had to deal with the taxation of foreign investments with the ownership of land, currency conversion, protection of intellectual property rights, and other measures. Another set of regulatory measures was related to accounting practices. In some countries, for example Russia, piecemeal approaches characterized the development of the necessary framework; in others, such as Hungary, there were more comprehensive legislative measures.

11. There are, of course, a number of multilateral agreements related to FDIs to which the former socialist countries joined or expressed their wish to participate in, such as the World Trade Organization's TRIM and arbitration system and its provision related to the protection of intellectual property rights, the Multilateral Investment Guarantee Agreement (MIGA).

12. The developments prompted Zbigniew Brezezinski to observe: "Current political life in Poland suffers from a large number of negative features, above all the fact that it is dominated by parochial political parties lacking a vision of modern society. Instead of such a vision they represent either narrow and sometimes anachronistic class interests or ideas derived chiefly from the early experiences of nineteenth century industrialization. Life in Poland cannot continue to be dominated by political parties which are either coffeehouse formations or of a doctrinaire persuasion or simply socially anachronistic. Poland needs modern integrating parties guided by a vision of post-industrial society, ones which combine knowledge of the modern world (which is the starting-point for any kind of agenda at all) with lasting moral values (the starting-point for choice of bearings)." "Polska scena obrotowa," *Polityka*, 1994; (44). The same could be even more characteristic of several other countries, such as Russia, Ukraine, Romania, and Bulgaria.

13. Richard Kozul-Wright and Paul Rayment, "Walking on Two Legs: Strengthening Democracy and Productive Entrepreneurship in the Transition Economies," *UNCTAD Discussion Papers No. 101*, August 1995, p. 15.

14. See Rodolfo Stavenhagen, *Problems and Prospects of Multi-Ethnic States* (Tokyo: The United Nations University Press, 1986).

9

Political representation and economic competitiveness: Is a new democratic synthesis conceivable?

Ian Marsh

Much of the literature on Western liberal democracy laments the seemingly intractable disjunction between the pluralization of political representation, on one hand, and the requirements for running a competitive economy, on the other.[1] One influential line of thought – public choice theory – even challenges the legitimacy of the patterns of interest representation that have emerged.[2] Moreover, past strategies for accommodating interest groups – corporatism, for example – have been discredited.[3]

The favoured paradigm for a competitive economy, at least amongst policy makers in the Anglo-American world, emphasizes market-based approaches. There has been a determined effort to reduce the role of government and to replace politically mediated by market-mediated relationships. The capacity of the state to influence the quality of its citizens' economic experience is held to have been curtailed by such factors as economic globalization, footloose finance, and the uncertainties of technological development.[4]

Are there alternatives? One comprehensive approach that prioritizes economic competitiveness and argues for the legitimacy of interest representation – "stakeholder capitalism" – has been proposed by Will Hutton.[5] In Hutton's analysis, economic efficiency has not one, but two, necessary and sufficient conditions: well-functioning markets *and* trust and commitment. The energy and dynamism that creates efficiency originates in, and is stimulated by, some combina-

formation of groups of providers and professional administrators, for example doctors, teachers, and economists. The state, because of its need for information and mediation, often encouraged group formation. Imitation also encouraged this process: those who could make a case for their special needs in the broader logic of the welfare state-managed economy could lobby for its benefits. Bidding between the parties for electoral support encouraged this trend. The net result was the development of interest organization on an unprecedented scale.[10]

These trends were further exacerbated by the emergence of issue movements after the 1960s. Their genesis was exogenous in the sense that they did not grow out of the project to secure material equality, embodied in the welfare state-managed economy.[11] Rather, their emergence signified the renewal of political romanticism, an important normative current in the liberal-democratic tradition. The genesis of the issue movements lay in a concern for a cause, rather than the defence of an interest. Contemporary issue movements recall political formations last seen in the nineteenth century – suffragette, temperance, anti-slavery, and the anti-Corn Law movements, for example. The nineteenth century formations either achieved their purposes and disbanded, or were absorbed into the major parties with the rise of collectivism. Their re-emergence at the end of the twentieth century is another mark of the recession of the collectivist project.

Major movements have emerged, at least in the Western liberal democracies, around nine issue areas: these are women, the environment, peace and the third world, gay rights, ethnic rights, Black rights, consumers, animal liberation, and the "new right" or neo-liberal movement. The precise formations can vary from country to country; this is the Australian list. In each case, the evidence of their organizational capacity and political capability is overwhelming. To state only the most obvious point, each major extension of the domestic political agenda over the past 20 years has been driven by one of these movements. The major parties may have ultimately mediated the development of legislation, but the original energy in identifying an issue, championing it for a sustained period, building public support, and mobilizing political pressure belongs with the movements.

Organized political formations are important because they are durable. They both represent and sustain an interest or a cause. The women's movement, the neo-liberal movement, the environment movement, the trade unions, business, and so on, all articulate the

139

more ambitious goals than either party, acting alone, would have judged feasible; and third, in relation to business production and export performance – collaboration required accountability, at least in relation to these outcomes.[16]

What are the formations of this collaboration? The literature on developmental states is quite clear. Commitment from relevant stakeholders has been sought in three phases, reflecting the different major stages in policy development: the first phase involves development of a longer-term vision; the second involves the development of sectoral and functional strategies; and the third involves scrutiny and oversight. These are considered in turn.

First, a longer-term vision of a desired economic future needs to be formulated.[17] This might cover a desired industry structure and/or foreseeable technologies in whose commercialization the nation's industries will, desirably, play a role. The East Asian states have put industry structure, not economic magnitudes, at the centre of their conversations about longer-term outcomes.[18] They have linked discussion of a desired future to current industrial, technical, and commercial competencies and capacities, as well as to skill development and employment. It could equally be linked to other desired social outcomes such as, for example, environmental quality. This vision might be set in an 8- to 12-year framework. Obviously, it would be cast at a fairly high level of generality. Examples are available from Japan and the other developmental states. The key point is to begin a conversation among relevant interests about the rationale for, and feasibility of, desired longer-term outcomes and to explore the extent to which purposes are shared and interdependent.

By such means, the process of building understanding of the realism of desired goals, of their implications for other social interests, and of the possible gains from cooperation might begin, at least among stakeholder élites. This exercise would be no less fruitful for political parties than for social interests, such as business, trade unions, welfare, research, educational, and environmental organizations. Agreement might be sought, although there would, clearly, often be a number of issues on which important interests might differ. As Charles Lindblom has noted, agreement may be far from the only, or most important, ground for cooperation and consent.[19] Other approaches, such as issue transformation, compensation, deferred opposition, or procedural acceptance, may provide grounds for acceptance of an outcome. Even if a sufficiently encompassing vision cannot be formulated, the process will have revealed the extent of conflict, thus alerting relevant actors to future potential political challenges.

Assuming that a sufficiently encompassing vision can be identified, it then needs to be translated into specific sectoral programmes affecting such areas as industry policy, research and development, education, and skill development. The literature on developmental states illustrates the dense institutional networks through which collaboration, particularly between business and government, is sustained and fertilized.[20] The fact that this occurs in the different political settings of Japan and the East Asian states complicates the task in a liberal-democratic society, although it does not alter the need for a framework of information collection, dissemination, and exchange and for collaboration between interests.

At a third level, parties need to be held to account for their commitments. This is partly to avoid the "capture" of programmes by beneficiaries. The public-choice literature holds this to be an unsolvable hazard in liberal states. The origin of much of this literature – the United States – where the institutional structure is largely frozen by the constitution, is relevant. In practice, the evidence is much more mixed than the public-choice proponents would have us believe.[21] Nevertheless, there needs to be confidence that public purposes have not been subverted, and there needs to be the capacity to change or refine programmes if circumstances have changed.

For example, government purchasing of information technology or of telecommunications might have been "bundled" in return for a commitment by one or several suppliers to build desired research capabilities. Specific incentives might have been introduced for a particular sector – such as pharmaceuticals – in return for a commitment to an export or research target. In another domain, the trade-off between employment levels and competitiveness might have persuaded the organized trade union movement and workers generally to agree to a wage norm. In all such cases, institutional arrangements need to be designed to permit scrutiny and review to ensure that beneficiaries meet commitments, free riders are identified, or – in the event of changed circumstances – programmes are modified in a way that is perceived to be fair to all parties, without subverting public interests.

These three dimensions of collaboration – the development of longer-term vision, the design of sectoral programmes, and adequate capacity for scrutiny and review – add up to a major institutional challenge in a liberal-democratic setting. Before considering the precise requirements to which it gives rise, there needs to be further discussion of the link between the structure of politics (the regime), the capacity to achieve particular policy outcomes, and the mobilization of interest-group consent.

Regime structure and consent

A description of the structure of politics and policy-making, if it is to be focused and useful for comparative and evaluative purposes, requires a template. Because this chapter is concerned with the educational – or tutelary or consent-mobilizing – possibilities of the state apparatus, particularly in the strategic dimensions of policy-making, the idea of political learning provides the appropriate framework.[22]

At a practical level, in a two-party adversarial regime, political learning occurs through such day-to-day occurrences as the comments on major political issues made by the individuals who dominate the media. The media naturally turn to senior ministers and the opposition leader or a senior opposition spokesperson. It can also be seen in the cast which has the institutional capacity to command media attention – typically, the leadership élite of the major parties. It can be seen in who has the capacity to introduce a new issue to the public agenda. It can be seen in the cast who initiate, or play leading roles in, the daily rituals of parliament and gain public attention through them. A moment's reflection will suggest the extent to which the leadership élite of the major parties dominates public awareness. It is hardly any wonder, then, that the media relish and foment leadership gossip. This accords with the reality of a most potent political power – commanding public awareness.

The characteristics of political learning can be seen in other areas, such as the horizon of political debate, for example. Generally, the electoral cycle defines the boundaries. In addition, such learning is involved in the information directed to citizens about specific issues that affect them in their roles as pensioners or trade unionists, perhaps directly through the media of the organizations to which they belong. In fact, in a two-party adversarial system, interest groups generally participate in policy-making only through "private" processes of consultation and advice established by ministers and officials, or through party committees. If they disagree with a government proposal, their only redress, apart from private lobbying, is public confrontation.

The characteristics of political learning can also be seen in the lack of any capacity for bipartisanship. On the contrary, the opposition typically declares black what the government asserts is white. These features are not the result of the nature of things or the malevolence of power-hungry politicians, although both these latter factors may also be present. They are, rather, the consequence of the particular pattern of incentives and opportunities created by the structure of the two-party adversarial regime. Political learning is thus a function of regime structure.

Stated more abstractly and dynamically, the idea of political learning suggests that the attitudes, expectations, and, ultimately, the behaviour of citizens is contingent on – and, in important aspects, influenced by – what they hear, see, and read. This occurs both directly, in their role as citizens, through the major political parties, and the formal structure of politics and policy-making; and indirectly, in and through the omnipresent interest groups and issue movements. These meso-level political formations represent particular aspirations and interests and mediate between particular and general interests.

Political learning is one mode of the "empire of opinion."[23] The scope, pattern, and dynamics of this process of communication and learning depends in important aspects on the structure of politics. A focus on political learning thus invites attention to the ways in which the formal structure of politics and policy-making builds awareness, mobilizes actors, constrains or fertilizes information flows, and thus shapes the attitudes, expectations, and behaviour of citizens and policy makers.

Political learning occurs partly through electoral contests, partly through parliamentary activity, and partly through the interaction between citizens and their representative groups that occurs in the development and implementation of public policy on particular matters. Various institutions – cabinet subcommittees, select committees, royal commissions, public inquiries, bureaucratic task forces – might mediate particular phases of this process. By such means, politics and policy-making occur with greater or lesser levels of transparency and access which, in turn, produce different effects on the dissemination of information and the mobilization and alignment of interests.

Various processes, such as those involved in the passage of the annual budget or of legislation, also mediate this activity. The media – whether national, local, or constituency – provide an important conduit, but other actors – such as governments, oppositions, interest groups, issue movements, political parties, and public institutions –

are mostly the initiators or constitute the primary settings. Political learning is a two-way process. Different approaches to policy-making can affect the "learning" of ministers and of the public service about policy options, interest-group attitudes, and the requirements for interest-group management as well as the understanding of public-policy needs, constraints, options, and trade-offs in wider society and its component interests. These linkages and effects are fundamentally a function of the regime structure.

Another way of considering the special characteristics and conditions of political learning is to contrast it with other deliberative and analytic processes. The mass scale of political learning is one singular characteristic; its inherently provisional character is another. The fact that outcomes, if they are reached, bind everyone, including those opposed or who stand to lose, is a third factor; a fourth is its unique fusion of power and justice. At one end, political learning draws on representation, of which one aspect is the brute power of interests through their capacity to mobilize and organize citizens; at the other, the metric of political learning is the public interest, which obliges interests to be accountable in terms of the common good. In other words, the weighting and balancing of concerns and the distribution of rights of access, decision, and redress is a collective intellectual and deliberative process that is suffused with power. For these reasons, political learning, in Stephen Breyer's insight, is inherently an expressive and dramatic activity, with an occasional descent to farce.[24]

In sum, two conclusions are pertinent to the argument of this chapter: first, in the perspective of political learning, the regime is the decisive unit of analysis – the experience of learning is grounded in a drama of power and the structure of power constitutes the *mise en scène* for this theatre; and second, the two-party adversarial regime has structural features which handicap its capacity to build a political consensus about longer-term issues or to mobilize interest-group consent. Before exploring institutional arrangements that might remedy these deficiencies, policy-making requirements arising from the earlier discussion of interest pluralization and competitiveness need to be specified more precisely.

Policy-making requirements

Specific policy-making requirements can be derived from earlier discussions of interest proliferation and competitiveness. First, in relation to the mobilization of interest-group consent, the pervasiveness of interest organization and the general requirements for establishing trust and commitment are both pertinent. Second, in relation to economic competitiveness, the requirements are shaped by the phases in the formulation and implementation of economic purposes, in which collaboration and commitment need to be sought. These considerations suggest at least five requirements for policy-making: first, a capacity to focus public attention on *both* longer-term (18–12 years) *and* current/medium-term (up to 5 years) issues; second, some capacity to explore the scope for bi(multi)partisanship; third, the separation of the strategic policy-making cycle from that concerned with current and medium-term issues; fourth, a strategic policy-making structure with equivalent formal "standing" to that concerned with current and medium-term issues (that is, the process led by ministers and cabinet); and fifth, a policy-making structure with a capacity for interest mobilization and coalition building. These five requirements are explored in turn.

Public focus on longer-term issues

The first requirement arises from the need to focus public attention on longer-term issues. This can occur only through parliament. This is because the drama of power in which the major parties engage – directly in elections and indirectly on the floor of parliament – is at the same time a theatre of political learning. As Bernard Crick has observed, parliament is the setting for a continuous election campaign. In the current system, much of the business of government occurs "privately" through "technical" arenas, such as departments and agencies and their various advisory panels and consultative councils. This works to separate the politics of policy-making from the struggle for office between the major parties. If attention to longer-term issues is to be generated, key elements of the process would need to be sited in the political arena – that is, in parliament. This is because of the special role of this institution in public education and its potential to achieve stakeholder mobilization.

Capacity for bi(multi)partisanship

The second requirement arises from the need to explore the degree of shared or overlapping purposes between the major parties around longer-term goals and outcomes. This is partly because of the over-arching representational role of the major parties and partly because

147

of the requirements for interest mobilization. Various pressures in contemporary society conspire to create considerable common ground between the major parties about desired longer-term economic outcomes. One is economic globalization: this constrains the room for manoeuvre available to national governments, as it encourages national governments to make competitiveness an explicit responsibility. Another pressure arises from electoral change: the older class-based foundations of party support are eroding. To an increasing degree, the major parties pursue common constituencies in their quest for electoral majorities.[25] The degree of tacit bipartisanship is clear in current circumlocutions.

The present adversarial system, in which electoral incentives encourage one party to declare to be black whatever the other declares white, distorts public opinion and reinforces disaffected interests. Shared purposes between the major parties on longer-term goals need to be made explicit to exploit their impact on public opinion. Tacit common ground between the major parties needs to be made explicit to enhance the pressure on interests to rethink their purposes or to restate their dissent, perhaps in more encompassing terms. Through such means, group learning about longer-term outcomes, their interrelationship, and implications might be advanced in the absence of a degree of agreement between the major parties. Explicit bi(multi)partisanship, to the degree that it can be mobilized, would provide focus, momentum, and "weight" to the task of mobilizing public and interest-group consent.

Separate strategic policy-making cycle

The third requirement reflects the need to "locate" responsibility for strategic issues in a separate policy-making cycle – largely independent of the management of current and medium-term issues on which the struggle for office between the principal protagonists might continue to turn. This means that an explicit political focus on strategic questions might be explored. At the moment, longer-term and current or medium-term issues are conflated: both are the responsibility of ministers. As a consequence, strategic issues are rarely raised; if they are brought forward, this will be typically in an adversarial context. The electoral cycle provides the political context in which major parties raise and respond to such issues. Their approach is unlikely to be consistent with the requirements for building understanding of the issues and the trade-offs between possible outcomes or for exploring the extent to which objectives are shared or overlap with their rivals. Again, electoral incentives invite one side to declare to be black whatever the other calls white; any other approach would likely be dysfunctional from a vote-building perspective. To avoid these outcomes, a separate policy-making capacity is required in the political arena which could "manage" the development of a strategic vision. Framing that process within an 8–12-year horizon, with reviews every fourth year, should separate such deliberation from electoral contests and, perhaps, enhance the quality of debate in those contests.

Equivalent formal standing to ministers/cabinet

Earlier discussion pointed to the array of actors who would need to be mobilized in defining, and building commitment to, longer-term economic and other outcomes – political parties, officials, interest groups, and individual experts. Significant conflict between any of these actors needs to be brought to public attention and the reasons ventilated in a forum to which all stakeholders have access and the right of representation. A focus for national and constituency media attention is also required. This points to a process with equivalent formal standing to that led by ministers and the cabinet. Its authority needs to draw on an equivalent democratic legitimacy. This is essential to its ability to elicit evidence and to achieve public, interest-group, and media impact. This is also essential to provide the means to highlight, and perhaps resolve, contentious issues. Finally, as policy-making unfolds into the administration of programmes, a capacity for scrutiny and review is required that can hold ministers, departments, agencies, and interests to account.

Capacity for interest-group mobilization and accountability

The fifth requirement for policy-making arises from the need to mobilize interests and to hold them to account for their commitments. A capacity to mobilize interest-group consent is central to the idea of stakeholding; a capacity to hold particular interests to account for commitments is essential for effective public policy. Neither of these capacities currently exists in any developed form. Interest groups have no legitimate independent standing in the policy-making system. They have no access to a political structure to ventilate their concerns. No political structure can routinely monitor their commitments. The scale of interest organization points to the realism of stakeholding as a policy-making norm. But interest mobilization, integration, and accountability requires an institutional structure of formal standing equal to that of ministers and departments: it needs to be able to shadow the policy-making process in departments and agencies, to provide access to stakeholders, and to call all parties to account. Such a structure should also be capable of producing the necessary "political learning" amongst interests – that is, of inducing reflection about the link between sectional concerns and larger national outcomes: for example, for trade unionists and employees generally, the links are between wage claims, business investment, inflation, and employment levels.[26] "Political learning" also needs to occur amongst all stakeholders to any particular issue, encompassing potential "winners" as well as "losers." Through processes of deliberation and the other arts and devices of politics, a process of ad hoc coalition building might become a routine element of policy-making. By such means, the mobilization of interest-group consent might be accomplished.

Competitiveness and consent: A role for parliamentary committees?

How might these five requirements be satisfied? The only possible candidate would seem to be a "strong" parliamentary committee system, which could be superimposed on existing patterns of executive government.[27] This would transfigure the existing two-party, adversarial, political structure. Parliamentary committees are the appropriate institutional mechanism because of their distinctive capacities and potential. For example, they have the capacity to explore the scope for agreement between the partisans; indeed, their capacities are already well demonstrated, at least in the UK House of Commons. Select committees can make policy-making more transparent, bringing the politics of policy-making into the open. As agents of parliament they draw on the democratic legitimacy, prestige and public standing of this institution. Select committees have a formal standing equivalent to that of ministers. In the event of a dispute with the current government, protagonists would have recourse to the voting power of the House. Finally, such a role for select committees is not without precedent in Westminster parliamentary history.[28]

What are the requirements for a "strong" system? There are at least four: first, it should be structured to cover the major departments of state and the major dimensions of public policy; second, it should have an independent capacity for technical analysis; third, it should have the capacity to mobilize media and interest-group attention; fourth, it should be composed of members of whom at least some share a "committee culture" – that is, they value the independent role of members of parliament (MPs) – qualified, but not quenched, by party allegiance – and value the independent role of parliament. Ideally, such committees will have demonstrated a capacity for bi(multi)partisanship, interest mobilization, and public impact.

Many of these requirements have been met by the current select committees in the British House of Commons. First, the structure is appropriate: the committees cover the major departments of state and they have demonstrated a capacity to cover the major phases of policy-making. It remains to be considered whether a special committee – perhaps a committee of committees – might need to be constituted to handle a periodic review of the longer-term vision. If that proved to be so, the Chairman's group is a possible candidate. Otherwise, the Treasury committee has a demonstrated capacity to undertake longer-term reviews, particularly of economic issues.

One or other of the present committees has demonstrated a capacity in relation to all the other criteria over the past 15 years. They have demonstrated a capacity to mobilize interest groups and to achieve impact on their views and attitudes. They have displayed considerable bipartisanship on non-contentious or longer-term issues. The government's failure to appoint them speedily after the 1987 election, and its endeavour to stack membership and to appoint tame chairs after the 1992 election, testifies to their potential. The late Stuart Walkland described the present committees as "a new House of Commons in waiting."[29] The idea of stakeholding and the policy frameworks associated with a developmental state offers the normative and substantive base for converting this possibility into actuality.

Are there other requirements? Clearly, the present committees in the House of Commons have been neutered by the overriding requirements of adversarial politics. The transfiguration envisaged here is inconceivable outside a "hung" parliament. Even in that context, it would require a new policy culture concerning the role of the state in economic competitiveness – a transformation in the climate of opinion similar to that accomplished by the neo-liberal movement in the 1970s. In addition, perhaps minor party coalition partners (presumably the Liberal Democrats) could be convinced of the special advantages for them in more transparent policy-making. This case has been argued elsewhere.[30]

But a hung House of Commons would seem to be the precondition for this mutation in the policy-making system, and this outcome is not beyond the bounds of possibility. A hung parliament would become routine with voting reform. In other Westminster states – Australia and New Zealand, for example – parallel developments are conditional on specific local factors. In New Zealand's case, as a consequence of electoral reform, a multi-party future is assured.[31] The precise changes that this might stimulate in the structure of policy-making will emerge after the pending general election, the first under the new system. In Australia's case, the constitution gives the upper house, the Senate, powers analogous to the similarly named chamber in the United States. This fact, coupled with the relatively small size of the Australian parliament, makes the upper chamber the logical site for a "strong" committee system. A minor party, of broadly similar persuasion to the British Liberal Democrats, a Green MP, and an independent currently hold the balance of power. This group has yet to convert its pivotal role into major structural changes in the policy-making system. There is a cameo precedent for the role of the Australian Senate envisaged here in the first decade of the twentieth century.[32]

Conclusions

This chapter has explored a possible mutation in the two-party regime. Liberal-democratic politics is perhaps the highest – perhaps the most benevolent – legacy of English-speaking culture. The transfiguration envisaged here would lift democratic practice to a new level and be tantamount to an experiment in citizenship. Can a liberal society, with a tradition of a "strong" state, tolerate wider participation in policy-making and still realize effective governance?[33]

The ultimate grounds for such development arise from the moral basis of the liberal-democratic project. At the deepest level, a more collaborative (or more participatory) political system would enrich the norm of citizenship and, through a public drama of power, realize more comprehensively the tutelary or educational role of politics – variously celebrated by Locke, Rousseau, Tocqueville, and Mill. In this world, the horizon of policy-making would be extended, contention would be focused to a greater extent on specific issues, the policy-making process would be more transparent and accessible, and ad hoc coalition building would be the key policy-making strategy.

Some see states inexorably driven to a common economic pattern under the influence of international economic forces. This seems at best a half-truth. In practice, in any particular society, culture, institutions, and markets coexist in a mutually conditioning, contingent pattern. The meanings realized in and through both institutions and markets are based in the surrounding culture. Anything more than partial convergence is thus unlikely. Perhaps more accurately, convergence on some dimensions will bring into sharper focus differences on others. If states seek to imitate what they perceive to be others' key success factors, they will mostly be able to do so only through functionally equivalent means.[34] This will foster variety, not convergence. The reality seems likely to be interdependence and the management of variety – not interdependence and progressive homogeneity.

At a practical level, the foregoing discussion of the possibilities of mutation in at least the Westminster versions of democratic politics is not wholly speculative, although it is remote from present conventional wisdom. The structure of politics is about to be reconfigured in New Zealand. A similar outcome would occur in the United Kingdom if the present campaign for voting reform achieves success. Similarly, in Australia's case, the erosion of the major parties in the electorate and the existence of a strong and chronically hung Senate provide a base for development in the character of the regime.

However, the precise form such developments might take depends on new conceptions of the economic role of the state and a new understanding of the significance of democratic pluralism. The conceptions outlined here suggest one path that synthesizes these apparently incompatible developments in and through a new democratic pattern. This way involves the reconciliation of representation and competitiveness through a transparent and participatory, potentially more collaborative, structure of politics. By such means, the liberal-democratic project might unfold at a new level. Whether a possible democratic configuration has been realistically envisaged – and whether present political forces and possibilities have been realistically portrayed – others, and time, can judge.

Notes

1. C. Maier, "Democracy and its Discontents," *Foreign Affairs* 1994; 77 (4): 48–64.
2. For example, Mancur Olson, *The Rise and Decline of Nations* (New Haven: Yale University Press, 1983); Samuel Brittan, "The Economic Contradictions of Democracy," *British Journal of Political Science* 1975; (5) 129–159.

3. See, for example, Martin J. Bull, "The Corporatist Ideal Type and Political Exchange," *Political Studies* 1992; 40: 255–272.

4. See, for example, Susan Strange, "The Limits of Politics," *Government and Opposition* 1995; 30(3): 291–311.

5. Will Hutton, *The State We're In* (London: Vintage Books, 1995).

6. Ian Marsh, *Beyond the Two Party System: Political Representation, Economic Competitiveness and Australian Politics* (Melbourne: Cambridge University Press, 1995).

7. See, for example, Peter Self, *Government by the Market? The Politics of Public Choice* (London: Macmillan, 1993).

8. Samuel H. Beer, *Britain Against Itself* (New York: W.W. Norton, 1982); also Marsh, op. cit., especially chapter 2, "A Pluralised Polity: The Rise of Interest Groups and Issue Movements."

9. Kalecki recognized these implications of Keynesianism in 1943 when he wrote that new levels of interdependence between trade unions, business, and governments would prove politically feasible only if matched by new procedural arrangements that recognized the new political role of the former: "Political Aspects of Full Employment", *Political Quarterly* 1943; (14): 322–331.

10. See, for example, Peter Drucker, *Post-Capitalist Society* (New York: Harper Business, 1990).

11. For a broader perspective on electoral change, see, for example, Ronald Inglebeart, *The Silent Revolution* (Princeton: Princeton University Press, 1977).

12. The Thatcher governments sponsored a range of measures designed to curb trade union power and reduce, if not eliminate, their influence in wage bargaining. One result was the abandonment of full employment as a goal of politics. Another was the abandonment of incomes policy. After 16 years it is possible to make some assessment of their success. John MacInnes ends a scrupulous appraisal of Thatcher's impact on the established wage-fixing system with the judgement: "There is every reason to believe that decentralisation (of wage fixing) when combined with workplace-based union organisation is the system most likely to maximise earnings differentials, maximise earnings for the best organised, and maximise unemployment and insecurity for the rest." *Thatcherism at Work* (Milton Keynes: Open University Press, 1987), p. 124. Writing in 1992, Andrew Oswald concluded: "There is only a little evidence that union power fell over (the past) decade. Trade union effects on wages appear to have remained unchanged." *Pay Setting, Self-Employment and the Unions: Themes of the 1980s, Discussion Paper No. 64* (London: Centre for Economic Performance, London School of Economics, 1992). In 1993 David Metcalf wrote: "The market solution to industrial relations difficulties has singularly failed to improve macroeconomic performance ... macroeconomic policy remains a shambles ... The market has failed to solve our wage fixing problem ... surely it is possible to devise a better system of industrial relations and collective bargaining than one which requires 3 million unemployed to get wage inflation under control." *Industrial Relations and Economic Performance, Discussion Paper No. 129* (London: Centre for Economic Performance, London School of Economics, 1993), pp. 34–35. Also in 1993, David Blanchflower and Richard Freeman conclude "the (Thatcher) reforms were premised on an incorrect understanding of the labour market. In particular, the reform package failed to recognise the power of insider pressures for rent sharing and related policies that segment decentralised labour markets in periods of less than full employment." *Did the Thatcher Reforms Change British Labour Market Performance? Discussion Paper No. 168* (London: Centre for Economic Performance, London School of Economics, August 1993).

13. Samuel H. Beer, op. cit. pp. 211–212.

14. Lester Thurow, "Asia: The Collapse and the Cure," *New York Review of Books* 5 February 1998; 22–26.

15. Mark Tilton, *Troubled Tiger*, revised edition (Singapore: Butterworth–Heinemann Asia, 1997).

16. See, for example, Linda Weiss and John Hobson, *The State and Economic Development: A Comparative, Historical Assessment* (Cambridge: Polity Press, 1995); Robert Wade, "Managing Trade: Taiwan and South Korea as Challenges to Economics and Political Science," *Comparative Politics* January 1993; 25(2): 147–167, and *Governing the Market: Economic Theory and The Role of Government in East Asian Industrialisation* (New Jersey: Princeton University Press, 1990); Chalmers Johnson, "Political Institutions and Economic Performance: The Government–Business Relationship in Japan, South Korea and Taiwan," in Frederick C. Deyo (ed.) *The Political Economy of the New Asian Industrialisation* (Ithaca: Cornell University Press, 1987); Michael Best, *The New Competition* (Cambridge: Harvard University Press, 1990); Alice Amsden, *Asia's Next Giant: South Korea and Late Industrialisation* (New York: Oxford University Press, 1989).

17. Ronald Dore has written thus of the difference in "political learning" between the British and Japanese political systems: "To a Japanese person surveying the British scene, it would seem incredible that there should not be a ... certain range of ideas and assumptions about the long-term future with which people – or, to be more specific, the readers of quality newspapers – are wholly familiar, the subject of sufficiently commonplace references in everyday political speech making, that they can be referred to in shorthand words. For example, the 'mid 90s problem', the 'manufacturing/trade balance problem', as the Japanese talk of 'the population/aging problem', 'the structural creditor nation problem', as taken-for-granted starting points for policy discussion. This kind of consensus ... provides legitimation for measures with long-term pay-offs, especially those likely to be bitterly opposed by people in declining industries, for example, who are likely to suffer dislocation in the short run." *Taking Japan Seriously* (London: Athlone Press, 1987), p. 187.

18. See, for example, Michael Best, *The New Competition* (Cambridge, Mass.: Harvard University Press; 1990); Bruce Scott, "Economic Strategy and Economic Performance," *Discussion Paper N9-792-086*, 6 September 1992 (Cambridge, Mass.: Harvard Business School).

19. Charles Lindblom, *The Intelligence of Democracy* (New York: 1965 Free Press, especially chapter 14; also Marsh, op. cit. 1995, especially chapter 8.

20. Daniel I. Okimoto, *Between MITI and the Market: Japanese Industrial Policy for High Technology* (Stanford: Stanford University Press, 1989).

21. Steven Kelman, *Making Public Policy: A Hopeful View of American Government* (New York: Basic Books, 1987).

22. This idea has a considerable genealogy. It can be found in Locke, was extended by Rousseau, and developed by Tocqueville and Mill. See, for example, Samuel Beer, "Two Models of Public Opinion," *Political Theory* 1974; 2(2): 162–180; Ronald Beiner, *Political Judgement* (University of Chicago Press: Chicago, 1983); Philip Selznik, *The Moral Commonwealth* (University of California Press: Berkeley, 1992). Other relevant literature includes that on the role of institutions in policy-making; see, for example, Peter Hall, "Policy Paradigms, Social Learning and the State," *Comparative Politics* 1993; 25(3): 275–296; J. Rogers Hollingsworth, Philippe Schmitter, and Wolfgang Streeck (eds) *Governing Capitalist Economies* (New York: Oxford University Press, 1994); and that on the role of ideas in public polity – see, for example, D. Yankelovitch, *Coming to Public Judgments* (New York: Syracuse University Press, 1992); Robert Reich, *The Power of Public Ideas* (Cambridge: Harvard University Press, 1988); Peter Hall (ed.) *The Political Power of Economic Ideas: Keynesianism Across Nations* (Princeton: Princeton University Press, 1989).

23. J.J. Rousseau, *Politics and the Arts*, translated by A. Bloom (Ithaca: Cornell University Press, 1977), p. 22.

24. Stephen Breyer, "Analysing Regulatory Failure: Mismatches, Restrictive Alternatives and Reform," *Harvard Law Review* 1979; 92(3): 544–609.

25. See, for example, Richard Rose and Ian McAllister, *The Loyalties of Voters* (London: Sage, 1990).

26. The possibility of building support for a wage norm is explored in Marsh, op. cit. 1995, chapter 11.

27. Marsh, op. cit. 1995, chapter 8; also *Policy Making in a Three-Party System* (London: Methuen, 1986).

28. Oliver MacDonagh describes policy-making in the early nineteenth century: "After 1820, and more particularly 1830, both (select committees and Royal Commissions) were used with a regulatory and a purpose quite without precedent. It is difficult to overestimate the importance of this development. Through session after session and through hundreds of inquiries and the examination of many thousands of witnesses a vast mass of information and statistics was being assembled. Even where (as was uncommonly the case) the official inquiry was in the hands of unscrupulous partisans, a sort of informal adversary system usually led to the enlargement of true knowledge in the end. A session or two later the counter-partisans would secure a counter-exposition of their own. All this enabled the administration to act with confidence, a perspective and a breadth of vision which had never hitherto existed. It had also a profound secular effect upon public opinion generally and upon parliamentary public opinion in particular. For the exposure of the actual state of things in particular fields was in the long run probably the most fruitful source of reform in nineteenth-century England." *Early Victorian Government* (New York: Holmes and Meir, 1977), p. 6.

29. In Gavin Drewry (ed.), *The New Select Committees*, 2nd edition (Oxford: Clarendon Press, p. ix).

30. Ian Marsh, "The Lib–Lab Pact and Policy Influence," *Parliamentary Affairs* July 1990; 43(3): 292–322.

31. Jonathan Boston, Stephen Levine, Elizabeth McLeay, and Nigel Roberts, *New Zealand Under MMP: A New Politics* (Auckland: Auckland University Press, 1996).

32. Marsh, op. cit., 1990, chapter 10.

33. Schumpeter's classic exposition of "workable" liberal democracy emphasizes the necessity for limited participation: *Capitalism, Socialism and Democracy* (New York: Harper Colophon Edition, 1976), esp. chapters 22 and 23.

34. J. Rogers Hollingsworth, Philippe Schmitter, and Wolfgang Streeck (eds) *Governing Capitalist Economies*, op. cit.; also Paul Hirst and Grahame Thompson, *Globalism in Question* (Cambridge: Polity Press, 1996).

10

A structure for peace: A democratic, interdependent, and institutionalized order

Bruce Russett

Three principles for a peaceful international order

As the Second World War drew to a close, leaders of the great powers drew up a set of landmark documents, including the Charter of the United Nations and the foundations for the Bretton Woods financial institutions. The inspiration for these documents stemmed primarily from democratic countries, notably the United Kingdom and the United States. In part, of course, the victors depended upon military strength. But their new structure for international relations encompassed much more: it used trade, economic assistance, foreign investment, and cultural instruments like the US Information Agency and the BBC. A key feature was that it was based not on unilateralism but multilateralism. Its multilateral instruments ranged far beyond NATO and the rest of the alliance system, depending heavily upon regional trade arrangements like the OECD, the World Bank, the IMF, GATT, and many UN specialized agencies. Central UN institutions, such as the Security Council, were also vital for blessing peace-enforcement action and managing dangerous confrontations.[1]

Initially, the hope was that the Soviet Union would be fully inside this structure. But the rise of the Cold War undermined the effectiveness of the institutions, and many operated without the active participation of the Soviet Union. Thus, it was only in part a fully global structure and, in important ways, principally a structure for managing and strengthening relations among the Western allies. For that purpose, on the whole it worked well. Now, with the end of the Cold War, we have seen an opportunity to broaden the earlier structure to encompass a much larger proportion of the world.

Contemporary policy formulation needs a similar central organizing principle. To promote its acceptance, that principle would be best rooted in the earlier experience. It should build on the principles which underlie the rhetoric and much of the practice, principles rooted in beliefs about the success of free political and economic systems. The first of these principles is democracy; the second – now buttressed by increasing evidence that economic interdependence promotes peace as well as prosperity – is free markets; the third is international law and organization. These ideas remain as strong as ever.

Consider a puzzle about the end of the Cold War. The question is not simply why did the Cold War end but, rather, why did it end before the drastic change in the bipolar distribution of power, and why did it end peacefully? In November 1988, Margaret Thatcher proclaimed, as did other Europeans, that "the Cold War is over"; by spring 1989, the US State Department stopped making official reference to the Soviet Union as "the enemy." The fundamental patterns of East–West behaviour had changed, on both sides, beginning even before the circumvention of the Berlin Wall and then its destruction in October 1989. All of this preceded the unification of Germany (October 1990) and the dissolution of the Warsaw Pact (July 1991). Even after these latter events, the military power of the Soviet Union itself remained intact until the dissolution of the USSR at the end of December 1991. None of these events was resisted militarily.

Understanding of the change in the Soviet Union's international behaviour before its political fragmentation, and in time reciprocated by the West, demands attention to the operation of the three principles.

1. *Substantial political liberalization and a movement toward democracy in the Soviet Union.* Consequently, there were improvements in free expression and the treatment of dissidents at home, in the East European satellites, and in behaviour toward Western Europe and the United States.
2. *The desire for economic interdependence with the West,* impelled by the impending collapse of the Soviet economy and the perceived need for access to Western markets, goods, technology, and capital, which in turn required a change in Soviet military and diplomatic policy.
3. *The influence of international law and organizations,* as manifested in the Conference on Security and Cooperation in Europe (CSCE) and human rights based on the Helsinki accords, which legitimized

and supported dissent in the communist states. Whereas the United Nations itself was not important in the process of penetrating domestic politics, the CSCE most certainly was, as were the various international non-governmental organizations devoted to human rights.

A vision of peace among democratically governed states has long been invoked as part of a larger structure of institutions and practices to promote peace among nation-states. In 1795, Immanuel Kant spoke of perpetual peace based partially upon states sharing "republican constitutions." His meaning was compatible with basic contemporary understandings of democracy. As the elements of such a constitution, he identified freedom, with legal equality of subjects, representative government, and separation of powers. The other key elements of his perpetual peace were "cosmopolitan law," embodying ties of international commerce and free trade, and a "pacific union" established by treaty in international law among republics.

Woodrow Wilson expressed the same vision for the twentieth century. It appeared that Kant was guiding his writing hand when he formed his Fourteen Points: they included Kant's cosmopolitan law and pacific union. Point three demanded

Removal, so far as possible, of all economic barriers and the establishment of an equality of trade conditions among all the nations consenting to the peace and associating themselves for its maintenance.

The fourteenth point stated that

A general association of nations must be formed under specific covenants for the purpose of affording mutual guarantees of political independence and territorial integrity to great and small states alike.

He did not explicitly invoke the need for universal democracy, since not all of America's war allies were democratic. But his meaning is clear if one considers the domestic political conditions necessary for his first point:

Open covenants of peace, openly arrived at, after which there shall be no private international understandings of any kind but diplomacy shall proceed always frankly and in the public view.

This vision once sounded utopian, but later in the twentieth century it was picked up again. Konrad Adenauer, Jean Monnet, and other founders of the European Coal and Steel Community (now the European Union) sought some way to ensure that the great powers,

159

who had repeatedly fought dreadful wars over the previous century, would finally live in peace with each other. To do so, they supported the restoration of democratic institutions in their countries, built a network of economic interdependence to make war unthinkable on cost/benefit grounds, and embedded their relationships in new structures of European organization.

Democracies rarely fight one another

The following discussion necessarily is merely an overview with references to detailed research. I discuss evidence supporting all three elements of this vision here, although for the purposes of this volume I focus more on democratization than on the other two elements. That is also appropriate because the most solid, extensive, and elaborated evidence is for the proposition that democracies do not engage in war with each other. Much of it is addressed in my book on this topic, although far more has accumulated since then.[2] In the contemporary era, "democracy" denotes a country in which nearly everyone can vote, elections are freely contested, the chief executive is chosen by popular vote or by an elected parliament, and civil rights and civil liberties are substantially guaranteed. Democracies may not be especially peaceful in general: we all know the history of democracies in colonialism, covert intervention, and other excesses of power. Democracies may be as violent in their relations with some authoritarian states as some authoritarian states are toward each other. But the relations between stable democracies are qualitatively different.

Democracies are unlikely to engage in militarized disputes *with each other* or to let any such disputes escalate into war; in fact, they rarely even skirmish. Since 1946, pairs of democratic states have been only one-eighth as likely as other kinds of states to threaten to use force against each other, and only one-tenth as likely actually to do so. Established democracies fought *no wars* against one another during the entire twentieth century. (Although Finland, for example, took the Axis side against the Soviet Union in the Second World War, it engaged in no combat with the democracies.)[3]

The more democratic a state is, the more peaceful its relations are likely to be. Democracies are more likely to employ "democratic" means of peaceful conflict resolution. They are readier to reciprocate each other's behaviour, to accept third-party mediation or good offices in settling disputes, and to accept binding third-party settlement.[4]

Democracies' relatively peaceful relations toward each other are not spuriously caused by some other influence, such as sharing high levels of wealth, or rapid growth, or ties of allowance. This has been established by statistical analysis of the behaviour of pairs of states in the international system since the Second World War.[5] Pairs of states that are democratic are more peaceful than others, even aside from these influences. The peace between democracies is not limited just to the rich industrialized states of the global North. It was not maintained simply by pressure from a common adversary in the Cold War, and it has outlasted that threat.

The phenomenon of democratic peace can be explained by the pervasiveness of normative restraints on conflict between democracies. That explanation extends to the international arena the cultural norms of live-and-let-live and peaceful conflict resolution that operate within democracies. The phenomenon of democratic peace can also be explained by the role of institutional restraints on democracies' decision to go to war. Those restraints ensure that any state in a conflict of interest with another democracy can expect ample time for conflict-resolution processes to be effective and that the risk of incurring surprise attack is virtually nil.

Non-industrial societies, studied by anthropologists, also show restraints on warfare among democratically organized polities that typically lack the institutional constraints of a modern state. Despite that absence, democratically organized units fight each other significantly less often than do non-democratic units. And political stability also proves an important restraint on the resort to violence by these democratically organized units. Finding the relationship between democracy and peace in pre-industrial societies shows that the phenomenon of democratic peace is not limited to contemporary Western democracies.[6]

The end of the Cold War ideological hostility is highly significant because it represents a surrender to the values of economic and, especially, political freedom. To the degree that the countries once ruled by autocratic systems become democratic, the absence of war among democracies comes to bear on any discussion of the future of international relations. By this reasoning, the more democracies there are in the world, the fewer potential adversaries democracies will have and the wider the zone of peace.

The *possibility* of a widespread zone of democratic peace in the contemporary world exists. To bring that possibility to fruition, several fundamental problems must be addressed – the problem

161

of consolidating democratic stability, the interaction of democracy with nationalism, the role of economic development and interdependence, and the prospects for changing basic patterns of international behaviour.

Strengthening democracy and its norms

The literature on the "prerequisites" of democracy is vast and has often been deeply flawed – ethnocentric and too enamoured with economic preconditions. Other contributors to this volume know that literature far better than I, and have contributed to making it much more subtle and far less ethnocentric. Most (but by no means all) of the influences on the successful consolidation of democratic transitions are largely domestic. For the sake of a general point, I refer only briefly to some of the international influences which, along with the domestic ones, are identified in Samuel Huntington's now-familiar work.[7]

Among changes that played significant parts in *producing* the latest wave of recent transitions to democracy, Huntington includes changes in some religious institutions (including transnational ones) that made them less defenders of the status quo than opponents of governmental authoritarianism; changes in the policies of other states and international organizations, to promote human rights and democracy; and "snowballing" or demonstration effects, enhanced by international communication, as transitions to democracy in some states served as models for their neighbours. Among his list of conditions that favour the *consolidation* of new democracies is a favourable international environment, with outside assistance. While internal influences are certainly prominent, the international conditions are impressive also. Favourable international conditions may not be essential in every case but they can make a difference, and sometimes a crucial one when the internal influences are mixed.

With economic conditions still so grim in much of the developing world, Eastern Europe, and the former Soviet Union, and the consequent dangers to the legitimacy of new democratic governments, external assistance – technical and financial – is especially important. New democracies will not survive without some material improvement in their citizens' lives. As a stick, aid can surely be denied to governments that regularly violate human rights and perpetrate blatantly anti-democratic acts, such as a military coup or an aborted election. As to the carrot of extending aid on a conditional basis, broader goals of developing democratic institutions require the creation of a civil society and are less easily made conditional. Recipients may see multilateral aid, with conditions of democratic reform attached, as a less blatant invasion of their sovereignty than aid from a single country.

A special complication, hardly unique to the current era but felt acutely now, is ethnic conflict. With its lines of inclusion and exclusion, nationalism readily conflicts with the quasi-universalistic ethos that "democracies do not fight each other." Hatreds, long suppressed, emerge to bedevil any effort to build stable, legitimate government. An irony is that the initial creation of democratic institutions can contribute to the explosion of ethnic conflicts, by providing the means of free expression, including expression of hatred and feelings of oppression:[8] people who have long hated each other can now say how much they hate each other.

Even if stable and established democracies are generally at peace with one another, the *process of democratization* is not always a peaceful one. A brand-new democracy may be unstable and may face fierce problems of restructuring its economy and satisfying diverse interests and ethnic groups. Under these, perhaps temporary, circumstances, nationalism and domestic problems may sometimes lead to conflicts with neighbouring states. Nearby autocracies may attack them because they see their shift to democracy as endangering the legitimacy of authoritarianism, or their period of transition as a moment of potential weakness to be exploited. But, importantly, *only* those democracies who have autocratic states as neighbours are more likely to get into military conflicts. One piece of good news is that democratizing states from the former Warsaw Pact countries have been substantially peaceful with democratic or democratizing neighbours. Furthermore, transitions from autocracy to democracy are no more dangerous to international peace than are failed democracies that revert to autocratic rule. The problem is one of instability and transition in both directions, not just of new democracies.[9]

The solution does not lie in less democracy; rather, it requires measures including external assistance and protection to assist and speed the transition. It also requires attention to devising institutions, and nurturing norms and practices, with respect for minority rights. If democratization is temporarily a problem, the establishment of stable democracy is key to the solution. The creation of institutions, norms, and practices to protect minorities has never been easy, but it presents the fundamental challenge of world political development in this

163

era. It is worth remembering that the most terrible acts of genocide in this century – from Turkey's slaughter of the Armenians through Hitler, Stalin, Pol Pot, and others – have been carried out by authoritarian or totalitarian governments, not democratic ones.[10]

Economic interdependence and international organizations

Ties of economic interdependence – international trade and investment – form an important supplement to shared democracy in promoting peace. Here is the second element of the Kantian/Wilsonian/EU vision, representing the role of free trade and a high level of commercial exchange. Economic interdependence gives countries a stake in each others' well-being. War would mean destruction, in the other country, of one's own markets, industrial plants, and sources of imports. If my investments are in your country, bombing your industry means, in effect, bombing my own factories. Just the threat of war inhibits international trade and investment. Economic interdependence also serves as a channel of information about each other's perspectives, interests, and desires on a broad range of matters not the subject of the economic exchange. These communications form an important channel for conflict management. Interdependence, however, is the key word: mutual dependence, not one-sided dominance.

Interdependence over the last 50 years has contributed to wealth, to alliances, and to reducing conflict among states so linked. When countries trade with each other (and this constitutes a substantial portion of their national incomes), violent conflict and war between them are rare. The combination of democracy and interdependence is especially powerful. Democracies trade more with each other than do non-democracies. States that are both democratic and economically interdependent are extremely unlikely to initiate serious military disputes with each other.[11]

New democracies and free markets should be supported financially, politically, and morally. Successful transitions in some countries can supply a model for others. A stable and less menacing international system can permit the emergence and consolidation of democratic governments, and peaceful economic growth and interchange. International threats – real or only perceived – strengthen the forces of secrecy, authoritarianism, and autarky in the domestic politics of states involved in protracted conflict. Relaxation of international threats to peace and security reduces the need, and the excuse, for repressing dissent and centralizing control of the economy.

The reliance on international law and institutions, and the need for strengthening them, constitutes the third element of the Kantian/ Wilsonian vision. As expressed in former Secretary-General Boutros-Ghali's *An Agenda for Peace*,[12] the United Nations has a new mission of "peace-building," attending to democratization, development, and the protection of human rights. The United Nations is newly strengthened and, paradoxically, also newly and enormously burdened.

International organizations, like other institutions, may serve a variety of functions. Their occasional role in coercing norm-breakers – for example, by the Security Council – is only one. In addition, they may mediate among conflicting parties, reduce uncertainty in negotiations by conveying information, expand material self-interest to be more inclusive and longer term, shape norms, and help generate narratives of mutual identification among peoples and states. Some organizations are more successful than others, and in different functions; but, overall, they do make a difference.

An extension of the quantitative empirical analyses referred to above makes the point. The same kind of analysis that first established an independent and significant influence of democracy in reducing conflict between countries, and then added evidence for an additional meliorative influence of economic interdependence, has been carried out on the effect of international organizations. We have collected information on the number of intergovernmental organizations (IGOs) in which both of any pair of countries are a member. This "density" of IGO membership varies from zero for some countries to over 100 for some pairs of European states. Adding this information to the previous analysis, we find that it, too, contributes an additional, independent, statistically significant effect in reducing the probability of international conflict: the thicker the network, the fewer the militarized disputes. We still need to know more about how this effect works, and under what conditions. Together, when two countries share democracy, interdependence, and numerous IGO memberships, they reduce by nearly 75 per cent the likelihood that they will experience any militarized disputes. Furthermore, a reinforcing feedback condition operates whereby countries at peace with each other typically participate in the same IGOs. But these results represent good evidence for the third and final leg of the Kantian/ Wilsonian/EU structure underlying peaceful international relations.[13]

Democratization and the role of international organizations

Understanding that democracies rarely fight each other – and why this is so – has great consequence for policy in the contemporary world. It should affect the kinds of military preparations believed to be necessary and the costs one would be willing to pay to make them. It should encourage peaceful efforts to assist the emergence and consolidation of democracy. But a misunderstanding of it could encourage war-making against authoritarian regimes and efforts to overturn them, with all the costly implications of preventive or hegemonic military activity such a policy might imply.

The successful defeat of adversaries can be misleading if one forgets how expensive it can be and especially if one misinterprets the political conditions of military defeat. The allies utterly defeated the Axis coalition during the Second World War. Then, to solidify democratic government, they conducted vast (if incomplete) efforts to remove the former élites from positions of authority. The model of "fight them, beat them, and then make them democratic" is no model for contemporary action. It probably would not work, anyway, and no one is prepared to make the kind of effort that would be required. Not all authoritarian states are inherently aggressive; indeed, at any particular time, the majority are not. A militarized crusade for democracy is not in order.

External military intervention, even against the most odious dictators, is a dangerous way to try to produce a democratic world order. Sometimes, with a cautious cost–benefit analysis and with the certainty of substantial and legitimate internal support, it might be worth while – that is, under conditions when rapid military success is likely *and* the will of the people at issue is clear. Even so, any time that an outside power supplants any existing government, the problem of legitimacy is paramount. The very democratic norms to be instilled may be compromised. At the least, intervention cannot be unilateral: it must be approved by an international body like the United Nations or a regional security organization. When an election has been held under UN auspices and certified as fair – as happened in Haiti – the United Nations has a special responsibility, even a duty, to see that the democratic government it helped to create is not destroyed.

Under most circumstances, international bodies are better used as vehicles to promote democratic processes at times when the relevant domestic parties are ready. Peace-keeping operations to help provide the conditions for free elections, monitor those elections, and advise on the building of democratic institutions are usually far more promising and less costly for all concerned than military intervention.

With the end of the Cold War, the United Nations experienced highly publicized troubles in Somalia and the former Yugoslavia, as it tried to cope with a range of challenges not previously part of its mandate. None the less, its successes, though receiving less attention, outnumber the failures: it emerged as a major facilitator of peaceful transitions and democratic elections in such places as El Salvador, Eritrea, and Namibia; its Electoral Assistance Unit has provided election monitoring, technical assistance, or other aid to electoral processes in more than 70 states.

Economic interdependence is also supported by international organizations. Increasingly, economic development is seen to be dependent upon open markets for goods and capital. Without the network of regional and global institutions to promote free and expanding trade, much of the world could readily slip back into protectionism and trade wars. The IMF and the World Bank have recently become instruments not just to create and strengthen free markets but also to ease the transition to democracy and to rebuild societies shattered by civil war.

The emerging order

Democracy and international peace can feed upon each other. An evolutionary process may even be at work. Because of the visible nature and public costs of breaking commitments, democratic leaders are better able to persuade leaders of other states that they will keep the agreements they do enter into. Democratic states are able to signal their intentions in bargaining with greater credibility than autocratic states. Democracies more often win their wars than do authoritarian states: in fact, they do so 80 per cent of the time. They are more prudent about what wars they get into, choosing wars that they are more likely to win and which will incur lower costs. With free speech and debate, they are more accurate and efficient information processors. In wars, democracies exhibit superior organizational skills and leadership. Authoritarian governments who lose wars are often subsequently overthrown and may be replaced by democratic regimes. States with competitive elections generally have lower military expenditures, which, in relations with other democracies, promotes cooperation. As the politically relevant international environment becomes composed of more democratic and internally stable states, democracies tend to reduce their military allocations and conflict involvement.[14]

The modern international system is commonly traced to the Treaty of Westphalia and the principles of sovereignty and non-interference in internal affairs affirmed by it. In doing so it affirmed the anarchy of the system, without a superior authority to ensure order. It also was a treaty among princes who ruled as autocrats. Our understanding of the modern anarchic state system risks conflating the effects of anarchy with those stemming from the political organization of its component units. When most states are ruled autocratically – as in 1648 and throughout virtually all of history since – then playing by the rules of autocracy may be the only way for any state, democracy or not, to survive.

But the emergence of new democracies with the end of the Cold War presents an opening for change in the international system more fundamental even than at the end of other major wars – the First and Second World Wars and the Napoleonic Wars. For the first time ever, in 1992, a virtual majority of states (91 of 183) approximated the standards for democracy that I employed earlier; another 35 were in some form of transition to democracy.[15] Democracy will not be consolidated in all these states. A subsequent report notes some backsliding in the number of people living in democracies, though still an increase in the number of democratic governments.[16] Yet states probably can become democratic faster than they can become rich. Some autocratically governed states will surely remain in the system. In their relations with states where democracy is unstable, or where democratization is not begun at all, democracies must continue to be vigilant and maintain military deterrence. But if enough states become stable democracies in the coming decade, then among them we will have a chance to reconstruct the norms and rules of the international order. We have already come a long way from 1648.

In time, the current quasi hegemony of the United States and its allies will fade, giving way to a more diffused distribution of global power. That diffusion will occur across some very different national cultures and experiences, in Asia, Latin America, the Middle East, and (perhaps) Africa. It could give rise to a highly fragmented, competitive, and dangerous international system, or to one in which conflicts of interest can be managed without an excessive frequency and severity of violence. For the latter, there must be agreements to disagree peacefully, and protection for minority needs and cultural distinctiveness – centrally associated with concepts of democracy – built into the structures of nation-states and, as well, into relations between states. Those relations will need to be further buttressed by linkages of economic interdependence and mediated by international (and, perhaps, supranational) institutions. Wide implementation of the Kantian/Wilsonian/EU vision offers the opportunity to manage global power changes in a constructive fashion. Indeed, it may well be the only alternative to catastrophic destruction.

Notes

1. G. John Ikenberry, "The Myth of Post-Cold War Chaos," *Foreign Affairs* 1996; 75: 79–91.
2. In part this chapter summarizes research reported in detail in Bruce Russett, *Grasping the Democratic Peace: Principles for a Post-Cold War World* (Princeton, NJ: Princeton University Press, 1993). See also Spencer Weart, *Never at War: Why Democracies Will Never Fight Each Other* (New Haven, CT: Yale University Press, 1998). The larger project that I lay out here, including the effects of interdependence and international organizations, is discussed in Russett, "A Neo-Kantian Perspective: Democracy, Interdependence, and International Organizations in Building Security Communities," in Emanuel Adler and Michael Barnett (eds) *Security Communities in Comparative Perspective* (Cambridge: Cambridge University Press).
3. My assertions have not gone uncontested, but the predominant evidence remains strongly in their favour. For a reply to some critiques see Bruce Russett, "Counterfactuals about War and Its Absence," in Philip Tetlock and Aaron Belkin (eds) *Counterfactual Thought Experiments in World Politics: Logical, Methodological, and Psychological Perspectives* (Princeton, NJ: Princeton University Press, 1996).
4. Russell Leng, "Reciprocating Influence Strategies and Success in Interstate Bargaining," *Journal of Conflict Resolution* March 1993; 37(1): 3–41; William Dixon, "Democracy and the Peaceful Settlement of International Disputes," *American Political Science Review* March 1994; 88(1): 14–32; Gregory Raymond, "Democracies, Disputes, and Third-Party Intermediaries," *Journal of Conflict Resolution* March 1994; 38(1): 24–42.
5. Russett, 1993, op. cit., ch. 4 reports much of this evidence, based on an analysis of nearly 100 pairs of states' international behaviour in each of the years from 1950 to 1985. Similar results over a longer period are reported independently by Stuart Bremer, "Dangerous Dyads: Conditions Affecting the Likelihood of Interstate War, 1815–1965," *Journal of Conflict Resolution* June 1993; 36(2): 309–341. One of the most persuasive recent studies is David Rousseau, Christopher Gelpi, Dan Reiter, and Paul Huth, "Assessing the Dyadic Nature of the Democratic Peace, 1918–1988", *American Political Science Review* September 1996; 90(3): 512–533.
6. In addition to Russett, 1993, op. cit., ch. 5, see Neta Crawford, "A Security Regime Among Democracies: Cooperation Among Iroquois Nations," *International Organization* Summer 1994; 48(3): 345–386.
7. Samuel P. Huntington, *The Third Wave: Democratization in the Late Twentieth Century* (Norman: University of Oklahoma Press, 1991).
8. Ted Robert Gurr, *Minorities at Risk: A Global View of Ethnopolitical Conflicts* (Washington, D.C.: U.S. Institute of Peace, 1993).
9. Edward Mansfied and Jack Snyder, "Democratization and War," *International Security* Summer 1995; 20(1): 5–38 have suggested the dangers of democratization, but their systematic evidence does not indicate that democratizing states are more likely to fight either mature democracies or other democratizing states. For the important qualifications about neighbours and autocratization, see John Oneal and Bruce Russett, "The Classical Liberals

Were Right: Democracy, Interdependence, and Conflict: 1950–1985," *International Studies Quarterly* June 1997; 41(2): 267–294, and William R. Thompson and Richard Tucker, "A Tale of Two Democratic Peace Critiques," *Journal of Conflict Resolution* June 1997; 41(3): 428–454.

10. R. J. Rummel, *Death by Government: Genocide and Mass Murder in the Twentieth Century* (New Brunswick, NJ: Transaction, 1994).

11. Harry Bliss and Bruce Russett, "Democratic Trading Partners: 1950–1986," *Journal of Peace Research* February 1996; 33(1): Ties of Interest and Community," in Gustaaf Geeraerts and Patrick Stouthuysen (eds) *Democratic Peace for Europe: Myth or Reality* (Brussels: Free University of Brussels Press, 1998); Oneal and Russett, 1997, op. cit.

12. New York: United Nations, 1993, paragraph 81.

13. Bruce Russett, John Oneal, and David Davis, "The Third Leg of the Kantian Tripod for Peace: International Organizations and Militarized Disputes, 1950–1985," *International Organization* Summer 1998; 52(3): forthcoming.

14. James Fearon, "Domestic Political Audiences and the Escalation of International Disputes," *American Political Science Review*, September 1994; 88(3): 577–592; David Lake, "Powerful Pacifists: Democratic States and War," *American Political Science Review* March 1992; 86(1): 37; Kenneth Schultz and Barry Weingast, *The Democratic Advantage: The Institutional Sources of State Power in International Competition* (Stanford, CA: Hoover Institution, 1996); Bruce Bueno de Mesquita, Randolph Siverson, and Garry Woller, "War and the Fate of Regimes: A Comparative Survey," *American Political Science Review* June 1992; 86(3): 639–646; Bueno de Mesquita and Siverson, "War and the Survival of Political Leaders: A Comparative Study of Regime Types and Political Accountability," *American Political Science Review* December 1995; 89(4): 840–855; Michelle Garfinkel, "Domestic Politics and International Conflict," *American Economic Review* December 1984; 84(5): 1294–1309; Zeev Maoz, *Domestic Sources of Global Change* (Ann Arbor: University of Michigan Press, 1997; Dan Reiter and Allan Stam III, "Democracy and Battlefield Effectiveness," *Journal of Conflict Resolution* June 1998; 42(3): forthcoming.

15. R. Bruce McColm and James Finn, *Freedom in the World: Political Rights and Civil Liberties 1991–1992* (New York: Freedom House, 1992), p. 47. These ratings are somewhat controversial, but a careful analysis found the Freedom House scores to have the least systematic bias on any major assessment. See Kenneth Bollen, "Liberal Democracy: Validity and Method Factors in Cross-National Measures," *American Journal of Political Science* November 1993; 37(4): 1207–1230.

16. R. Bruce McColm and James Finn, *Freedom in the World: Political Rights and Civil Liberties 1994–1995* (New York: Freedom House, 1995).

Regional characteristics of democracy

11

Asian-style democracy?

Takashi Inoguchi

The past quarter-century has seen a quadrupling globally of the number of countries that can be considered to be democracies, from 25 to around 100. As a consequence of this democratic proliferation, the world has acquired new ways of assessing and analysing democracy. In this context, a significant new perception is to approach democracy as a regional or cultural phenomenon, reflecting historical evolutionary tracks that differ from those of the Westminster model of parliamentary democracy and its American variant of federalism. This chapter discusses the components that make up a hypothetical Asian "variant" of democracy, sometimes called "Asian-style" democracy.

Behind the new tendency to particularize or localize varying "cultures" or systems of democracy is an important theoretical shift from substantive to a procedural definition of democracy.[1] The classical definition of democracy by Seymour Martin Lipset is based on the assumption that a single value system is inherent to all democracies. Lipset asserts that democracy has to meet two basic conditions – legitimacy and good governance. Democratic governments, according to Lipset, must be based on popular representation coupled with effective management of the economy and administration. But the Lipset definition corresponds closely only to Western democracies: American democracy is its point of departure; other democracies are measured by their proximity to or distance from the American norm.

The contemporary view of democracy departs radically from Lipset: rather than focusing on values, it views democracy as a set of procedures through which a regime achieves legitimacy. Under this definition, the minimum test for a democracy is that it incorporates free elections and a multi-party system, and guarantees the confidentiality of the electoral process. Even such a minimalist definition of democracy does not leave out the notion of democracy as a normative value structure. Increasingly, however, democracy and market liberalization are lumped together as general values to be sustained by the international system.

Yet, when we try to analyse the substantive or value components of an individual democracy, the tendency is to be overwhelmed by a bewildering array of cultural, social, and economic variants. Some analysts argue that the contemporary era of democratic proliferation is also the "end" of democracy, as form races beyond any effort to establish prescriptions or norms.[2]

Democracy in Pacific Asia

Here, I define "Pacific Asia" as the countries that ring the western shores of the Pacific, from Japan to Indonesia, including China, the Korean Peninsula, Taiwan, the Philippines, Singapore, and mainland South-East Asia. Before discussing the nature and features of Asian democracy, a brief discussion of the history of democracy in Pacific Asia is in order.[3]

The region's first two democracies, after the Second World War, were the Philippines and Japan, both through the agency of the United States. The United States granted independence to the Philippines in 1946, after a "trial" period of democracy had been interrupted by the Japanese Occupation. Democracy was introduced forcibly to Japan during the American Occupation, from 1945 to 1952, and sustained in the context of the San Francisco Treaty of 1952 and the US–Japan Mutual Security Treaty.

None the less, Pacific Asia was a bastion of authoritarianism during most of the post-war period, through the 1980s. After 1955, Japan effectively adopted a one-party system under the Liberal Democratic Party (LDP), in which the economic bureaucracy made many of the important decisions of the Japanese state. In 1972, Philippine President Ferdinand Marcos declared martial law, bringing an end to Philippine democracy until it was restored by the "People Power" movement in 1986.

The image of Asian authoritarianism was reinforced by the developmental strategies of a number of Asian states from the 1950s to the 1980s. These states – Japan, South Korea, Taiwan, Singapore,

Malaysia, Indonesia, and Thailand – participated in the emerging global free-market system but justified authoritarian practices on the grounds that the state needed to be able to act flexibly and forcibly in order to spur economic growth.

Most of these nations emerged from the Second World War in dire poverty and disorder, and only a few – notably Japan, Korea, and Taiwan – had begun the industrialization process prior to the wars of national liberation that swept the region immediately after the end of the war. These "developmental authoritarian states" occupied an economic middle ground between capitalism and Soviet- or Chinese-style command economies, but were tolerated by the West because they allied themselves politically with the anti-communist camp.[4]

In the mid-1970s, a new tide of democratization began in the Mediterranean, spreading swiftly to Latin America. Starting in the late 1970s and early 1980s, the wave of democratization permeated Pacific Asia as well.[5]

With the end of the Cold War, Pacific Asia was a showcase of democracy. Of the post-war "developmental authoritarian" states, all except Malaysia and Indonesia had experienced major political restructuring. South Korea and Taiwan deliberately introduced their first free presidential elections in the early to mid-1990s. Singapore's authoritarian-minded Prime Minister Lee Kuan Yew voluntarily stepped down. In the Philippines, the People Power movement toppled the Marcos dictatorship in 1986 and was succeeded by two democratically elected presidents. In Japan, the monolithic rule of the LDP came to an end in 1993, followed by a period of political restructuring and public debate over the nature of the Japanese democracy.

In 1996, almost all of Pacific Asia is under some form of democracy. Only the remaining Communist states – China, North Korea, and Viet Nam – and the military dictatorship in Myanmar and Brunei's monarchy fail to meet the description of democracy.

The subsequent discussion of "Asian-style" democracy is restricted to the following political systems: Japan, South Korea, Taiwan, the Philippines, Malaysia, Singapore, Indonesia, and Thailand. Obviously, the diversity of these democracies is immense. The discussion has as its framework three aspects of "Asian-style" democracy – its emphasis on economic performance, its legitimizing values, and its institutional framework. In each case, I seek to generalize the common themes of "Asian-style" democracy, without insisting that any one of these themes is represented in each of the eight political systems.

The East Asian Miracle

Good economic performance is an important component of Asian-style democracy. Even in the Lipset definition of democracy, economic performance is an indispensable pillar of democracy. Good economic performance helps to sustain the legitimacy of democratic rule. In Pacific Asia, however, there is an additional twist, associated with higher levels of social discipline and a greater propensity to sacrifice individual consumption to collective welfare goals. In discussing this aspect of Asian-style democracy, the World Bank's 1993 *East Asian Miracle* report offers a useful starting point for discussion.[6]

According to the World Bank study, the "high-performing Asian economies" followed "a combination of fundamental and interventionist policies." It argues that the basis of East Asian success was "getting the fundamentals right," by following sound macroeconomic practices, investing in human capital, minimizing price distortions, and remaining open to foreign technology (if not always to foreign investment). At the same time, the report argues that governments played a vital role in early stages of development by acting as a market intermediary, providing information, and setting targets for private business in ways that were, in Stanford economist Masahiko Aoki's phrase, "market-enhancing."[7]

According to the report, East Asian leaders established their legitimacy by adhering to a principle of "shared growth," and East Asian economies are unique in the developing world for relatively small income gaps between rich and poor. Finally, the World Bank report recommends that policy makers in developing countries learn from export-promotion strategies in East Asia: these gave local manufacturers initial help in the form of subsidies, domestic market protection, and other market-distorting incentives, but threatened to withdraw them from unsuccessful exporters. This "export contest" helped to keep companies on their toes and put the government in the role of referee, rather than judge.

The East Asian Miracle is by no means propaganda for the Asian developmental state. If anything, the volume seeks to marginalize certain key economic strategies of the developmental states by incorporating such notions as industrial policy, government–private-sector cooperation, and directed credit policies into the Bank's intellectual mainstream. It is not a book that directly challenges the orthodox neoclassical views of the World Bank.

None the less, Japanese officials, notably Masaki Shiratori, a vice-president of the Overseas Economic Cooperation Fund, and Isao Kubota of the Ministry of Finance, instigated the research effort that produced *The East Asian Miracle*. Shiratori, who was Japan's Executive Director at the World Bank from 1989 to 1992, challenged the Bank to examine the experience of East Asia, a process that he believed would validate both the East Asian record of industrial policy and Japanese foreign-aid practice. Shiratori hoped that the Bank would modify its orthodox views and prescriptions in a way that would be more in line with the realities of East Asian development.

This, as we have observed, did not happen, but *The East Asian Miracle* is a well-written and synthetic work. Even though it reflects the Bank's neoclassical orthodoxy, it presents the chief elements of East Asia's successful economic growth strategies in a clear fashion. Moreover, these elements correspond closely to those proposed by a prominent Japanese government official and economist, Eisuke Sakakibara, as the basis of Japanese capitalism.

Sakakibara, currently Vice-Minister of Finance in charge of International Finance, asserted in a 1990 book, *Beyond Capitalism*, that Japan has created a new form of capitalism, distinct from American and European forms of capitalism.[8] According to Sakakibara – and echoed by the World Bank's *East Asian Miracle* report – the chief elements of Japanese capitalism include a strong emphasis on human resource development, high propensity to save, social trust, and a small and agile government. All these have contributed to high levels of economic performance in East Asia, as well as Japan, according to Sakakibara. Let me deal briefly with each of these characteristics of Japanese or East Asian capitalism in relation to "Asian-style" democracy.

Human resource development concerns the quality and quantity of manpower resources made available to economic activities. High literacy rates are a testimony to this: Japan, Viet Nam, Korea, and Taiwan have among the highest literacy rates in the world, with 95–98 per cent literacy rates in the adult population. East Asian culture is distinctly oriented to high achievement, and both families and the education systems reinforce the tendency.

A high savings rate is a *sine qua non* for economic development. Without high levels of savings, capital accumulation cannot occur, and capital accumulation is one of the key ingredients for economic development. Japan was known for its high savings rate for a good part of the mid- and late twentieth century.

In East Asian societies, social trust provides a foundation for

177

profit-making activities. The nature of social trust differs from one culture to another. But social networks and kinship ties have not broken down, despite industrialization in much of East Asia – a fact which has given additional impetus to development.[9]

Throughout East Asia, there is a marked preference for small and agile government. This might also be called a preference for a strong state.[10] But I have deliberately avoided the use of the adjective, strong, because of the ambiguity of its connotations: strong may mean large and powerful; strong may mean authoritarian and imposing. East Asian governments tend to be small in terms of staffs and budgets, agile in terms of their orientation to the market. Economic decisions are pragmatic and guided by the market. The Japanese central government's staff size is about one-half that of the United States and one-quarter that of France, for instance.

The "market-conforming" characteristic means that governments formulate economic policy with few ideological or moral considerations. This is in sharp contrast to the policies of some West European governments and the United States. In East Asia, pragmatic and market criteria tend to override imperatives based on ideology or moral values. Such East Asian pragmatism also has consequences for the institutional framework of Asian-style democracy.

All of these characteristics emerged in the context of authoritarian regimes and have somehow survived the transition to democracy. This, of course, is partly a matter of culture. Respect for education, social preference for relations based on trust rather than contract or law, and proactive governments, with a strong sense of social responsibility, stretch way back, particularly in Confucian Asia.

Somehow, these elements have become part of the popular notion of what constitutes good governance in Pacific Asia. There will be those who object to the proposition that economic strategy is central to the legitimacy of Pacific Asian governments. But it is appropriate to emphasize that spectacular economic performance has given East Asian leaders confidence in their approach, which involves higher levels of government intervention – and a more intimate relationship between government and business – than in the West.

Rather than fade away with the introduction of democracy, the interventionist strategies associated with developmental states have gained new life as Pacific Asian governments begin to turn their attention away from development to the provision of less-quantifiable public goods, such as improving the environment for technological creativity and recreation.

Asian values

The explosion of democratic growth in the last quarter-century has been accompanied by a quest for values, particularly values reflecting indigenous history and sensibilities. Not all of these value systems are significant beyond the communities which generate them: a Tokyo neighbourhood may exercise a particularly vigorous form of local participation and representation, reflecting either the older traditions of Shitamachi or the brand-new community practices of Tama City; but such values and ideals say little to villagers in rural Thailand, or to teenagers in Singapore, or to the South Korean company worker.

Asian values are, if anything, a broad spectrum of moral preferences arising from the ancient religions that unite the region, as well as from characteristic patterns of family and social structure. Not everyone agrees that these values exist, or are shared in common. Those who argue that they do exist describe Asian values as a set of widely shared principles and practices with regard to community, order, hierarchy, individualism, mutual help, thrift, social deference, self-sacrifice, and so on. They claim that the particular mix of values that exists in Pacific Asia is highly distinctive and differs from value systems associated with other world civilizations, such as the Anglo-American value system or the complex of values associated with Islam.

The most vocal and articulate proponents of Asian values are from Malaysia and Singapore.[11] But Japan has its share of critics who espouse Asian values, such as the diplomat Kazuo Ohura and Susumu Nishibe, a magazine editor.[12] There are advocates of Asian values in Korea and China as well.

Almost all formulations of Asian values assume a dichotomy between Asian and Western, particularly American, values. Indeed, the debate often assumes aspects of a "declaration of independence" from American cultural values. Thus, Asian values are identified as values neglected (or even despised) by Americans – communitarian ties with neighbourhood, workplace, and the state; respect for the elderly; an emphasis on education; collective over individual welfare; and so on.

Singapore's former Prime Minister Lee Kuan Yew has spoken about the difference between Asian and Western values. If Pacific Asia attempts to practise American-style individualism, Lee says, it will collapse into chaos.[13] Hence, the Singaporean government offered no apologies for the caning of an American teenager, Michael Fay, in the early 1990s for violating Singapore's laws against the defacement of private property. Fay had gone on a spree, painting graffiti on cars.[14] At about the same time as this incident, the South Korean government denied a visa to one of America's most famous rock musicians, Michael Jackson, fearing that he might corrupt the morals of Korean youth.

An even more dramatic example of Asian values is Singapore's introduction of legislation that makes it a crime for children to fail to support their parents, except in instances of egregious child abuse.[15] This is communitarianism in action, Singapore style. The legislation has two major purposes: one is to uphold the sanctity of family ties and respect for age – both important components of the Asian value structure; the second is to place the onus on the public to support the elderly, removing the burden from the government to the extent possible.

It is important to note that the Asian values debate is a subset of a larger argument about the existence and relevance of major systems of culture, embodied in civilizations. The Harvard political scientist Samuel Huntington has been the major proponent in the United States of the notion that value systems play an important role in international relations.[16]

A non-Westminster institutional model

The Lipset framework makes it possible to discuss Asian democracy without ever looking at political institutions. But the political institutions common to democracies in Pacific Asia do have characteristics that differ from – and are even at odds with – Western democracy. Let us look at some of them.

Asian democracies are not based on the Westminster model. To generalize the features of political institutions in Asian democracies, most combine a small and agile government with a system of one-party rule or coalition rule. Pacific Asia's small, lean bureaucracies tend to be endowed with considerable authority, which enables them to adopt highly efficient strategies both to conform to markets and to anticipate them.[17] Asian political parties tend to reinforce bureaucratic rule because they bring many social groups under their umbrella.[18] The fact that political parties represent a consensus view makes it easier for bureaucracies to act: they can be confident that they reflect the majority view, as expressed by the dominant party or coalition. On the other hand, the political party structure typical of Pacific Asia works against any attempt to focus on single issues, or to take decisive action, because such an attempt would break the hard-won consensus. The political parties cede single issues and decision-making to the non-elected bureaucrats.

Political institutions in Pacific Asia have the following features. In the first place, the typical political party in Pacific Asia is a catch-all organization. Its policy tenets are vague, but it constructs and operates through extremely strong personal networks. The main function of political parties is to recruit support for the government at the grass-roots level.

There are few instances of two-party systems with regular alternation of the governing party in Pacific Asia.[19] There is also a noticeable absence of parties based on ideological or religious tenets. Ideology normally hampers a party's ability to achieve power, in the Pacific Asian context.

A second feature of Pacific Asia political institutions is the relatively high prestige and morale of the bureaucracy. The bureaucracies of Pacific Asia tend to believe in themselves as protectors of the people. However patronizing and self-serving such a conception may be, the bureaucracies of Pacific Asia tend to be less constrained by vested interests – unlike the politicians – and to associate themselves and their role with the pursuit of national interest.[20] As long as the political parties are doing their job, placating grass-roots interests and personalities, the bureaucracies are able to conduct their business free from "distraction."

So far, there has been little attention paid to the complex of political institutions associated with Asian democracy. Perhaps this aspect will be played up only if a debate begins over whether Western democracies should act to restrain the two-party system. Interestingly, the trajectory of political reform in Japan since 1993 has been to return to a system of one-party dominance, or rule by coalition, after a period of party reorganization.[21]

One must be cautious in rendering the characteristics of democracy in the Pacific Asian region. All too often, "Asian-style" democracy has been associated with developmental dictatorship, cultural Orientalism, and political authoritarianism.[22] This chapter has attempted to analyse the major components of Pacific Asian democracy and place these in a broader context.[23]

Notes

1. Do Chul Shin, "On the Third Wave of Democratization: An Evaluation and Synthesis of Recent Theory and Research," *World Politics* October 1994; 47(1): 135–170.
2. Jean-Marie Guehenno, *La fin de la democratie* (Paris: Flammarion, 1993).
3. Robert H. Taylor (ed.) *The Politics of Elections in Southeast Asia: Delusion or Necessity?* (Cambridge: Cambridge University Press, 1996); Anek Laothamatas (ed.) *Democratization in Southeast and East Asia* (Singapore: Institute for South-East Asian Studies, 1996).
4. A number of scholars have contributed to the idea of the developmental state in East Asia. See Chalmers Johnson, *MITI and the Japanese Miracle* (Stanford: Stanford University Press, 1981); Alice Amsden, *Asia's Next Giant: South Korea and Late Industrialization* (New York: Oxford University Press, 1989); Richard Rosecrance, *The Trading State* (New York: Norton, 1985); Robert Wade, *Governing the Market: Economic Theory and the Role of Government in Taiwan's Industrialization* (Princeton: Princeton University Press, 1990). See also Takashi Inoguchi, "Japan: Reassessing the Relationship Between Power and Plenty," in Ngaire Woods (ed.) *Explaining International Relations Since 1945* (Oxford: Oxford University Press, 1996), pp. 241–258.
5. James Cotton, "Consolidation versus Containment in East Asian Democracy," paper presented at the Seminar on Economic Change, Political Pluralism and Democratic Reform in the Asian Region, Adelaide, Australia, 21–22 April 1996.
6. *The East Asian Miracle* (Oxford: Oxford University Press, 1993).
7. Masahiko Aoki, Kevin Murdock, and Masahiro Okuno-Fujiwara, *Beyond the East Asian Miracle: Introducing the Market-enhancing View*, CEPR Publication No. 442 (Stanford University: Center for Economic Policy Research, October 1995).
8. Eisuke Sakakibara, *Shihonshugi o koeta Nihon* (Japan Has Surpassed Capitalism) (Tokyo: Toyo keizaishimposha, 1990).
9. Francis Fukuyama, *Trust: Social Virtues and the Creation of Prosperity* (New York: Free Press, 1996). The seminal work relating social trust or social capital to the deepening of democracy is Robert Putnam, *Making Democracy Work: Civic Traditions in Modern Italy* (Princeton: Princeton University Press, 1993).
10. C. Johnson, op. cit.
11. Kishore Mabubhani, "The West and the Rest," *The National Interest* Summer 1992; (28): 3–13. Bihari Kausikan, "Asia's Different Standard," *Foreign Policy* Fall 1993, (92): 24–41. From Malaysia, Mahathir Mohamad, Noordin Sophie, and Chandra Muzaffar are among those arguing broadly in similar directions. See also Takashi Inoguchi, "Human Rights and Democracy in Pacific Asia: Contention and Collaboration between the U.S. and Japan," in Peter Gourevitch, Takashi Inoguchi, and Courtney Purrington (eds) *United States–Japan Relations and International Institutions After the Cold War* (La Jolla: University of California Graduate School of International Relations and Pacific Studies, 1995), pp. 115–153.
12. Kazuo Ohura, *Tozai bunka masatsu* (East–West Cultural Conflict) (Tokyo: Chuokoronsha, 1990). Susumu Nishibe, Editor of *Hatsugensha*, a monthly magazine, registers the voice of preserving/resuscitating some Japanese norms, values, and practices presumably conducive to Japan's dynamic adaptation to the changing environment firmly anchored with its cultural identity.
13. Takashi Inoguchi, "The Political Economy of Conservative Resurgence under Recession: Public Policies and Political Support in Japan, 1977–1983," in T. J. Pempel (ed.) *Uncommon Democracies* (Ithaca: Cornell University Press, 1990), pp. 189–225. Also see *The Economist*, "Freedom and Prosperity," 29 June 1991, pp. 15–18.
14. The irony is that, according to a public opinion poll in the United States, some 60 per cent of respondents agreed with the punishment.
15. This observation comes from Shad S. Faraqui, MARA Institute of Technology, Malaysia, at the Human Rights Seminar, United Nations University, 4–5 July 1996.
16. Samuel Huntington, "Clash of Civilizations?" *Foreign Affairs* Summer 1993; 72: 22–49.

17. Takashi Inoguchi, "The Political Economy of Conservative Resurgence under Recession," op. cit.
18. Under my editorship, the University of Tokyo Press published six volumes under the East Asian states and societies series (Japan, Taiwan, China, South and North Korea, and Viet Nam). *Japan: The Governing of a Great Economic Power*, my own volume, was published in 1993 and will be published in English by Routledge in 1998.
19. Arend Lijphart, *Democracies* (New Haven: Yale University Press, 1984); Ian Marsh, *Beyond the Two Party System: Political Representation, Economic Competitiveness and Australian Politics* (Sydney: Cambridge University Press, 1995).
20. Takashi Inoguchi, "The Pragmatic Evolution of Japanese Democratic Politics," in Michelle Schmiegelow (ed.) *Democracy in Asia* (Frankfurt: Campus-Verlag, and New York: St Martin's Press, 1997, pp. 217–231; "The Japanese Political System: Its Basic Continuity in History's Eye," *Asian Journal of Political Science* December 1997; 5(2): 65–77.
21. See Takashi Inoguchi, "The Rise and Fall of Reformist Governments: Hosokawa and Hata, 1993–1994," *Asian Journal of Political Science* December 1994; 2(2): 73–88.
22. David Williams, *Japan: The End of History* (London: Routledge, 1993); *Japan and the Enemies of the Open Political Science* (London: Routledge, 1995).
23. A recent special issue of *World Development* examines the East Asian miracle theories, and the social capital theories of Putnam and others are examined carefully both conceptually and empirically. Peter Evans, "Introduction: Developmental Strategies and the Public–Private Divide," and other articles in *World Development* 1996; 24(6): 1033–1037.

12

Post-communist Europe: Comparative reflections

Alfred Stepan and Juan J. Linz

The continuing tumultuousness of events in post-communist Europe, especially in the former Soviet Union and the former Yugoslavia, demonstrates the proximity between democracy and conflict. This region reflects conflicts over power, the state, and citizenship. The question is whether, through these contests, democratic practice can become "the only game in town." From this perspective, all the countries of post-communist Europe can and should be (at least, briefly) compared. Without doubt, in some of the 27 post-communist countries – such as Turkmenistan, Uzbekistan, or the Serbian-dominated rump Yugoslavia – a realistic evaluation must lead to the conclusion that democracy has barely been established and that few weighty actors are even trying to put democracy on the agenda.[1] However, in some other countries in post-communist Europe – for example the Czech Republic, Hungary, and possibly even Lithuania – democratic practices are near to becoming "the only game in town." Thus, it is indeed appropriate to focus upon democracy, but it is necessary to develop the critical categories, frames of reference, and evidence that will allow a comparison within post-communist Europe.

As a contribution to the development of such critical categories, frames of reference, and evidence, three points are developed. First, is the danger of "inverting the legitimacy pyramid" by activists and analysts who believe that the market will legitimate democracy. The history of successful democratization indicates that the reverse nor-

This chapter is reprinted, with changes, by permission of the authors and the Johns Hopkins University Press from Juan J. Linz and Alfred Stepan, *Problems of Democratic Transition and Consolidation: Southern Europe, South America, and Post-Communist Europe*, 1996.

mally occurs: democracy legitimates the market, especially capital-ism. Second, many activists and analysts also argue that not only is there the well-known simultaneity problem but also that economic and political results must be achieved simultaneously or poor eco-nomic results will rapidly derail support for democratization; this is a questionable argument. We give empirical data and a theoretical explanation to support our cautiously optimistic hypothesis concern-ing support for democracy as it relates to East Central Europe and our much less optimistic hypothesis for democratization in the non-Baltic countries of the former Soviet Union. Third, much of the pop-ular press saw the return to power of former Communist political leaders and parties in such vanguard transitions to democracy as Poland, Hungary, and Lithuania as a "return to communism" and as a major reversal of democracy. Such an analysis is faulty, both con-ceptually and politically.

The danger of an inverted legitimacy pyramid

The Spanish sequence of political reform, socio-economic reform, and then economic reform was probably optimal for the consolida-tion of democracy in that country. Generally, it is problematic to insist on any sequence because, historically, quite different sequences have, in fact, worked.

Most analysts of post-communist Europe, especially policy advo-cates, implicitly rejected a Spanish-like sequence as infeasible because of the perceived need for *simultaneous* economic and political change. Indeed, despite frequent obeisance to this simultaneity imperative, domestic and foreign activists and advisors often privileged economic change first. Solid research is just beginning on the question of sequence in post-communist politics, but, on theoretical (and now historical) grounds, more consideration should have been given in the post-communist cases to the cost of neglecting political reforms, especially state reconstruction. Why?

Theoretically, because the issue for modern democracies is not the creation of a *market*, but the creation of an *economic society*. Further, logic implies that a coherent regulatory environment and the rule of law is required to transform command economies into economic societies. If this is so, then a major priority must be to create demo-cratic regulatory state power.[2] In this respect, two empirical extremes are Spain and the former USSR: attention to electoral sequence and constitutional change contributed to effective power creation and state reconfiguration in Spain; inattention to electoral sequence – by Gorbachev – and constitutional change – by Gorbachev and Yeltsin – contributed to power erosion and a decomposing state in the USSR and Russia.

Empirically, *post hoc* studies – as opposed to *ex ante* doctrinal advocacy – of privatization and structural economic change are just beginning to appear for the region. However, the best studies of the region are confirming a pattern about state power already documented in Latin America – that effective privatization (often mistakenly equated with "state shrinking") is best done by relatively strong states that are able to implement a coherent policy. The essence of a rich body of research on privatization and state restructuring shows that effective privatization entails less state *scope* but greater state *capacity*.[3] In the context of a post-communist, post-command economy, a state with a rapidly eroding capacity simply cannot manage a process of effective privatization.[4]

It is important to note that the key is a strong state and not necessarily a democracy. A strong non-democratic state in Chile privatized reasonably effectively. However, in a post-communist setting such as Russia, where the old communist party-state has imploded or is no longer effective, privatization can proceed in an orderly way only after the state has been *reconstructed*. Once the totalitarian or post-totalitarian state, with its extensive command economy, has collapsed, given up, imploded, or disintegrated, state structures must be put in place. But many of the non-democratic ways of restructuring the state are less available as alternatives than normally thought.

Some people argue – particularly in Russia – that a Pinochet is needed. But in Russia and many other countries of the former Soviet Union a coherent state and a unified military organization of the sort that supported Pinochet no longer exist.[5] An authoritarian, or perhaps a semifascist, party-state in Russia is also sometimes held up as a powerful alternative ruling model. However, a single party with ideological legitimacy and the resources to assume and implement non-democratic power would require the emergence and construction of a state-wide hegemonic semifascist movement, and this also seems unlikely. Even an authoritarian or semifascist Russia would still be an example of what Ken Jowitt describes as a polity with a weak state and a weak society.[6] The quiescence of Franco's post-Civil War Spain is a less-likely outcome of a Russian Fascist government than is a series of Chechnyas and Afghanistans. Some people argue for a China-type solution, but the Chinese model, which could possibly have been a pre-perestroika alternative, is also no longer available as an option in Russia. Unlike in Russia, the Chinese non-democratic regime and state never broke down. Indeed, the Chinese regime never initiated or even considered a process of democratization and underwent only a very selective and partial process of liberalization.

For Russia, the cost of a weak democratic state is high but, at the same time, many of the non-democratic solutions either are not available or would probably entail a repressive but still weak state. In Steven Lukes' useful formulation, such a state might have repressive power over more people but still lack the power to reconstruct a prosperous and peaceful Russia.[7] Thus, in a context where the party-state has imploded and a command economy is no longer feasible, the state must be reconstructed. Far from being an irrelevance, some degree of democratic legitimacy can be a way of helping in this state reconstruction.

This leads to the central point about legitimacy and privatization. In their rush to move away from state-controlled economies, some free-market enthusiasts have endorsed privatization as the most important component of the post-1989 process. Privatization, *however it is accomplished*, is often seen as creating the key structural prerequisite for market democracies and the economic foundations for new democracies; this is highly questionable. Repeated surveys in democracies show that at the apex of a hierarchy of democratic legitimacy are the overall democratic processes – elections, multiple parties, and free speech. At a lower level in the legitimacy hierarchy are incumbents, such as parliamentarians. Political institutions related to democracy are normally more legitimate than such economic institutions in market economies. Furthermore, economic institutions – market economies – are always more legitimate than capitalist actors.[8] Thus, on theoretical grounds, the endeavour to legitimate the post-1989 democracies by the efficacy of the new capitalists and thus to increase – by whatever means – the number of new capitalists, is to invert the legitimacy pyramid.

Such an inverted legitimacy pyramid is especially problematic in those countries, such as Russia, where privatization has been virtually unregulated, highly unequal, and often illegal.[9] In such contexts, the former holders of political power – such as the "red bourgeoisie" in the state enterprises or state financial or trading institutions – have been in a privileged position to transform their former political power into new types of economic power by numerous forms of "spontaneous" privatizations or thefts. Comparative surveys repeatedly show

187

that in most societies some legitimacy is given to earned or inherited private property and to entrepreneurship. However, the new Russian capitalists of the former red bourgeoisie cannot draw upon these principles of legitimation. Indeed, the origins of their new wealth are often condemned as an illegitimate appropriation of public property and may leave a legacy of distrust both of market economies – which will be seen as mafia economies – and of the democracies that tolerated, or even created, these mafia economies. Much more political, theoretical, and research attention should be given to evaluating the democratic consequences of attempting to build new democratic polities and economic societies on this inverted legitimacy pyramid. The essence of the empirical findings and historical studies of Western democracies has always been that political systems of democracy legitimate market economies, not the reverse. This is because, as long as a democratic majority does not question private ownership of the means of production when it can do so legally, that property is protected.[10]

Simultaneity of results versus the comparative politics of deferred gratification

The assumption that economic reform – the market and privatization – can legitimate the new democracies is also based on the dubious assumption that economic success and the creation of greater wealth can be achieved simultaneously with the installation and legitimation of democratic institutions. In fact, for imploded command economies, democratic polities can and must be installed and legitimized by a variety of appeals *before* the possible benefits of a market economy actually materialize fully. Many analysts and political advisers dismiss the argument for prior state restructuring because of their assumption that, because of people's demands for material improvements, economic and political gains must not only be pursued but must *occur*, simultaneously. Some even argue that, though simultaneous economic and political reforms are necessary, such simultaneity is impossible.[11] We can call these two perspectives about the relationship between economies and democratization the *tightly coupled* hypothesis and the *loosely coupled* hypothesis, respectively.

Loosely coupled does not mean that there is no relationship between economic and political perceptions, but only that the relationship is not necessarily one to one. For at least a medium-range time horizon, people can make independent (and even opposite) assessments about political and economic trends. Furthermore, if assessments about politics are positive, they can provide a valuable cushion against painful economic restructuring.[12] What evidence is there concerning the relationship between economics and democratization in the first five years of post-communist Europe? In terms of relatively hard economic data, of the 27 countries in post-communist Europe, no country except Poland experienced positive growth in 1992. Indeed, all post-communist countries in 1993 were still well below their 1989 industrial output levels (table 12.1).

If we look at the subjective perception of economic well-being in the six East Central European Warsaw Pact countries, the mean positive rating (on a scale of +100 to −100) among those polled between November 1993 and March 1994 for the Communist economic system was 60.2. But the mean positive rating of the post-communist economic system was only 37.3, a drop of almost 23 points. The "tightly coupled" hypothesis would predict that the attitudes toward the political system would drop steeply, even if not the full 23 points. What does the evidence show? In the same survey, the mean positive ranking of the Communist political system was 45.7. A one-point drop in political evaluation for every point drop in economic evaluation (a perfectly coupled correlation) would yield a positive evaluation of the political system of only 22.6. However, positive ranking for the post-communist system did not fall as the "tightly coupled" hypothesis would predict (table 12.2).

How can we explain such incongruence? First of all, human beings are capable of making separate and correct judgements about a basket of economic goods (which may be deteriorating) and a basket of political goods (which may be improving). In fact, in the same survey, in *all* six countries of East Central Europe the citizens polled judged that, in important areas directly affected by the democratic political system, their life experiences and chances had overwhelmingly improved, even though in the same survey they asserted that their personal household economic situation had worsened (table 12.3).

Such incongruence cannot last for ever; however, it indicates that, in a radical transformation such as is occurring in East Central Europe, the deterioration of the economy does not necessarily translate rapidly into erosion of support for the political system.[13]

Table 12.3 indicates that the perceived legitimacy of the political system has given democratic institutions in East Central Europe an important degree of insulation from the perceived inefficacy of the new economic system.[14] Indeed, most of the people in East Central

Table 12.1 **GDP, industrial output, and peak inflation rates in post-communist countries: 1989–1995**

Country	Measure	GDP (percentage change)							Industrial output 1993 (1989 = 100)	Inflation rate (at peak year during 1989–1993)
		1989	1990	1991	1992	1993	1994 (estimated)	1995 (projected)		
Albania	GDP	9.8	−10.0	−27.1	−9.7	11.0	7.0	5.0	52	237 [92]
	Industrial production	5.0	−7.6	−36.9	−44.0	−10.0	na^a	na		
Armenia	GDP	14.2	−7.4	−11.0	−52.0	−15.0	0	na	na	10,900 [93]
Azerbaijan	GDP	na	−11.7	−0.7	−22.6	−13.0	−15.0	−10.0	na	1,174 [92]
Belarus	GDP	8.0	−3.0	−1.2	−9.6	−11.6	−26.0^a	−10	76	2,775 [93]
	Industrial production	na	na	−6.8	−10.2	−6.0	na	na		
Bulgaria	GDP	0.5	−9.1	−11.7	−5.6	−4.2	2	4	na	339 [91]
	Industrial production	−1.4	−16.5	−27.3	−22.0	−10.0	4	na		
Croatia	GDP	−1.6	−8.6	−14.4	−9	−3.2	1	6	57	1,150 [92]
	Industrial production	na	−11.3	−28.5	−15.0	−6.0	−3.0	6		
Czech Republic	GDP	na	−0.4	−14.2	−7.1	−0.3	3	6	57	52 [91]
	Industrial production	na	−3.5	−22.3	−10.6	−6.3	0	na		
Estonia	GDP	−1.1	−8.1	−11	−14.2	−3.2	5.0	6.0	54	965 [92]
Macedonia	GDP	na	−9.9	−12.1	−14.0	−14.1	−7.2	0	na	1,691 [92]
	Industrial production	na	−10.6	−17.2	−16.1	−17.2	na	na		
Georgia	NMP	−4.8	−12.4	−20.8	−43.4	−40.0	−35.0	na	na	na
	Industrial production	−6.9	−29.9	−24.4	−43.4	−21.0	na	na		
Hungary	GDP	0.7	−3.5	−11.9	−4.3	−2.3	3.0	3.0	69	
	Industrial gross output	−1.0	−9.6	−18.2	−9.8	−4.0	9.0	6.0		
Kazakhstan	GDP	−0.4	−0.4	−13.0	−14.0	−12.0	−25.0	na	68	1,925 [93]
Kyrgyzstan	GDP	3.8	3.2	−5.0	−25.0	−16.0	−10	1.5	53	1,354 [93]
	Industrial production	na	na	0.0	−27.0	−25.0	na	na		
Latvia	GDP	6.8	2.9	−8.3	−33.8	−11.7	3	3	38	958 [91]
	Gross mfg output	na	na	0.4	−48.7	−32.6	na	na		

Country	Measure	1989	1990	1991	1992	1993	1994	1995	1993 output (1989=100)	Inflation [year]
Lithuania	GDP	1.5	−5.0	−13.1	−37.7	−16.2	4	4	na	1,175 [92]
	Industrial production	na	na	na	−50.9	−42.7	na	na		na
Moldova	GDP	8.8	−1.5	−11.9	−25.0	−14.0	−20.0	0	69	837 [93]
Poland	GDP	0.2	−11.6	−7.6	1.5	3.8	4.5	5.0		640 [89]
	Industrial production	−1.4	−26.1	−11.9	3.9	5.6	na	na		na
Romania	GDP	−5.8	−5.6	−12.9	−13.6	1.0	2.0	3.0	47	296 [93]
	Industrial output	−5.3	−23.7	−22.8	−21.9	1.3	2.0	na		na
Russia	GDP	na	na	−13.0	−19.0	−12.0	−15.0	−7.0	60	2,138 [92]
	Industrial production	na	−0.1	−8.0	−18.8	−16.0	−21.0	−12.0		−7.0
Slovakia	GDP	1.4	−0.4	−14.5	−7.0	−4.1	3.5	3.0	55	58 [91]
	Industrial production	−0.7	−3.6	−17.8	−14.0	−10.6	5.5	na		3.0
Slovenia	GDP	−1.8	−4.7	−8.1	−5.4	1.0	5.0	6	46	247 [91]
	Industrial production	−0.1	−10.3	−11.3	−12.0	−2.6	6.6	5.1		6
Tajikistan	NMP	−2.9	−1.6	−12.5	−33.7	−28	na	na	56	7,344 [93]
	Industrial production	1.9	1.9	−7.4	−35.7	na	na	na		na
Turkmenistan	GDP	na	2.0	−4.7	−5.3	−7.6	−10.0	−5.0	90	1,875 [93]
Ukraine	GDP	4.1	−3.4	−12	−17.0	−14.0	−23.0	−5.0	79	10,155 [93]
	Industrial production	2.8	−0.1	−4.8	−6.5	−8.0	−30.0	na		na
Uzbekistan	GDP	3.7	1.6	−0.5	−11.1	−2.4	−2.6	2.0	94	927 [93]
	Industrial output	3.6	1.8	1.8	−12.3	−8.3	na	na		2.0
Yugoslavia	Industrial output	na	na	na	na	na	na	na	35	3.72×10^{13} [93]

Source: The yearly 1989–1995 data were supplied by the European Bank for Reconstruction and Development, London, January 1995. The figures for 1994 are estimates; those for 1995 are projections. A common method was used in the data collection. The 1993 industrial output data in relation to a baseline of 100 for 1989 are from Jacek Rostowski, *Macro-economic Instability in Post-Communist Countries* (Oxford: Clarendon Press, forthcoming). No data were available for Bosnia. The data on inflation rates are also from Rostowski. The figure for inflation in Yugoslavia (3.72 times 10 to the 13th power) computes to one of the all-time world hyperinflation rates of over 37 trillion.

a. na, not available.

Table 12.2 **Percentages expressing positive attitudes toward communist versus post-communist economic systems and political systems: Responses from six East Central European countries**

Question	Country	Percentage of positive responses for 1989	Percentage of positive responses for 1993–1994
"Here is a scale ranking how the *economy* works: the top, plus 100 is the best; the bottom, minus 100 the worst."	Bulgaria	66	15
	Czech	42	66
	Hungary	75	27
	Poland	52	50
	Romania	52	35
	Slovakia	74	31
	Mean	60	35
"Here is a scale ranking how *government* works: the top, plus 100 is the best; the bottom, minus 100 the worst."	Bulgaria	51	59
	Czech	23	78
	Hungary	58	51
	Poland	38	69
	Romania	52	60
	Slovakia	50	52
	Mean	46	62

Source: Richard Rose and Christian Haerfer, "New Democracies Barometer III: Learning from What Is Happening," *Studies in Public Policy* 1994; 230: questions 22–23, 32–33. Percentages are rounded off. The polls were administered in these countries between November 1993 and March 1993.

Europe in 1993 had a fairly long time horizon and expressed optimism that by 1998 *both* the performance of the new democracy *and* the performance of the new economic system would improve significantly (fig. 12.1).

In East Central Europe the evidence is thus strongly in favour of the argument that deferred gratification and confidence in the future is possible, even when there is an acknowledged lag in economic improvements. Simultaneity of rapid political and economic results is, indeed, normally extremely difficult but, fortunately, as figure 12.1 shows, the citizens of East Central Europe did not perceive such simultaneity as necessary. The overall implication of the tables and figures presented thus far seems to be further evidence of the potential danger of policies based on the inverted-legitimacy pyramid.

Before returning to the former Soviet Union, we should note briefly two other factors that help to explain the surprisingly high degree of political support for the new political regime – political

Table 12.3 **Incongruent perceptions of the economic basket of goods versus the political basket of goods in the communist system and the current system: Six East Central European countries**

Question	Percentage of respondents answering "better now" versus those answering "worse now"					
	Bulgaria	Czech	Slovakia	Hungary	Poland	Romania
Economic Basket:						
"When you compare your overall household economic situation with five years ago, would you say that in the past it was better, the same, worse?"	16/58	23/49	18/62	6/76	17/62	21/65
Political Basket:						
"Please tell me whether our present political system by comparison with the Communist is [better, the same or worse] in the following areas:"						
"People can join any organization they want."	95/5	90/1	88/3	81/2	79/2	94/1
"Everybody is free to say what he or she thinks."	90/11	84/3	82/4	73/8	83/4	94/2
"People can travel and live wherever they want."	95/5	96/1	87/2	75/4	75/7	90/2
"People can live without fear of unlawful arrest."	88/11	73/4	62/5	59/4	71/5	81/1
"Each person can decide whether or not to take an interest in politics."	97/3	84/0	81/1	n/a	69/5	92/1
"Everybody is free to decide whether or not to practise a religion."	98/2	94/0	96/1	83/1	70/6	95/1

Source: Same as for figure 12.1, questions 26, 35, 36, 37, 39, 40, 42. Where the percentages do not add up to 100 the respondents answered "equal."

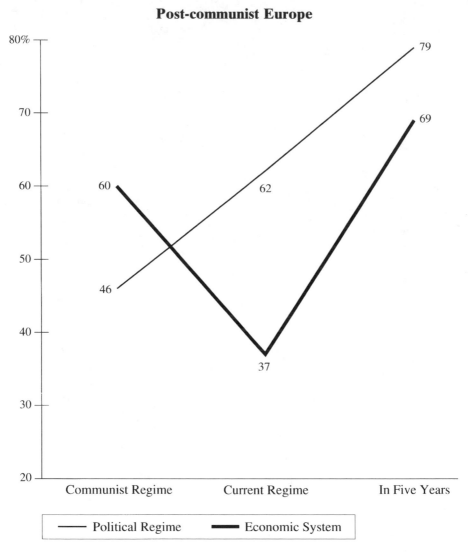

Post-communist Europe

Fig. 12.1 **Percentage of people giving a positive rating to the economic system and to the political regime in the communist system, the current system, and in five years: Six East Central European countries (source: Richard Rose and Christian Haerpfer, "New Russia Barometer III,"** *Studies in Public Policy* **1994; 228: questions 24 and 34**

regime, not necessarily political *incumbents* – despite economic hardship. None of the former Warsaw pact countries of East Central Europe, unlike the former USSR, experienced widespread bloodshed over stateness problems. Also, unlike Russia, there is no ambivalent legacy about the loss of an empire or the disintegration of the USSR.

How do the non-Baltic countries of the former Soviet Union compare with the countries of East Central Europe on the same set of dimensions concerning satisfaction with the pre- and post-communist economies and political systems? Unfortunately, there are data only for Russia, Ukraine, and Belarus; but the differences are striking, especially in the substantially lower ranking accorded to current support for the post-communist political system (fig. 12.2).

A panel of outside observers also notes a set of very different patterns within countries of East Central Europe, in contrast to the former Soviet Union, with respect to their political development. An annual publication of Freedom House developed a common method to evaluate political rights and civil liberties for almost all of the countries of the world. Freedom House uses a seven-point scale to rank countries concerning political rights and a seven-point scale to rank political liberties. A score of 1 indicates the highest rights and liberties and 7 the lowest. For the purposes of this argument, if a country is ranked no lower than 2 on political rights and no lower than 3 on civil liberties, it is labelled as *above* the democratic threshold for that year; if a country is given a score of 4 or lower on political rights and/or 5 or lower on civil liberties, it is considered as *below* the democratic threshold for that year; countries between the two categories are labelled as on the *border* of the democratic threshold. In short, the lower the number the better the results for democracy. How does post-communist Europe rank on this scale? See table 12.4.

To make table 12.4 more useful for a comparative analysis of post-communist Europe, let us separate these 26 countries into three broad categories – East Central Europe, the former Soviet Union, and the former Yugoslavia. Within the former Soviet Union, we will make a further subdivision between those countries that had been a part of the former Soviet Union since the early 1920s and that are now, with Russia, a part of the Commonwealth of Independent States (CIS), and those countries that became a part of the Soviet Union only after 1940 (Estonia, Latvia, and Lithuania) and that refused to join the CIS. The classification results are presented in table 12.5.

The implications of the numerous tables and figures presented will have to be elaborated and analysed more fully by the new generation of comparativists conducting research into European post-communist politics. However, we can at least note some patterns.

Respondents in the six former Warsaw Pact countries of East Cen-

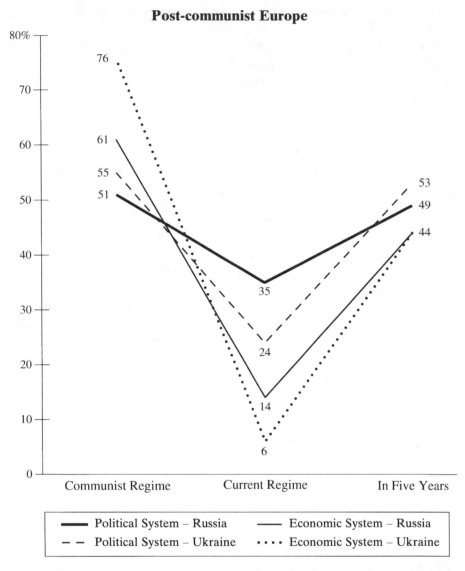

Post-communist Europe

Fig. 12.2   **Percentage of people giving a positive rating to the economic system and to the political system in the communist regime, the current regime, and in five years: Russia, Ukraine, and Belarus (source: for Russia see Richard Rose and Christian Haerpfer, "New Russia Barometer III,"** *Studies in Public Policy* **1994; 228: questions 15–17 and 27–29; for Ukraine see Rose and Haerpfer, "New Democracies Barometer III," questions 22–24, 32–34; the data for Belarus are roughly similar to those for Ukraine; positive evaluations of the economic system under communism, in the present, and in five years are 78, 11, and 47, respectively, and positive evaluations for the political systems in these three periods are 64, 28, and 56, respectively; sources same as cited for Ukraine)**

196

Table 12.4 **Rating of 26 countries of post-communist Europe on the Freedom House scale of political rights and civil liberties for the year 1993**

Country	Political rights	Civil liberties	Democratic threshold rating: "above," "below," or "border"
Armenia	3	4	Border
Azerbaijan	6	6	Below
Belarus	5	4	Below
Bosnia–Herzegovina	6	6	Below
Bulgaria	2	2	Above
Croatia	4	4	Below
Czech Republic	1	2	Above
Estonia	3	2	Border
Georgia	5	5	Below
Hungary	1	2	Above
Kazakhstan	6	4	Below
Kyrgyzstan	5	3	Below
Latvia	3	3	Border
Lithuania	1	3	Above
Macedonia	3	3	Border
Moldova	5	5	Below
Poland	2	2	Above
Romania	4	4	Below
Russia	3	4	Border
Slovakia	3	4	Border
Slovenia	1	2	Above
Tajikistan	7	7	Below
Turkmenistan	7	7	Below
Ukraine	4	4	Border
Uzbekistan	7	7	Below
Yugoslavia (Serbia and Montenegro)	6	6	Below
Summary			6 of 26 Above
			7 of 26 Border
			13 of 26 Below

Source: Raymond D. Gastil (ed.) *Freedom in the World: Political Rights and Civil Liberties, 1993–1994* (New York: Freedom House, 1994), pp. 677–678.

tral Europe gave a mean positive rating of 62 to the post-communist political system – an *increase* of 16 points over the positive rating they gave to the Communist political system. In sharp contrast, in the three former Soviet Union countries – Russia, Ukraine, and Belarus – a mean of only 29 gave the post-communist political system a positive rating – a *decrease* of 26 points from those who gave the Communist system a positive rating.[15]

Table 12.5 **Comparative democratic threshold rating of post-communist Europe: The countries of East Central Europe, the former Soviet Union, and the former Yugoslavia (1993)**

Classification	Country	Political rights	Civil liberties	Democratic threshold rating ("above," "border," or "below")
East Central Europe	Czech Republic	1	2	Above
	Hungary	1	2	Above
	Poland	2	2	Above
	Bulgaria	2	2	Above
	Slovakia	3	4	Border
	Romania	4	4	Below
Summary				4/6 Above
				1/6 Border
				1/6 Below
The former Soviet Union (since the 1940s, not CIS members)	Lithuania	1	3	Above
	Estonia	3	2	Border
	Latvia	3	3	Border
Summary				1/3 Above
				2/3 Border
				0/3 Below
The former Soviet Union (since the 1920s, now CIS members)	Russia	3	4	Border
	Armenia	3	4	Border
	Ukraine	4	4	Border
	Kyrgyzstan	5	3	Below
	Belarus	5	4	Below
	Moldova	5	5	Below
	Kazakhstan	6	4	Below
	Azerbaijan	6	6	Below
	Georgia	6	6	Below
	Tajikistan	7	7	Below
	Turkmenistan	7	7	Below
	Uzbekistan	7	7	Below
Summary				0/12 Above
				3/12 Border
				9/12 Below
The former Yugoslavia	Slovenia	1	2	Above
	Macedonia	3	3	Border
	Croatia	4	4	Below
	Bosnia–Herzegovina	6	6	Below
	Yugoslavia (Serbia and Montenegro)	6	6	Below

Table 12.5 **(cont.)**

Classification	Country	Political rights	Civil liberties	Democratic threshold rating ("above," "border," or "below")
Summary				1/5 Above
				1/5 Border
				3/5 Below

Source: Same as table 12.4 The only country of post-communist Europe not included is Albania, which did not start its transition until quite late. It also does not fit easily into any of the three geographical–historical categories utilized in the table. In our judgement, Albania as of mid-1995 would score "below" the democratic threshold.

Another finding is that *none* of the twelve CIS countries that had been part of the Soviet Union were above the minimal threshold of democratic practices, according to the 1993 annual Freedom House poll. In fact, three of the twelve countries – Turkmenistan, Uzbekistan, and Tajikistan – received the lowest possible scores of 7 on political rights and 7 on civil liberties.[16] In contrast, four of the six East Central European countries were above the threshold. Romania received the lowest scores of the six former Warsaw Pact countries of East Central Europe, with 4 on political rights and 4 on civil liberties. Thus, it seems accurate to say that, in 1993, both the "ceiling" and the "floor" of democratic practices in East Central Europe were substantially higher than those in the CIS countries.

We must also note that, in contrast to the six East Central European countries, economic and political judgements are more tightly coupled in the CIS countries. There is thus a much lower propensity for deferred gratification in the non-Baltic parts of the former Soviet Union than in East Central Europe.

What explains such sharp contrasts between East Central Europe and the non-Baltic countries of the former Soviet Union? Let us begin with the question of deferred gratification. No doubt the pattern of difference is partly due to the extreme severity of the drop in positive economic assessments. In East Central Europe the mean positive evaluation dropped only from 60 to 37, whereas the post-Soviet mean of Russia, Ukraine, and Belarus dropped from 71 to 10. Timing and perception of the future were also probably important. According to table 12.1, the worst year in East Central Europe in

199

terms of economic decline was 1991. The worst year in Russia, Ukraine, and Belarus was 1994, *after* the poll. The year 1995 was probably economically somewhat better than 1994, but in late 1993 people might not have seen any light at the end of the tunnel.

It is almost certain that the severity of the stateness problem in the USSR and the subsequent state disintegration and widespread armed conflict played an independent role in objectively deepening economic disarray. The continuation of such conflicts in 1995 in some CIS countries inevitably also decreased the subjective confidence as to whether deferred gratification was merited. After all, a politics of deferred gratification is rational only if some signs of potential gratification can be discerned. In a context of very weak and contested states, the confidence of the future that was an important ingredient reinforcing the "politics of deferred gratification" in East Central Europe was understandably weaker in the former Soviet Union and in much of the former Yugoslavia. To be sure, Czechoslovakia had a stateness problem, but, because of the orderly and reasonably well-planned velvet divorce, no armed violence was involved and no significant economic downturn occurred in either the Czech Republic or Slovakia.[17]

Stateness problems, and not just economic problems, critically affect democratic outcomes. This becomes clear when we note that, of the 22 independent countries that emerged out of the disintegration of the former Soviet Union and the former Yugoslavia, only 2 – Lithuania and Slovenia – are *above* the democratic threshold rating (see table 12.5). Both of these countries are exceptions that prove the rule concerning the importance of stateness problems for democratization. Lithuania's economy is not as robust as that of Estonia, but Lithuania was the *only* Baltic country to grant inclusive citizenship to all residents, whether they were ethnic Balts or not. This policy has enabled Lithuania to manage its potential stateness problem in a more democratic fashion than Latvia or Estonia and, thus, Lithuania has, correctly, received a higher score for "political rights" than has Latvia or Estonia.

Of the five countries in the former Yugoslavia, Slovenia is the *only* country not to have a significant stateness problem. Slovenia does not have a significant ethnic minority population, so it has not been embroiled in actual or potential conflicts over a Serbian (or Albanian) irredenta of the sort that have occurred in Croatia, Bosnia–Herzegovina, and rump Yugoslavia, where armed conflicts have contributed to widespread curtailment of political rights and civil liberties. Macedonia, more than Slovenia, has potentially severe stateness problems – with Albania *and* Serbia, and even Bulgaria and Greece – and this has contributed to its less-than-inclusive citizenship and language policies.

Another factor that has, no doubt, contributed to greater support for the post-communist regimes in East Central Europe, in contrast to Russia and (to some extent) Belarus, is that Russian citizens may be happy to be independent but feel, none the less, a sense of geopolitical loss and anger about the way in which the USSR disintegrated. Among other things, the disintegration of the USSR has left 25 million Russians as often beleaguered, and sometimes stateless, minorities in other countries. Also, unlike the citizens of the Czech Republic, who believe that the velvet divorce improved Czech standards of living, the Russians are convinced that the dissolution of the USSR contributed to the decline of their standard of living (table 12.6).

We can infer that, in contrast to Russian citizens' sense of geopolitical loss over 1991, the citizens of the "outer empire" in countries such as Poland no doubt feel a sense of geopolitical gain due to the events of 1989. This is one of the reasons why citizens in Poland have a much stronger preference for the present political system than do those in Russia, and thus have more willingly accepted the politics of deferred gratification (table 12.7).

We do not want to overstress the preference for the old system in Russia, however. Many people in Spain believe that they lived better under Franco but would not like to return to that political system. The key question in politics is the desired future *alternative*. Russians, in fact, see the political basket of goods reviewed in table 12.2 as *better* under the new political system, but they feel this by a smaller margin than do respondents in East Central Europe.[18] Thus, despite their sense of ambivalence and loss concerning the dissolution of the USSR, only a small percentage say that they would like to return to communism and an even smaller percentage prefer military rule as a desired future alternative (table 12.8).

Other important explanatory factors for democratization differences in post-communist Europe for future researchers to explore are, of course, those related to time, prior regime types, and the presence or absence of a usable democratic legacy. The USSR lasted for about 75 years, during much of which totalitarian practices predominated. East Central Europe was a part of the Soviet subsystem for only 40 years. In Poland for much of this period, authoritarian, not totalitarian, political realities predominated. In Hungary, mature

Table 12.6 **Russian attitudes in 1994 about the dissolution of the USSR in 1991**

Question	Percentage response in age-group (years)			
	18–29	30–59	60+	Total
"In December 1991 leaders of Russia, Belorussia and the Ukraine decided to dissolve the USSR and found the CIS. What do you think of that now?"				
It was the right decision.	16	12	8	12
It was the wrong decision.	57	70	75	68
Difficult to answer.	28	18	17	20
"How has the disintegration of the USSR affected Russian living standards?"				
For better.	5	4	3	4
For worse.	68	76	83	76
No change.	11	8	5	8
Difficult to answer.	16	12	9	12

Source: Rose and Haerfper, "New Russian Barometer III," questions 57–59. We believe a similar phenomenon is at work in Belarus as in Russia. The *only* deputy in the Belarus parliament to vote against independence, Aleksandr Lukashenko, was elected president in 1994. In May 1995 he sponsored a referendum in which he argued. "If people call for it, we will also have a political union that is even closer than the Soviet Union was. For the moment I am talking about economic union." See Matthew Kaminski, "Belarussians Seek the Future in the Past," *Financial Times* 17 May 1995, 3. Lukashenko won support for all questions on the referendum. In the same article the *Financial Times* correspondent noted that "over three-quarters of Belarussian voters in a national referendum chose to bring back Soviet-era national insignia, make Russian the state language, and support economic integration with Russia."

Table 12.7 **Preferences for old and new political systems in Russia and Poland in January–February 1992**

Preference	Percentage response in age-group (years)				Percentage preferring present system over old system
	≤29	30–59	60+	Total	
In Russia					
Present system better	43	39	21	36	−18
Old system better	45	52	71	54	
Don't know	12	9	8	10	
In Poland					
Present system better				74	+51
Old system better				23	
Don't know				3	

Source: Irina Bolva and Viacheslav Shironin, "Russians between State and Market," *Studies in Public Policy* 1992; 205: 19–22.

Table 12.8 **Russian attitudes toward restoring the former communist system: April 1994**

Agreement with statement. "It would be better to restore the former communist system."	Percentage response in age-group (years)			
	≤29	30–59	60+	Total
Completely agree	5	8	18	9
Generally agree	8	14	19	14
Generally disagree	30	29	23	28
Completely disagree	41	36	22	34
Difficult to answer	16	13	19	15

Source: Rose and Haerfpfer, "New Russia Barometer III," question 31a. In the same poll, only 3 per cent competely agreed and only 7 per cent generally agreed with the statement that "the army should rule" (Question 31b). The army is thus clearly not a desired alternative.

post-totalitarianism evolved. Finally, pre-communist history must be analysed comparatively. Czechoslovakia, for example, was democratic from independence in 1919 until the Nazi interventions of 1938. There is virtually no such usable pre-communist democratic past in the non-Baltic countries of the former Soviet Union. This does not mean that democracy is impossible in these countries; it does mean, however, that there will be longer and more perilous journeys toward constitutionalism and state reconstruction before democracy becomes, if ever, the only game in town.

The astute reader has no doubt noted that religion has not been built into this explanation of the comparatively weaker progress toward democratization in the CIS countries and the former Yugoslavia. This is so for two reasons. First, it is becoming increasingly popular among analysts to make certain religions – such as Orthodox Christianity, Islam, or Confucianism – a major explanation for difficulties in democratization in many parts of the world.[19] However, the factors mentioned in this chapter, *in themselves*, are sufficient to explain the sharply different results of democratization in the non-Baltic countries of the former Soviet Union versus East Central Europe. Second, religions differ in the range of their autonomously controlled resources and their relationship to the state. Roman Catholicism, as a transnational, hierarchical organization, can potentially provide material and doctrinal support to a local Catholic church to help it resist state oppression. To the extent that a Catholic church might resist the state, it could be considered a support for more robust and autonomous civil society.

Empirically, in the resistance state of democratization, the Catholic church played a supportive role in Poland and Lithuania, as well as in Chile and Brazil, and in the last years of Franco in Spain. Protestantism, with its emphasis on individual conscience and its international networks, can also play a role in supporting civil society's opposition to a repressive state, as in East Germany and Estonia. Concerning civil society and resistance to the state, Orthodox Christianity is often – although not always – organizationally and doctrinally in a relatively weak position because of what Max Weber called its "caesaropapist" structure, in which the church is a *national* as opposed to a *transnational* organization. In caesaropapist churches, the national state normally plays a major role in the national church's finances and appointments. Such a national church is not an autonomous part of civil society because there is a high degree, in Weber's words, of "subordination of priestly to secular power."[20] Having acknowledged this, Orthodox Christianity is not an inherently anti-democratic force. That is to say, if the leaders of the state are committed to democracy and follow democratic practices, the caesaropapist structures and incentives should lead to loyal support of democracy by the Orthodox Christian church, as in Greece since 1975. However, if the leaders of the state and political society are anti-democratic, the democratic opposition in civil society will not normally receive substantial or effective support from a national Orthodox church. The role of the world's religions in democracy and democratization is an important and interesting dimension.[21]

Democracy and the return of communism

Some interpreters have seen the "return of communists" to power in Poland, Hungary, and Lithuania – countries that played a vanguard role in democratic transitions – as proof that economics and politics are so tightly linked that economic decline means democratic decline. For countries where there has been at least one legitimate victory by democratic electoral forces – and in many countries there has never been such a victory – we believe that a more nuanced judgement is appropriate.

The return to power of reformed Communist Party-led coalitions in Lithuania in 1992, in Poland in 1993, and in Hungary in 1994, although a set-back for some policies that were deepening democracy – such as local government reform in Poland – was not in itself an example of non-democratic regime change. By almost all reliable accounts, the reform Communist coalitions accepted the democratic rules of the game in how they contested the election and, later, in how they ruled. Also, very importantly, they were accepted as legitimated victors and rulers by the parties they defeated. In this sense there was not a *regime change* away from democracy, as political scientists normally use the term: strictly speaking, in comparative terms, the Lithuanian, Polish, and Hungarian elections represented a peaceful democratic alternation of power.

From a long historical perspective, it may even turn out that these elections actually strengthened democracy in Lithuania, Poland, and Hungary in one important respect: they indicated to victors and losers alike that democracy was becoming the only game in town. In fact, precisely because democracy was perceived in 1992–1994 as the only game in town, the reform Communists in Lithuania, Poland, and Hungary were extremely eager to demonstrate that they would govern as democratic parties. Their calculation was that, by so governing, they would be perceived (when they in turn were out of office) as part of the loyal democratic opposition and thus as a legitimate alternative government.[22] To make this point they are holding themselves in some respects to somewhat higher standards of civil liberties than did their predecessors in Hungary and Lithuania, who occasionally violated civil liberties in the name of their nationalist and anti-communist "mandates." For example, the reform Communists in Hungary are in coalition with the liberal Free Democrats and the coalition's overall policy toward the media has been less flawed than that of the first democratically elected government. In Lithuania, the leader of nationalist independence, Vytautas Landsbergis, pursued his anti-communist nationalism to such an extent that Anatol Lieven, in his excellent book, referred to him as a "backward-looking, religious-colored nationalist ... [who] left the nation more divided than when he became its leader."[23] His reform Communist successor, Algirdas Brazauskas, has paid somewhat more attention to providing a "political roof" of individual rights to all citizens and pursuing a politics of inclusion.

Conceptually and politically, what does the phrase "the return of communists" mean in Central Europe in the mid-1990s? In the full sense of the meaning, a Communist regime in Central Europe before 1989, even in mature post-totalitarian Hungary or authoritarian Poland, meant a powerful, dependent alliance with a non-democratic hegemonic world power. In the mid-1990s there is no such alliance and Russia is not a hegemonic world power. In this new geopolitical context, the reform Communists' best chance for power is to present themselves as – and to be – "social democrats."[24] Even if some of the reform Communists might not actually have undergone profound changes in their mentality (and many, of course, have not), the external reality to which the reform Communists must respond has changed profoundly. As long as democracy is the only game in town, the incentive structure of those who seek governmental power is derived from the democratic context.

Finally, since voters play a crucial role in weighting the incentive system, what did they actually want? Did they actually want a return to communism?[25] The Polish voters, two months after the elections that had supposedly "returned" the former Communists to power, believed, correctly, that they had not actually returned the old Communists to power. Polish respondents recognized the fundamental discontinuity in global and national power relations between 1988 and 1993. To the question, "Does the formation of the SLD–PSL [the reform Communist Party and their old Peasant Party ally] government coalition signify the return to power of persons who ruled prior to 1989?", 63 per cent answered "no," 13 per cent said "difficult to say," and only 24 per cent of the population answered "yes."[26] This answer is geopolitically, politically, and historically correct. An observation from the Spanish case may clarify this reasoning. If sometime in the 1990s – as seems probable – the Partido Popular (a party that is perceived by a segment of the electorate as representing a continuity with the right wing that governed with Franco) wins control of the government after an election, their victory in the changed Spanish environment would not signify a "return to franco-ism" as much as an alternation in power, in which a modern democratic conservative party has won the election with a mandate to rule democratically.[27]

It is possible to end on a somewhat optimistic note concerning the future of democracy in East Central Europe, although this is not to embrace a geopolitical or philosophical perspective of democratic immanence. It is probable that, in some of the countries, democracy will never be consolidated. In other countries, democracy might become consolidated but will eventually break down. Some countries will consolidate democracy but will never *deepen* democracy in the spheres of gender equality, access to critical social services, inclusive citizenship, respect for human rights, and freedom of information; they might, indeed, occasionally violate human rights.

All serious democratic thinkers and activists are now also aware that the much-vaunted democratic Third Wave has already produced some dangerous undertows, not only in post-communist Europe but also in Western Europe.[28] In the United States, influential ideologues of liberty are at times too simplistic and mean spirited for a healthy democratic polity. In this context, democratic triumphalism is not only uncalled for but dangerous. Democratic institutions have to be not only created but crafted, nurtured, and developed. It is abundantly clear that to create an economic society supportive of democracy requires more than just markets and private property. It is time to problematize and transcend "illiberal liberalism" and also to theorize and construct socially integrative identity politics, as opposed to endlessly fragmenting identity politics. Further, to argue that democracy is better than any form of government once alternatives have been in crisis is not sufficient. Democracy has to be defended on its own merits. Clearly, more research should also be devoted to learning about the great variety of democratic regimes that actually exist in the world. Most important, new political projects, as well as research endeavours, must be devoted to improving the quality of consolidated democracies.

Notes

1. However, while it is true that rump Yugoslavia (Serbia, Montenegro, and the former province of Kosovo), as presently constituted is non-democratic, it is useful to recognize that there are more pressures for democracy there than Western policy makers and public opinion normally recognize. According to Tibor Varady, the Minister of Justice in the Milan Panic government in the rump Yugoslavia, when Prime Minister Panic challenged Milosevic in the December 1992 presidential election, the West sent fewer than 30 election observers, and most arrived just days before the election. In contrast, in the plebiscite in Chile in 1988 that led to the defeat of Pinochet, the West sent thousands of observers, many of whom were involved months before the election. Why this difference? Commentary in the West in essence assumed that Serbia was univocally for Serbian expansionism and that "primordial nationalism" was so strong that Slobodan Milosevic was unbeatable. But, even with the abstention of the Muslims of Kosovo (about 10 per cent of the potential electorate), election day technical fraud by Slobodan Milosevic of possibly 5–10 per cent of the vote, and the lack of election observers and financial and technical support from the West, Panic still won 43 per cent of the vote. In December 1992 Milosevic was not politically unbeatable. Some analysts, when confronted with the Chilean–Serbian comparison, shrug their shoulders and say, "So what? Milosevic never would have respected the elections." This again misses the point. Power is always relational. If Milosevic had actually lost and then annulled the election, he would have been domestically and internationally weakened in relation to democratic opponents and the myth of univocal support for aggressive nationalism would have been unmasked.
2. In addition, it is debatable that the privatization of all or most of publicly owned property is necessary for the creation of a functioning market economy. Post-Second World War Austria and Italy immediately come to mind as countries that retained a large public sector but were more or less efficient democratic market economies.

3. Four important studies of this phenomenon are Albert Fishlow, "The Latin American State," *Journal of Economic Perspectives* 1990; 4(3): 61–74; Hector Schamis, "Re-forming the State: The Role of Privatization in Chile and Britain" (Ph.D. diss., Columbia University, Department of Political Science, 1994); Peter Evans, "The State as a Problem and Solution: Predation, Embedded Autonomy, and Structural Change," in Stephan Haggard and Robert R. Kaufman (eds) *The Politics of Economic Adjustment: International Constraints, Distributive Conflicts, and the State* (Princeton: Princeton University Press, 1992), pp. 139–181; and Joan M. Nelson (ed) *Intricate Links: Democratization and Market Reforms in Latin America and Eastern Europe* (New Brunswick: Transaction Publishers, 1994), especially the article by Jacek Kochanowicz, "Reforming Weak States and Deficient Bureaucracies". China in the first half of the 1990s allowed the emergence of a robust private sector in some areas while maintaining a strong command economy in other sectors and overall near-totalitarian practices concerning politics, the media, and even family reproductive decisions.

4. We need more comparative studies of variation in state capacity *vis-à-vis* privatization and economic restructuring. Such variation could range from significant state reconstruction that increases state capacity and efficacy *vis-à-vis* privatization, to states that have had modest but unsatisfactory state reconstruction that has led to the creation of new post-reform problems and the threat of a low-level equilibrium trap, to the extreme case of state near-disintegration and virtually no state capacity for structuring change. East Central Europe and the former Soviet Union provide examples of all these possible variations. The most popularly supported privatization in Central and Eastern Europe has been the Czech Republic, which was also the case, despite some corruption, of the greatest transparency and where the freely elected government worked longest at such socio-economic reforms as job retraining and state restructuring. In contrast, in a country like Romania, where the state has not been reconstructed, some non-transparent privatization has occurred but there is a danger of a low-level equilibrium trap. In the Ukraine and parts of Russia, a new state had not been constructed, but the old state manifested strong disintegrative tendencies and low capacities in the 1992–1993 period. See, for example, the empirically grounded comparative analysis of the Czech Republic and Romania by Olivier Blanchard, Simon Commander, and Fabrizio Coricelli, "Unemployment and Restructuring" (World Bank, 1993), mimeo. Also see the chapter on Czechoslovakia in Roman Frydman, Andrzej Rapaczynski, and John Earle (eds) *The Privatization Process in Central Europe* (Budapest: Central European University Press, 1993), pp. 40–94, and Roman Frydman, Andrzej Rapaczynski, and John Earle (eds) *The Privatization Process in Russia, Ukraine and the Baltic States* (Budapest: Central European University Press, 1993). The case studies of Ukraine and Russia underscore the difficulties of orderly, effective, and non-mafia privatization if the state is in disarray. See also Roman Frydman and Andrzej Rapaczynski, *Privatization in Eastern Europe: Is the State Withering Away?* (Budapest: Central European University Press, 1994).

5. In frequent visits to Russia in 1991–1995, the subject of a Pinochet or a Chinese alternative frequently came up as possible alternatives for Russia in conversations with Russian analysts and policy makers. But, in fact, even before the disorderly behaviour of the Russian military in Chechnya, only 3 per cent of Russian respondents in an April 1994 poll "completely agreed" and only 7 per cent "generally agreed" with the statement that "the army should rule" as an alternative political formula for Russia. See Richard Rose and Christian Haerpfer, "New Russian Barometer III: The Results," *Studies in Public Policy* 1994; 228; question 31b.

6. Ken Jowitt, *New World Disorder: The Leninist Extinction* (Berkeley: University of California Press, 1992), especially pp. 249–331.

7. For this important approach to power, see Steven Lukes, *Power: A Radical View* (London: Macmillan, 1974).

8. For a detailed analysis and ample documentation of this phenomenon, see Juan J. Linz,

"Legitimacy of Democracy and the Socioeconomic System," in Mattei Dogan (ed.), *Comparing Pluralist Democracies: Strains on Democracy* (Boulder, Colorado: Westview Press, 1988), pp. 65–113.

9. See, for example, Stephen Handelman, "The Russian Mafiya," *Foreign Affairs* March–April 1994; 73(2): 83–96.

10. See Linz, "Legitimacy of Democracy," op. cit.

11. The title of a widely disseminated article by Jon Elster captures this perspective, "The Necessity and Impossibility of Simultaneous Economic and Political Reform," in Douglas Greenberg, Stanley N. Katz, Melanie Beth Oliviero, and Steven C. Wheatley (eds) *Constitutionalism and Democracy: Transitions in the Contemporary World* (New York: Oxford University Press, 1993). The reasons for the impossibility of simultaneity are not necessarily those advanced by Elster but may be the fact that the time necessary for successful economic change is inherently longer than the time needed to hold free elections and even draft a democratic constitution. An important survey-based critique of the Elster hypothesis and an argument for the empirical reality of respondents' multiple time horizons and their "political economy of patience" are given by the Hungarian political scientist László Bruszt in "Why on Earth Would East Europeans Support Capitalism?" (paper presented at the XVth World Congress of the International Political Science Association, Berlin, 21–24 August 1994).

12. The voters might, because of the negative economic performance, vote incumbents out of office, but the overall economic policies of their successors might well continue to be roughly the same. Poland in 1993–1995 and Hungary in 1994–1995 (especially after the reform acceleration of 1995) come to mind. Democratic alternations of governing coalitions in fact give more time to the policies of economic change while at the same time giving some valuable room for accommodation to the political sentiments and fears of those most hurt by the fundamental changes being undertaken by the new democratic regime.

13. In fact, in a regression model of their data, William Mishler and Richard Rose conclude that "our regression model shows that it takes a four point fall in either current or future economic evaluation to produce a one point fall in evaluations of the [political] regime." Their major explanation of this result is that East Europeans have a fairly long time horizon. See their "Trajectories of Fear and Hope: The Dynamics of Support for Democracy in Eastern Europe," *Studies in Public Policy* 1993; 214: 27.

14. Juan Linz, in a study of the breakdown of democracies – particularly in Europe in the interwar years – posed a more direct relationship between efficacy and legitimacy without data to prove that relationship. In fact, some of the data assembled later showed that the relationship was true for only a few countries, particularly for Germany and Austria, but not for Norway and the Netherlands. Why the apparent difference today? We could call attention to the presence in the interwar years of alternative "legitimate" models for the polity: the Soviet-Communist utopia, the new Fascist Italian and later German model, the corporatist–authoritarian–catholic "organic" democracy, the pre-war bureaucratic–monarchical authoritarianism, and even (in Spain) the anarchist utopia. They all appealed as alternative answers for inefficacious democracy. There are no such appealing alternatives to "difficult democracies" today. See Juan J. Linz, *The Breakdown of Democratic Regimes: Crisis, Breakdown, and Reequilibration* (Baltimore: Johns Hopkins University Press, 1978).

15. Even here we should note a partial confirmation of loosely coupled hypothesis in that the positive evaluation of the current post-communist political system was 18.7 points higher than the evaluation of the current post-communist economic system.

16. Turkmenistan, Tajikistan, and Uzbekistan are significantly less pluralistic in regard to democratic opposition electoral activity than in rump Yugoslavia. In contrast to the latter, where the opposition presidential candidate received 43 per cent of the vote in December 1992, open democratic contestation in Turkmenistan, Tajikistan, and Uzbekistan was de facto insignificant in 1994. According to the *Economist*'s useful political synopsis of the 12 members of the Commonwealth of Independent States, Turkmenistan is described as a

"one-party state. All members of the parliament, elected in December 1994, were unopposed. In February 1994, 99.99% voted to extend [President] Saparmurat Niyazoc's term of office until 1999. Only 212 Turkmen voted No, officially." The *Economist* summarizes politics in Uzbekistan thus: "Main opposition parties banned; media under state control. Ruling party won over 80% of seats in parliamentary elections in December 1994; 99.96% of the electorate voted on March 26 [1995] to extend [President] Islam Karimov's term of office until 2000." The *Economist* notes of Tajikistan: "Imamali Rakhmonov confirmed as president last November [1994] in an election at which most opposition parties were banned. Widespread vote-rigging alleged." See "Less Poor, Less Democratic," The *Economist* 22–28 April 1995; 48. Clearly, no serious theorist could consider that these three countries are involved in any form of democratic transition.

17. In fact, positive GNP growth in the Czech Republic was projected to be 3 per cent and 6 per cent for 1994 and 1995 and to be 3.5 per cent and 3 per cent for Slovakia. In contrast, for the same years the Russian figures were −15 per cent and −7 per cent and the Ukrainian figures were −23 per cent and −3 per cent.

18. For example, the better/worse ratio concerning freedom to travel was 95/5 in the Czech Republic, 75/7 in Poland, and only 41/28 in Russia. The better/worse ratio for freedom from unlawful arrest was 73/4 in the Czech Republic, 71/5 in Poland, and only 23/15 in Russia. These results, among other things, accurately reflect the stresses for individuals due to the continuing stateness crisis in Russia. Data are from table 12.2 and Rose and Haerpfer, 1994, op. cit., questions 30c and 30e.

19. For an argument concerning the tension or even hostility between Orthodoxy, Confucianism, Islam, and democracy, see Samuel P. Huntington, "The Clash of Civilizations," *Foreign Affairs* 1993; 72(3). Also see his *The Third Wave: Democratization in the Late Twentieth Century* (Norman: University of Oklahoma Press, 1991), pp. 298–311.

20. For Max Weber's discussion of caesaropapism, see Guenther Roth and Claus Wittich (eds), *Economy and Society* (Berkeley: University of California Press, 1978).

21. Islam (unlike Confucianism) is an important value system in parts of post-communist Europe. A complete argument concerning Islam would be much more complex than that argument concerning Orthodox Christianity. However, we note that Weber's fear of fundamentalism has frequently contributed to its shoring up of (and even legitimating) anti-democratic governments or movements that are seen as bulwarks against the spread of fundamentalism. This is so even when the Islamic parties were elected democratically and had not violated democratic practices. Nowhere was this clearer than in the West's implicit (and even explicit) endorsement of the military coup in Algeria after Islamic forces had won the first electoral round in 1991. Thus, for geopolitical reasons, authoritarian governments in the former Soviet Union that share borders with Iran and/or Afghanistan (e.g. Turkmenistan, Uzbekistan, and Tajikistan) are to some extent treated by Western policy makers and commentators with a democratic "double standard."

22. This was stressed in a conversation between the author and Jerzy Wiatr, who chairs an important congressional committee for the former Communists in the Polish parliament. Wiatr stressed that "the most important thing we should accomplish in our government is that we prove we are a legitimate democratic alternative." Conversation in Warsaw, 5 November 1993.

23. Anatol Lieven, *The Baltic Revolution: Estonia, Latvia, Lithuania and the Path to Independence* (New Haven: Yale University Press, 1993), p. 274.

24. In 1989–1990 the social-democratic political space in post-communist Europe was not effectively occupied in elections. The historic social democrats were too tarnished and too weak and the neo-liberal discourse was too hegemonic. In 1992–1994, some reformed Communist parties who were out of power partially restructured themselves to fill this space as the reaction to neo-liberalism set in. Also, with the collapse of communism, the

Socialist International sought new allies in post-communist Europe. The reform Communist parties could gain Socialist International certification and support only if in fact they ruled as democrats. In December 1994, the Council of the Socialist International, meeting in Budapest, recommended that the reform Communist party in Hungary, the Hungarian Socialist Party, be admitted as a full member of the Socialist International. For an astute analysis of the political and structural reasons for the social democratic turn, while out of office, of the Hungarian and Polish post-communist parties, see Michael Waller, "The Adaptation of the Former Communist Parties of East-Central Europe: A Case of Social Democratization?" (paper prepared for a conference on Political Representation: Parties and Parliamentary Democracy, Central European University, Budapest, 16–17 June 1995). At the same Central European University conference, the president of the Lithuanian Political Science Association, Algis Krupavicius, wrote that, for the Lithuanian post-communist party that came to power in 1992 (the Democratic Labour Party), "the period in opposition was an extremely favorable opportunity to renew their membership [which dropped from 200,000 in 1989 to 8,000 in 1995], organizational structures, and ideological identity." The quotation is from his conference paper, "Post-Communist Transformation and Political Parties," 12–13.

25. In both Poland and Hungary, the electoral laws resulted in the reform Communist parties or coalition receiving many more seats than votes. Seats therefore were not a solid indicator of voters' intentions. In Poland in 1993, 35.8 per cent of the votes for the reformed Communists and their coalition peasant allies yielded 65.8 per cent of the seats. In Hungary in 1994, the reform communist party, the Hungarian Socialist Party, received 33 per cent of the vote in the first round but an absolute majority of seats after the second round.

26. Poll published by the Polish Public Opinion Service, Centrum Badania Opinii Spolecznej, in November 1993, p. 1. Moreover, in late 1993 and early 1994, when a random sample of the population in Poland and Hungary was asked to comment on the statement, "We should return to Communist rule," 47 per cent of those polled in Poland "strongly disagreed" and 35 per cent "somewhat disagreed" with this statement. The sum total of respondents in Hungary who disagreed was an identical 82 per cent. See Rose and Haerpfer, 1994, op. cit., question 43. The highest percentage of respondents in East Central Europe who "strongly agreed" with the statement was in Bulgaria, with 9 per cent. The next highest was Romania, with 4 per cent.

27. For many readers the November 1995 victory in Poland of a former Communist Party leader, Aleksander Kwasniewski, in the second round of the presidential elections might seem a clearer victory for communism. From the viewpoint of democratic consolidation, the two most important questions for Poland's future are: (1) will the post-communists (who as a result of the 1993 and 1995 elections had a two-thirds majority in the parliament and controlled the presidency) rule democratically and (2) will the anti-communist forces accept the legitimacy of the free re-election results? While not happy with the November 1995 elections, Timothy Garton Ash was more worried about the second question than the first: "Morally, as well as aesthetically, the triumph of the post-communists in Poland is deeply distasteful, but is it dangerous? Not, I believe, so far as their aims and policies are concerned ... Kwasniewski and his friends want desperately to be seen not as eastern post-communists but as regular western social democrats." Concerning the second question, Garton Ash cites a number of post-election declarations by the Polish episcopate and Lech Walesa and concludes that the greatest danger in Poland is "a large right-wing extra parliamentary movement around Lech Walesa, supported by the Church and Solidarity, and simply not accepting President Kwasniewski as the legitimate head of Poland's Third Republic." See Timothy Garton Ash, "Neo-Pagan Poland," *New York Review of Books* 11 January 1996; 10–14, quotes from pp. 12 and 14.

28. Three excellent articles in a special issue of *Daedalus* called "After Communism: What?"

(Summer 1994) are devoted to the unexpected crisis that Western and European democrats began to experience after they had lost their legitimating enemy or "other" after the collapse of communism. Many problems that had long been deferred or denied came on the agenda. For this new and challenging "paradigm lost" situation, see Tony Judt, "Nineteen Eighty-Nine: The End of *Which* European Era?," 1–20; Elemér Hankiss, "European Paradigms: East and West, 1945–1994," 115–126; and István Rév, "The Postmortem Victory of Communism," 157–170. Claus Offe, *Der Tunnel am Ende des Lichts: Erkundungen de politischen Transformation im Neuen Osten* (Frankfurt: Campus Verlag, 1994) throughout the book, and particularly in chapter 10, raises similar questions.

13

Religion and democracy: The case of Islam, civil society, and democracy

Saad Eddin Ibrahim

Religion is a system of beliefs, rituals, and practices which deal with the "sacred," the "metaphysical," the "eternal," the "other-worldly," and the "absolute." Even when a religion deals with the "worldly," it is for the ultimate service of the "other-worldly." Religions, of course, vary in many ways and in many aspects, but they nearly all share these features. Being "sacred" and "absolute" has made it difficult for religions to tolerate, or coexist with, others in the same community or polity. One's sacred and absolute truths set a real or symbolic boundary with the other's sacred and absolute truth. If taken too seriously and passionately, such boundaries can become bloody. History is full of religious wars and sectarian conflicts, especially in Europe, the latest of which are still alive in Ireland and Bosnia–Herzegovina.

By the same token, being sacred and absolute makes it difficult for people who take religion too seriously and passionately to tolerate another system of ideas or beliefs that claims similar qualities to itself; that is, other man-made dogmatic ideologies such as Marxism. Again, modern history is replete with tragic tales of conflict among religious and non-religious – but equally dogmatic – ideologies. It is the exclusive nature of such belief systems which implies the negation of the different "other."

Democracy, in contrast, is based upon the completely opposite premise – the inclusion of all human beings within the community or the polity as equals, regardless of their religion, race, or creed. Whatever definition of democracy one opts for, it ultimately revolves around the peaceful management of "differences." Accepting the different other – whether on the basis of religion, class, interest, gender, or ethnicity – is central to political and legal equality. Moreover, such equality before the law is a necessary condition for democracy. In other words, democracy may be conceived of as a system for managing differences among legal–political equals, to attain their optimum well-being. Such differences are managed in the context of a set of rules agreed upon by those different equals. Though not as sacred as religious commandments, the rules of the democratic game are to be respected by all players. Unlike religious commandments, the rules of the democratic game – the constitution and laws – can be changed or amended. Thus, the fundamentals of democracy are both "worldly" – formulated by humans for humans on earth – and "relativistic" – temporally, culturally, and politically bound.

The inclusive worldly and relativistic nature of democracy puts it into potential conflict with any dogma which claims a monopoly on absolute truth, including religious dogma. This actual or potential conflict is what led to the separation between the "state" and the "church" in the early democracies of the West. Later democratic societies have followed suit. Such separation is neither a total divorce nor a hostile coexistence; rather, it has been a mutual respect for the autonomy of each other's sphere in regulating human affairs. Depending on a given society's pre-democratic history, the relationship between religion and politics is classifiable into modalities – ranging from working harmoniously together to being totally oblivious to each other. In either case, the religious dogma has been toned down or the passions often accompanying it seem to have subsided. One way to achieve this accommodation is through the reinterpretation, selectivity, or reformulation of sacred texts. The famous saying attributed to Jesus Christ, "Pay Caesar what is due to Caesar, and pay God what is due to God," is a case in point. It is the epitome of such a selective reinterpretation which backs up the principle of the separation of state and religion.

The problematic of such separation is more complicated and dramatized during periods of sociopolitical transition. In this respect, non-Western societies are going through transitions similar to – or more severe than – those that their Western counterparts went through a few centuries earlier. It is typical, during the transition, to encounter spokespeople in the name of a particular religion, giving their own idealized and simplistic (but often attractive) interpretation of sacred texts to suit the needs, deprivations, and aspirations of the marginalized and powerless – the ethos and idioms of restoring the "paradise lost." I demonstrate here that all religions, but especially Islam, lend themselves to diverse interpretations when it comes to politics and governance; and the prevailing socio-economic conditions make some of these interpretations more acceptable than others.

Let us start with a leaf of Western history. On 25 February 1534, in the German town of Münster, Anabaptist zealots staged an armed uprising and installed a radical dictatorship. All who refused to undergo re-baptism into the new faith were driven from the city without food or belongings during a snowstorm. The new regime impounded all food, money, and valuables and cancelled all debts. Mobs burned the financial records of all local merchants. The housing of the fleeing well-to-do was reassigned to the poor. Former beggars capered in the streets, decked in plundered finery. The religious positions of the new regime were equally radical. Under the new moral order that it had imposed, all books other than the Bible were burned. All "sins," including swearing, backbiting, complaining, and disobedience, were to be punished by instant execution. Soon, the regime instituted polygamy: unmarried women were ordered to marry the first man who asked them – and 49 women were executed and their bodies hacked into quarters for failing to comply. Before long, however, the outside world reacted: Münster was soon besieged by its bishop, who had escaped and recruited an army of mercenaries. Surrounded and cut off, the city was beset by growing confusion.

Then, out of the rebel ranks in Münster, there arose a new and absolute leader – John Bockelson, who assumed the name of John of Leyden and claimed to have been appointed by God to be king during the final days. A "this-worldly" rebellion now became firmly "other-worldly." The rebels did not need to win victory over their temporal rulers, for all was now in the hands of God in these days before the Last Judgement, announced by John of Leyden to be coming before Easter 1535. Anyone in Münster who opposed or expressed doubt on this prophecy was executed. On 24 June 1535, the bishop's troops made a surprise assault in the night and took the city. John of Leyden was arrested. Over the next few months, he was led by a chain from town to town and, in January 1536, back to Münster, where he was tortured to death with a red-hot iron in front of large crowds. His body was put in an iron cage and suspended from the church tower. The cage still hangs there today.[1]

There was nothing very unusual about the rebellion in Münster, or that it took the form of a religious movement. Similar events were commonplace in Europe at the time, especially in the growing commercial towns. The few decades preceding and following the Münster episode were replete with intense "worldly" discontent, shrouded in religious discourse and conflict. A quick glance at the annals of the first half of the sixteenth century would substantiate this proposition. Eighteen years before the Münster uprising, Sir Thomas More wrote his *Utopia* (1516). A year later, in protest against the sale of "indulgences," Martin Luther posted his 95 theses on the door of Palast Church in Wittenberg, beginning the infamous Reformation. In fact, by the time of the Münster rebellion, Martin Luther had completed the first translation of the Bible into German, and two years later he had his "Table Talks" in 1536. Two years after the execution of John of Leyden, Calvin was expelled from Geneva to settle in Strasbourg (1538). In 1542, Pope Paul III established the Inquisition in Rome, and, a year later, the first Protestants were burned at the stake in Spain. In 1544, Pope Paul III called a general council at Trent. The council met a year later to discuss reformation and counter-reformation.

This was a period of great transformations, ushered in by dramatic geographic explorations, scientific discoveries, and sprouting capitalism. By the time of the Münster uprising, the Americas had been discovered; some 25 universities had been founded throughout Europe; the printing presses had already turned out some 10 million copies of published books in various European languages. Before the mid-sixteenth century, religious reformation and counter-reformation would sweep Germany, France, Switzerland, England, Scotland, Poland, Spain, and Sweden.

Viewing sixteenth century Europe in retrospect is very instructive in understanding what is happening in the Arab Muslim world in the late twentieth century. The so-called Islamic revival is as much an expression of "worldly" concerns as it is a religious quest for "other-worldly" salvation.

The seizure of the Grand Mosque of Mecca at the end of 1979 by a group of Muslim zealots led by a young man, Juhiman al-Outiabi, resembles in many ways the Münster rebellion. The leader and his followers were all in their twenties and early thirties. They were of Bedouin tribal origin, newcomers to the rapid urbanizing centres of Saudi Arabia. In their youthful lifetime they had already witnessed the profound but confusing socio-economic transformation of their country, resulting from the oil boom. In the 10 years preceding their rebellion, Saudi Arabia had doubled its total population, tripled its urban population, and increased its money wealth tenfold. There were as many expatriates as native Saudis in the country. The expatriates poured into the country in unprecedented numbers, especially after 1973. They came from as many (and as far) lands as Korea, Australia, Scandinavia, and America. While Saudis may have been used to Arabs and Muslims coming in for the pilgrimage, the oil-boom's waves of expatriates had nothing (or very little) in common with the Saudi natives. Different in languages, religions, and lifestyles, the expatriates were running much of the economic life of Saudi Arabia. Meanwhile, the sudden wealth from sky-rocketing oil prices was not being equitably distributed, nor was political power equitably shared. The estrangement or alienation of Saudis in their own country was growing as rapidly as the oil wealth in those years. Like youth everywhere, young Saudis, and especially those with some education, felt the brunt of such estrangement more than others. With restricted participation in socio-economic life because of the limited skills and training for modern institutions being built, and with no political participation under the autocratic Saudi regime, long allied with the religious monopoly of the *Wahabbi* establishment, young Juhiman al-Outiabi and his fellow zealots must have felt the same way as John of Leyden did four and a half centuries earlier. The end result was nearly the same: the Grand Mosque of Mecca was soon besieged by Saudi government troops; the necessary pronouncements of condemnation were quickly issued by Sheikh Ben-Baz, the head of the *Wahabbi* religious establishment. However, unable to dissuade the rebels to surrender, and with the Saudi troops unable to storm the Grand Mosque, the Saudi regime called on French mercenaries to do the job. Several of the zealots were killed in the process; the others were arrested, quickly tried, and beheaded. Ultimately, the uprising was crushed and whole incident had ended in three weeks.

Although somewhat different in detail, similar episodes have taken place in Egypt in 1974 and 1977, in Tunisia just few months prior to the Grand Mosque seizure in 1979, and in Tehran at nearly the same time. The zealots in all of these cases were not the poorest of the poor, nor were they the scum misfits of the earth. They were all young and among the relatively better educated in their societies. They were all newcomers to the big city who had come from tribal and rural origins. Like their counterparts in Münster, their tocsin was against "king and pope"; in the Arab-Muslim world, that reads "against repressive political regimes and allied religious establishment". The counter-weapon of the discontented zealots is equally a combination of the political and the religious.

217

More than Christianity and other religions, Islam lends itself to be a mobilizing political weapon. In its precepts and dicta, Islam is as much a "worldly" as an "other-worldly" religion. In the latter, it promises a glorious life on earth to the believers who adhere to its teachings in letter and spirit – hence, the battle-cry of today's activists, "Islam is the Solution." The idealized history that Muslims learn in school and hear about in the mosque has a simple unidimensional message: Islam in the days of the Prophet Mohammed and the Guided Caliphs (610–661) enabled Muslims to be virtuous, just, prosperous, and strong; the true believers conquered the world and built the greatest civilization humanity had ever known.

Young Muslims are told in schools that the normative dimensions of Islamic teachings are second to none. Right from the start, Islam educated its adherents to accept differences among human beings. The Holy Qur'an addressed the believer unequivocally.

O Mankind! We [God] created you from a single pair of a male and a female; and made you into peoples and tribes, that ye may know each other (not that ye may despise each other). Verily the most honored in the sight of God is [he who is] the most religious among you.... (Hujurat or the Inner Apartments: 13)

If the Lord has so willed, He could have made mankind One Nation: but they will still differ. (Hud or the Prophet Hud: 118)

Among his [God's] Signs is the creation of the heavens and the earth, and the variations in your languages (tongues) and your colors .... (Rum, or the Roman Empire: 22)

These verses spoke about and embraced multiculturalism more eloquently and unequivocally than any twentieth century UN or European document of a similar nature. In more than 100 places in the Holy Qur'an we encounter clear and detailed verses teaching and preaching the norms, values, and virtues that are now considered essential for civil society.

On freedom of religious belief, the Holy Qur'an is no less equivocal. The following verses suffice:

Ye may believe in it (the Qur'an) or not.... (Bani Israel: 107)

Say, 'The Truth is From your Lord': Let him who will, Believe, and let him Who will reject (it). (Kahf: 29)

Let there be no compulsion in religion: Truth stands out Clear from Error. (Baqara or the Heifer: 256)

If it had been thy Lord's Will, They would all have believed, All who are on Earth! Wilt thou then compel mankind, Against their will to believe! (Yunus, or Jonah: 99)

Therefore do thou give Admonition, for thou art One to admonish. Thou art not one to manage (men's) affairs. But if any turn away And reject God, God will punish him With a mighty Punishment.

For to Us will be Their Return; Then it will be for Us to call them to account. (Gashiya, or the Overwhelming Event: 21–26)

This last verse laid down the Islamic principle of religious coexistence and tolerance. God spared the Prophet and all Muslims the trap of fruitless debate on who has the monopoly over religious truth. The Faithful's duty is to advocate, but not to admonish or coerce. It is only God who can hold people accountable in the thereafter in matters of beliefs. This fundamental point is repeated over and over again. Addressing the Prophet, God commands:

If they do wrangle with thee, Say: "God knows best What it is ye are doing." God will judge between you on the Day of Judgment Concerning the matters in which Ye differ. (Hajj or The Pilgrimage: 68–69)

Equally, the Qur'an adjoins the Prophet and the Faithful to be always gentle in addressing, dialoguing, or arguing with others in general, and Peoples of the Book (Jews and Christians) in particular:

Speak fair to people. (Baqara, or the Heifer: 83)

Invite (all) to the Way of thy Lord with wisdom and beautiful preaching; and argue with them, In ways that are best And most gracious: For thy Lord knoweth best, Who have strayed from His Path, And who received guidance. (Nahl, or the Bee: 125)

One could continue to give numerous illustrations of Islam's respect of differences and its advocacy of peaceful and civilized management of diversity. But this may, in fact, be said of nearly all great religions. The question remains: how seriously have Muslims taken their Glorious Commandments? For that we turn to some leaves of Muslim sociopolitical history.

The first Muslim state of Medina set up by the Prophet Mohammed and his four Guided Caliphs (successors) lasted for only 40 years (622–661 A.D.). For the following 14 centuries, the imagination of successive generations of Muslims has been galvanized by the purified glorious tales of those four decades. The history of Islam since 661 A.D. is replete with religious–social movements in quest for the "paradise lost." Not all such movements succeeded in seizing power, and none has managed to restore the "paradise lost." The political successes, rise of dynasties, religious failures, and the fall of those dynasties, had always sown the seeds of new religious–social movements.

Ibn Khaldoun, the great Arab social thinker, noted the cyclicality and the success prerequisites of such movements in seizing political power and establishing dynasties of their own. According to him, it is always a combination of *asabiya – esprit de corps –* and a "religious mission." The *asabiya*, a primordial form of solidarity, is often embodied in a strong tribe or a tribal coalition, providing the muscles of political–military success. The religious mission provides the spiritual *raison d'être* and legitimacy for success. To put it in other terms, every new movement has to provide an alternative "king and pope" to the decaying "king and pope." The last literal manifestations of the Khaldounian paradigm were the nineteenth century Saudi–Wahabbi movement in the Arabian Peninsula, the Sanusi movement in North Africa, and the Mahadist movement in the Sudan.

In the Khaldounian times of the fourteenth century, the would-be "tribe-religious movement" was often initiated in the hinterland, at an unreachable distance from the seat of political power. That hinterland was dubbed in the times of Ibn Khaldoun as *bilad al-Siba* or the unruly country – in contrast to *bilad al-Maghzin* or the ruly and tax-paying country. As the central power weakened, the *Siba* country expanded and inched closer to the capital until the right moment came for the *coup de grâce* against the decaying ruling élite. A new "tribe-dynasty," legitimated and empowered by a religious vision, then takes over to restore the "Islamic paradise lost." The rest of the cycle unfolds over three to four generations (about 100 years), until another *Siba* hinterland tribe and another religious vision coalesce into a new movement.

This elegant Khaldounian paradigm accounted for much, if not all, of medieval Arab-Muslim history. However, with sociocultural changes and the growing integration of the region into the world system since the late eighteenth century, the paradigm no longer accounts for the march of modern Arab-Muslim history. But some of its internal logic may still be operative. The mobilizing power of an Islamic vision in quest of the "paradise lost" still appeals to the marginalized, the relatively deprived, and the powerless.

In this century, the "tribe" alone may no longer be a viable organizational base for a religious–social movement. In the Yemeni elections of 1993 and the civil war of the following year we note an alliance between the *Mashid* Tribe and the Islamic *Islah* (Reform) Party. A year later, the same alliance would march with modern North Yemeni army units to expel the South Yemeni ruling élite and consolidate their hold throughout Yemen. More often, however, it is now the "underclass" that substitutes for tribe in fuelling religious–social movements in the Arab-Muslim world. Algeria and Egypt are striking cases in point: in both, one-party populist regimes ruled for 30–40 years before they were forcefully challenged by sprouting Islamic movements.

Initially, the single-party populist regimes had attractive visions of their own. Their visions promised tremendous worldly rewards – consolidation of newly gained independence, rapid development, economic prosperity, social justice, and cultural authenticity. Though not quite paradise on earth, the populist vision promised something very close to it. There were implicit conditions, however, for delivering on the populist promises: the "masses" were to work hard without demanding liberal political participation. With no firm tradition of participatory governance, anyhow, this populist trade-off seemed acceptable to the vast majority. For the first decade or two, the populist social contract seemed to be working. Remarkable expansion in education, industrialization, health, and other service provisions were effected. With these real gains, a new middle class and a modern working class grew steadily under state tutelage.

However, there were unintended and adverse consequences of populist policies – rapid growth of population, urbanization, and bureaucratization. In the first 20 years of Algeria's populist regime (1962–1982), its population had doubled, its urbanization tripled, and its bureaucracy quadrupled. In Egypt, it took slightly longer – about 27–30 years – for the same process to occur. By the third decade of populist rule, the regimes in both countries were no longer able to manage their society or their state effectively. A new socio-economic formation rapidly grew. For lack of a better term than Marxist, this is the "urban lumpenproletariat." With high expectations but little or no employable skills, capital, or civic norms, the swarming millions of rural newcomers to the cities formed this proletariat. They crowded the older city quarters or, more often, created their own new slum areas. Called *bidonevilles* in Algeria and *ashwaiyat* in Egypt, these densely overpopulated slum areas would become the late twentieth century equivalent of the Khaldounian *Siba*. Their human content is proving to be the most flammable material in Arab-Muslim society today. In Egypt and Algeria they constitute between 25 and 35 per cent of the total population. The youth of these communities are easy prey for manipulation by demagogues, organized criminals, *agents provocateurs*, and Islamic activists.

Other compounding factors have made the situation even worse for populist regimes. The lower rungs of the new middle class have been steadily alienated as a result of dwindling opportunities for employment or upward sociopolitical mobility. They began a mass desertion, in the 1970s in Egypt, and in the 1980s in Algeria. From their ranks, Islamic activists and other dissidents would sprout. They would manipulate the urban lumpenproletariat of the new *Siba* in staging their challenge against the now ageing and decaying populist ruling élite. To use the Khaldounian analogy, a typical armed confrontation between an Islamic-led new *Siba* and the Egyptian state – new *maghazin* – took place in December 1992. By official count, some 700 shanty areas (*ashwaiyat*) have sprung up, in or around Egypt's major urban centres, over the previous two decades (1970–1990). At present, their total population is estimated to be between 10 and 12 million. Western Munira is one of them: located on the north-western edge of Imbaba in Greater Cairo, it is less than three kilometres across the Nile from the aristocratic upper-class district of Zamalek, the residential area of most of the *maghazin* élite. At two square kilometres, less than one-fifth of the territorial size of Zamalek, Western Munira has nearly one million dwellers, 10 times the population of Zamalek. With nearly 50 times the density of Zamalek, at the time of the 1992 confrontation, dwellers of Western Munira had no schools, hospitals, sewage system, public transportation, or a police station within walking distance. For many years, this area represented a "Hobbesian world," run by thugs, criminals, and drug dealers and infested with every known vice. With no state presence, Western Munira was also used as a hide-out for many Islamic militants on the run. In the late 1980s, one of them, Sheikh Gaber, felt safe enough to operate in the open. He preached to, and recruited, several followers and, in a very short time, he emerged as a "community leader." He began to weed out the vice lords, impose order, veil women, arrange marriages, and collect "taxes." The Egyptian state did not take note of him, until a Reuters reporter filed a story with the provocative title "Sheikh Gaber, the President of the Republic of Imbaba." Angered and embarrassed, the Egyptian authorities ordered the Reuters reporter out of the country and staged an armed expedition to arrest Sheikh

Gaber. By official count, some 12,000 armed security forces laid siege to Western Munira, then stormed the place. The operation took three weeks before Sheikh Gaber and 600 of his followers were killed, wounded, or arrested.

Similar confrontations have been frequent in both Egypt and Algeria since 1991. The casualty toll has escalated in Egypt from 96 in 1991, to 322 in 1992, and to 1,106 in 1993 – more than a tenfold increase in three years. In 1994 and 1995, however, the number of casualties decreased to about 700. In Algeria, the toll has rapidly been escalating, from less than 1,000 in 1992, to about 10,000 in 1993, and about 20,000 in 1994. In April 1995, the Algerian Minister of the Interior, Mr. A. Mezian Sherif, announced that the total number of casualties has topped 30,000 persons and material losses over 2.2 billion US dollars in three years between January 1992 and January 1995.[2] This amount of money, according to him, was more than enough to build 400,000 housing units for more than 2.4 million people. A war of attrition has been the order of the day in both countries. It is a war between an Islamic-led new *Siba* and a semi-authoritarian state, timidly trying to democratize.

The profile comparisons between typical militants and the challenged populist rulers are stark. Of average or superior formal education, an Islamic militant is usually less than 40 years of age. Nearly 90 per cent of those militants arrested or killed in armed confrontations with the Algerian state in the four years between 1992 and 1996 were born after independence in 1962 – that is, after the present populist regime came to power. Some of the Egyptian militants who were recently arrested, tried, and sentenced to death were under 18 years old – born after President Mubarak came to power as Vice-President in 1975, and after the beginning of the uninterrupted tenure of at least four of his present cabinet members.

Not only did the populist authoritarian regimes fail to renew their ranks by infusing new blood and new ideas but, worse, for a long time they repressed or circumvented other social forces from sharing the public space. The middle and upper rungs of the middle class, both men and women, have not been allowed a sufficient margin of freedom to create, and get involved in, autonomous civil-society organizations. Had such a civil society been in place during the period of populist state retreat in the 1970s and 1980s, both Egypt and Algeria could have weathered the militant Islamic-led *Siba* storm. Egypt has nearly stood still with its timid democratization since the early 1980s;

Algeria rushed clumsily into it in the early 1990s. Nevertheless, the situation in both countries could be markedly improved, as we shall shortly see.

Surprisingly, what Michael Hudson calls the "modernizing monarchies" of the Arab-Muslim world have been more able to weather the Islamic-led *Siba* storms. Different in many ways from their populist neighbours, modernizing monarchies in Morocco and Jordan faced similar structural socio-economic problems during the 1980s – growing population, urbanization, bureaucratization, huge external debts, and a shrinking state resource base. They had their share of urban lumpenproletariat, the new *Siba*, and food rioting in the 1980s. But instead of repression, resisting change, or attempting to precipitate dramatic change, the two monarchs have carefully engineered a gradual and orderly democratization: they initiated public debates on governance and constitutional issues in which all political forces participated; a "national pact" or a "new social contract" was implicitly or explicitly formulated; municipal and parliamentary elections were held, with a marked degree of fairness; the secular opposition in Morocco and the Islamic forces in Jordan won an impressive number of seats; women were elected to national parliaments for the first time in both countries.

Morocco and Jordan are not constitutional monarchies and may not be for some time to come. Nor are there any illusions about their participatory experiments of governance soon becoming a Westminster-style democracy. But their sociopolitical march in the last decade has been far more orderly than that of Algeria and Egypt: there has been no politically motivated violence, killing, or rioting in either country; Islamic militancy hardly exists in Morocco and is fairly tamed, or under complete control, in Jordan.

In Kuwait (1992), Lebanon (1992), and Yemen (1993), Islamists participated in parliamentary elections. They came second in Kuwait and Yemen, and had an impressive showing in winning several of the seats assigned to both Shiite and Sunni Muslims in Lebanon. Even in Egypt, though not officially recognized as a legal party, the Muslim Brotherhood ran for parliamentary elections under the banner of other parties in 1984 (with the Wafd) and 1987 (with the Labor Socialist Party). In both elections, the Muslim Brotherhood won several seats and came out in third place among nine contending parties.

Beyond the Arab world, Islamists have regularly run for elections in Pakistan, Bangladesh, and Turkey since the 1980s. In Indonesia, Malaysia, and the Islamic republics of the former Soviet Union,

Islamists have been peacefully engaging in local and municipal politics and are petitioning for recognition and the expansion of pluralistic politics on the national level. It is important to note that in three of the largest Muslim countries – Pakistan, Bangladesh, and Turkey – women have been elected to the top executive office in the land, dispelling the stereotype about an inherent anti-democratic or anti-feminist Islamic impulse. Moreover, in Turkey the most religious Islamic Rafat Party and the most secular Straight Path Party formed a coalition government in July 1996. It is also noteworthy that Islamic-based parties in both Pakistan and Bangladesh have appealed to no more than 10 per cent of the electorate. In the fair elections in Turkey, the religious Rafat Party won only about one-fifth of the popular vote in the 1995 parliamentary elections. The important point in all these recent examples is that Islamic parties have accepted the rules of the democratic game and have played them peacefully and in an orderly manner.

There are a number of lessons to be drawn from the contrasting cases of Algeria and Egypt, on the one hand, and the rest of the Arab-Muslim world, on the other. These lessons also serve to elucidate the intricate relationship between religion and politics in general and that of Islam in particular.

First, political Islam has grown and spread in the last two decades as an idiom of protest against repression, social injustice, the hardening of political arteries, and the threat to collective identity. Its radicalism is commensurate with the degree to which these ills are felt or perceived by the young, educated lower-middle-class Muslims. Political Islam has not been the only appealing vision to these young Muslims: they have responded strongly to secular visions in this century, such as Arab nationalism, Turkish nationalism, inter-war liberalism, and socialism.

Second, despite their initial radical messages and/or actions, Islamic militants are tameable, through accommodative politics of inclusion. Running for office, or once in it, they recognize the complexities of the real world and the need for gradualism and toleration. The "worldly" concerns increasingly impinge on the "other-worldly" in their consciousness, language, and actions. The Islamists of Iran are a case in point: starting as "pro-natalist," Iran's Islamic Revolution is now feverishly pursuing an "anti-natalist" population policy. In this respect, Islamic activists are no different from their Chinese Communist counterparts: recognizing that their ideological rhetoric led to a rapid population increase that undermined their other socio-

225

economic policies, they were willing to perform a complete policy reversal.

Third, people in Muslim societies, like people everywhere, may give new visions and promised solutions a chance when the old ones fail. But, ultimately, they will judge these new ones by their results. The Islamists in Jordan lost one-third of the number of seats between the 1989 and 1993 elections. Despite the majority of seats won in the last aborted parliamentary elections, Algeria's Islamic Salvation Front (FIS) lost one million net votes between 1990 and 1991. In both Jordan and Algeria, the initial flare of the "Islamic Alternative" lost some of its attraction once Islamists were tried in office. On the contrary, in Turkey the Islamic Rafat Party has been gaining steadily in national parliamentary elections, doubling its popular vote from less than 10 per cent to more than 20 per cent between the mid-1980s and the mid-1990s. This surge of popularity is due to its impressive performance in running large urban municipalities (e.g. Istanbul and Izmir). The slum areas around major Turkish cities could have led to bloody confrontations similar to those of Algeria and Egypt.

Fourth, peoples of the Muslim world have increasingly been integrated in the international system. The radical Islamists among them cannot ignore this fact. Even their anti-Western rhetoric is an idiom of protest against other worldly grievances. Once fairly or equitably addressed, cooperation becomes not only possible but also desirable. In this respect, Islamic radicals are no different from their nationalist counterparts of an earlier generation. The problem of the Muslim peoples in relation to the West parallels their problems with their own repressive and corrupt regimes. Not only does the legacy of Western colonialism lurk in Muslims' collective memory, but it is easily invoked with every contemporary Western act or policy that smacks of double standards. Recently, the reaction of the West to the massacres of Muslims by non-Muslims in market-places of Bosnia, mosques in Palestine, or civilian refugee camps in Lebanon (Qana, April 1996) seemed muted at best. The Western pressure on Arab and Muslim countries to sign an unlimited nuclear non-proliferation treaty without asking their arch-enemy Israel to do the same is, to them, a blatant double standard. Equally, Algeria's short-lived experiment with pluralistic politics was a test of whether Islamists could be reconciled to democracy, but it was as much a test of whether the West could be reconciled to Muslim democracy. The West has long been on the best of terms with Muslim despots, such as Saudi Arabia and many Gulf states, Iran's Shah, and Pakistan's Zia'ul-Haq.

Once these inconsistencies are seriously and credibly addressed, not only militant Islamists but most of the Arab-Muslim people would have no legitimate misgivings *vis-à-vis* the West.

Fifth, as a thoughtful Western observer recently noted, Islamic societies now find themselves in the opening rounds of what the West went through in the sixteenth and seventeenth centuries in redefining the relationship between God and man, among human beings, and between themselves and the state.[3] We believe that Muslim societies will emerge from this process as more rational and more democratic. The process, however, could be much shorter and less costly if external actors lend an honest hand on the side of democratic forces. The West has recently been interfering militarily in the affairs of Muslim societies, from Libya to Somalia and from the Gulf to Kurdistan. It has also been interfering economically, directly or through the IMF–World Bank-prescribed structural adjustment policies. The West is yet to do the same politically in support of democracy. Even if it brings into office some radical Islamists, they would soon lose either their "radicalism" or "Islamism." Muslims everywhere have taken note that the Islamic Afghani mujahidin are fighting each other for worldly gains – power – as their counterparts had previously done in post-Shah Iran. Muslims recognize that the Islamists are not saints; but they may be less devilish than their present old repressive rulers.[4]

I conclude with a plea to continue to engage in a serious analysis and deconstruction of the complex processes now unfolding in various regions of the world, which embrace religion and politics. It is a renewed plea for the rehabilitation of the concepts of cultural diversity and the practice of "cultural relativism" as a requisite for the "bridging," not the "clashing," of civilizations. Boundaries will always exist as long as human groups continue to exist, but they need not be hostile boundaries. We do not need another Great Wall of China nor another Berlin Wall: neither stood the test of time; their remnants in China and Germany are now just tourist attractions. Let us hope that Samuel Huntington's *Clash of Civilizations* will transpire not to be a self-fulfilling prophecy but merely a intellectual tourist attraction.

Notes

1. Abridged from a full account in Rodney Stark and Williams Bainbridge, *The Future of Religion: Secularization, Revival and Cult Formation* (Berkeley and Los Angeles: University of California Press, 1985).
2. Quoted in *Al-Ahram* (Cairo Arabic daily,) 8 April 1995.

3. Robin Wright, "Islam, Democracy, and the West," *Foreign Affairs*, Summer 1992; 71: 133.
4. See the results of a recent multi-country survey in the Muslim world: David Pollock and Elaine El-Assai (eds) *In the Eye of the Beholder: Muslim and Non-Muslim Views of Islam, Islamic Politics, and Each Other* (Washington, D.C.: Office of Research and Media Reaction, U.S. Information Agency, August 1995).

Further reading

Mohammed Selim, Al-Awwa. 1989. *On the Political System of Islamic State*, 6th edition (in Arabic). Cairo: first Dar El-Shrouk edition, 1989.

Salah, El-Sawey. 1993. *Political Pluralism in the Islamic State*, 2nd edition (in Arabic). Cairo: Dar El Eilam El-Dawli.

Saad Eddin, Al-Hussainy. 1993. *Why Islamic? Features of the Coming State* (in Arabic). Dar All-Bayyena.

Polk, David, and Elaine El-Assali (eds). 1995. *In the Eye of the Beholder: Muslim and Non-Muslim Views of Islam, Islamic Politics, and Each Other*. Washington, D.C.: Office of Research and Media Reaction, U.S. Information Agency.

Invigorating democratic ideas and institutions

14

The Philadelphia model

John Keane

On 19 April 1775, red-coated British troops nervously opened fire, without orders, on a group of American militiamen who had gathered near the meeting house on Lexington Green in Massachusetts, watched by a large crowd frightened into silence by whiffs of gunpowder and the redcoats' cries of "Disperse ye villains, ye rebels! Lay down your arms!" Eight militiamen were killed and ten wounded. News of the massacre ballooned through the colonies, kept aloft by couriers and newspapers and the savage indignation of those who concluded that from here on the world would have to be changed. After conflicts like Lexington, many colonists saw life in a fundamentally different way. The British parliamentary monarchy now seemed miserly, aggressive. America felt larger, more confident, and capable of governing itself, even lighting the path to liberty with new principles that the world could follow.

Two centuries after their invention, and especially during parades and picnics on 4 July, the popular memory of these founding principles is vivid. Most Americans summarize them in one simple word – "freedom" – yet they are not easy to detail, because the shared sense of unorthodoxy and mistrust of power of these principles has spawned endless controversies about the nature of liberty itself. The principles of American freedom are, nevertheless, discernible in what might be called the Philadelphia model of democracy. It began to crystallize after battles like Lexington and first appeared in such documents as the Declaration of Independence, read out to cheering crowds in Philadelphia after Congress approved its revised wording on 4 July 1776 and, two months later, in the new Pennsylvania constitution, which abolished property qualifications for voting and office-holding and, for its time, was easily the most democratic in the world.

Many Americans remain proud of the Philadelphia model, and with good reason. It was entirely novel: for the first time in human history, a two-tiered federated system of republican government elected by, and responsible to, its citizens was created. This "compound republic," as James Madison called it, stressed the need for a written constitution, based ultimately on the consent of citizens. This specified the powers accorded to government and the powers accorded to citizens in the form of such entitlements as the liberty of the press, the right to vote, and (twisting Hobbes' maxim that covenants unprotected by the sword are worthless) the right to bear arms. The new American system was designed to destroy the pomp and power of monarchy, exemplified by the corrupt Crown-in-Parliament system of the British. Moreover, resistance to tyranny, it was argued, required a rejection of the old fiction that the people resemble a body crying out for an all-powerful sovereign head which enjoyed the right to muzzle and blindfold its subjects and to speak and act on their behalf. Sovereignty in this sense, the Philadelphia revolutionaries insisted, treated "the people" as mere dross. It also overvalued unified power.

In perhaps their boldest move, the Philadelphians unpicked the classical republican assumption that "the people," like an earthly God, are the unified source of all political authority. From the time of the Articles of Confederation in 1778, in particular, the revolutionaries – stretching from Hamilton to Paine on the political spectrum – cut a path into the unknown by insisting that Americans could only become citizens of a subdivided polity. The Philadelphians refused to see the relationship between the state and federal tiers of power in zero-sum terms; they were, instead, adamant that the new elected federation, by dividing and clearly limiting the jurisdiction of the two tiers of government, would help tame the arrogance of elected representatives, ensuring that those who govern do not stand above the law, violate the rights of citizens, or suffocate the public spirit of the commonwealth.

Public virtue was central to the Philadelphian model. It insisted that freedom is not freewheeling individualism; rather, it is the unhindered ability of (male) citizens to act in concert with others and so to govern themselves within a written constitutional framework. This idea of freedom as self-government implied the need to restrain selfishness and the shabby morals of politicians and men of wealth, who should not be allowed to manipulate the laws to grind down the poor

– or to own slaves. Republican principles should be stretched into the sphere of economic life; property and its corresponding "liberal" values of private property, competition, and moneymaking must be subject to the principles of civic virtue. Few republicans thought that public spirit could, or should, eliminate disparities of wealth. And the question of slavery remained a permanent embarrassment. But most were agreed that the availability of citizenship rights to all adult White male citizens – not just property owners – would ensure ongoing public discussion about how to divide the divisible, and thus guarantee that the existing patterns of wealth and inequality would not be seen as natural, as reflecting the will of God, or as a brutal fact of "market forces."

A remarkable feature of the revolutionaries' affection for public spirit is the continuing power to attract strong support in contemporary America as well as in those countries – stretching from France and Turkey to China and Australia – touched in some way by the spirit of the Revolution. Operating as a 220-year-old utopia, it still moves people to tears and stirs up heated disputes about democracy. This spirit is certainly among the principal themes heating contemporary American political debate, sometimes to boiling point, especially within the ranks of the so-called communitarians. This ragged coalition of New Deal Democrats, community organizers, academics, city officials, along with those from the right, such as Pat Buchanan, speak for new forms of public regulation of the economy and dislike "liberalism" and its image of the unencumbered self. According to communitarian thinkers like Michael Sandel, Reaganite/Thatcherite "liberalism" is, on balance, foul political thinking.[1] Its appeal to the image of the free and independent self is seductive: who could be opposed to the principle that we should respect persons as persons, and that we should strive accordingly to secure their equal right to live the lives they choose within a framework of government and laws that are neutral with respect to competing moral values? However, it ignores the elementary fact that people are regularly attached to others through bonds of love and affection, workplace and neighbourhood solidarity, and familial and religious duty. Such "civic obligations," the latter-day Philadelphians insist, are normally not freely chosen on a contractual basis. "Liberalism" is therefore self-contradictory: it cannot grasp that the kind of civic engagement that liberty requires is actually not thinkable within the "liberal" language of individual rights. The flip side of this point is that "liberalism" is slowly destroying the Philadelphian conception of the good life: "liberalism" is responsible for the "moral void" within the American polity. Now, more than ever, the republic needs republicanism – the old Philadelphian spirit of active citizenship, public spirit, and solidarity in the face of adversity.

In practical terms, the communitarians come out in support of the politics of "soulcraft" – a favourite term of Michael Sandel; they are for a range of centre-left, Mario Cuomo-style policies designed to forge a common sense of citizenship among the American population. Community development corporations; citizens' opposition to supermarket-driven sprawl; federal spending on job training and education; and an emphasis on the character-forming role of families, neighbourhoods, and churches; these, say the communitarians, must be among the ingredients of the uphill struggle to defend and extend the Philadelphia model of liberty against its "liberal" enemies. The confident energy of their case is reminiscent of the spirit of 1776. It serves as a reminder that the American revolutionaries were the first successful modern radicals to universalize the principles of their revolution, which they portrayed as the harbinger of world citizenship, good government, and peace on earth. But how viable is this Philadelphian image of democratic freedom? Is it anything more than post-revolutionary nostalgia; is it merely a cool *fin-de-siècle* perspective that keeps the conference circuit talking; or does it have real intellectual and political potential?

Time and politics will tell. So, too, will its intellectual strengths and its weaknesses, both of which need careful examination. Its intellectual strengths are obvious. The Philadelphian model appeals to significant parts of America precisely because it scores telling points against the blind spots, contradictions, and misdoings of intellectuals, politicians, and policies favouring a "Reaganite" vision of America. It correctly protests against such facts of American life as crass commercialism, the degradation of urban areas, and the disempowerment of citizens. It rightly cries out against the maltreatment of Blacks, government corruption, and the run-down of the public infrastructure. It traces these ailments in the body politic to the abusive exercises of power by selfish oligarchs. This keeps alive the old republican presumption that power, understood as the domination by some men over the lives of others, is a permanent temptation in human affairs and that, consequently, the wielders of power must be subject to effective checks to ensure its responsible exercise. This call for vigilance in the presence of power remains as pertinent today as it was during the eighteenth century. Yet – the caveat is important – the intellectual confidence with which latter-day Philadelphians object to American decadence should not blind them to the dangers of *republican fundamentalism* – the unthinking, dogmatic presumption that the basics of the Philadelphia model remain intact over two centuries after its birth in battles like Lexington.

The contribution of republicanism to modern democratic principles and institutions is considerable. From a democratic point of view, it is a tradition well worth supporting, but only after the meaning in theory and practice of republican liberty is first thoroughly scrutinized with an open mind. Among the paradoxes presently surrounding the Philadelphia model, its rising popularity is overshadowed by gathering clouds of intellectual doubt regarding some aspects of the republican project as a whole. Most obvious is the point that eighteenth century republicanism actively ignored women's right not to be ignored. It certainly criticized old-fashioned patriarchalism and championed the resistance of adult men to what Jefferson and others dubbed the "fatherly" government of monarchy. But republicanism, despite its sensitivity to citizens' freedom, stopped short of questioning the power of "fathers" by *preserving* the conventional imagery of women as (potentially) seductive, fickle prostitutes. Women were seen as creatures marked by their unvirtuous disregard for reason and hence fit only for the "private" realm of family life. This presumption is still alive and well and serves to constrain, and frustrate, and physically exhaust many women whose complicated daily lives of juggling partners, children, friends and relatives, employment, and civic involvements are hopelessly at odds with the symbolic association of "women" with "home."

Furthermore, in an era of growing awareness of multicultural and other *differences*, orthodox republicanism's call for strait-jacketing everyone within "the common good" seems moralizing, at best, and potentially authoritarian, at worst. Just as early modern republicanism actively resisted the "seditious" or fracturing effects upon political communities by the emergent party systems – "If I could not go to heaven but with a party, I would not go there at all," quipped Jefferson – so contemporary republicanism seems morose in the face of political and social divisions. Certainly, orthodox republicanism is today out of step with a basic feature and precondition of the democratic project – namely, its commitment to building and preserving institutional systems guided by a "higher amorality" that discourages moralizing politics and refuses to judge opponents as "enemies."[2] This revised understanding of democracy is, admittedly, at odds with the fact that, for the past two centuries, virtually every democratic thinker in Europe and elsewhere has attempted, with varying degrees of confidence, to justify democracy by referring back to a substantive grounding principle. Many examples come to mind: the argument of Georg Forster, Thomas Paine, and others that democracy is grounded in the natural rights of men and citizens; the belief of Mazzini that the growth of democracy is a law of history; the Benthamite assumption that democracy is an implied condition of the principle of utility; the (Marxian) claim that the triumph of authentic democracy is dependent upon the world-historical struggle of the proletariat; and the conviction of Theodor Parker and others that democracy is a form of government.

Belief in these obviously contradictory first principles has today crumbled. Within the old and new democracies, the salient "philosophical" themes contained within most controversies about power are the insistence on the horizoned and biased character of human life, the emphasis on the cognitive intransparency of the world, and awareness of the impossibility of substituting knowledge of the "independent" structures of the "real world" for uncertain and tentative theoretical interpretations and revisable public judgements. Democratic theory cannot ignore this trend, and that is why, in my view, democracy is no longer understandable as a self-evidently desirable norm. Democracy is now suffering a deep (if less than visible) crisis of authority that cannot be cured by concocting imaginary foundations such as national argumentation, principles of autonomy, or knowledge of a "good which we can know in common" (Sandel).

The key question is whether democratic theory can live without foundationalist assumptions such as "the common good." Following a clue provided in Hans Kelsen's *Vom Wesem und Wert der Demokratie* (1929), one can suggest that the sense of common purpose of pre-modern societies cannot non-violently and democratically be re-created under modern conditions. The philosophy of democracy cannot become a universal language game, capable of knowing everything, refuting all its opponents, and pointing to the practical synthesis of all differences of opinion and identity. Furthermore, democracy is best understood as an implied precondition and a practical effect of philosophical and political pluralism, which is not itself a philosophical first principle but instead understandable through the logic of occasion, as practised among the pre-Socratics. I have reached the tentative conclusion that the separation of civil society from state institutions, as well as the public monitoring of power in each domain, are both among the necessary conditions for enabling a genuinely rich plurality of individuals and groups openly expressing their solidarity with, or opposition to, others' ideals and forms of life.

This revised understanding of democracy addresses the objection that the very term "democracy" is polluted by its diverse and contradictory meanings. Paradoxically, it insists, against Sartori and others,[3] that what is viewed as "democratic" at any given time and place can be maintained and/or contested as such only through these democratic procedures. These normatively inclined procedures are the condition *sine qua non* of post-foundationalism; whoever rejects them falls back either into the trap of foundationalism and its pompous belief in truth and ethics or into a cynical and self-defeating relativism that insists that there are no certain or preferable guidelines in life, thereupon displaying the same logical incoherence as the Cretan Epimenides, who truthfully declared that all Cretans were liars. It is, indeed, possible to escape the twin traps of relativism and foundationalism by viewing the democratic project as equivalent to the struggle against trans-historical ideals, definite truths, and other allegedly safe high roads of human existence.

The most alert contemporary defenders of the Philadelphia model try to deal intellectually with the objection that the principle of the common good is undemocratic by emphasizing, correctly in my view, the political importance of cultivating civil society. This is, in effect, trying to "modernize" the Philadelphia ideals, just as de Tocqueville's *Democracy in America* attempted to do by praising local associations of citizens as the best way of resisting tyrannies of both public opinion and government. However, this spells trouble for the old republican belief in an ultimately unified polity in which citizens can happily disagree because they agree on the political basics. That this foundational belief in "the common good" is today no longer fully accepted – or even understood – in parts of multicultural America is illustrated by the bitter struggles over the merits of multiculturalism in such areas as the teaching of history and matters of religious orthodoxy. It is hard to know just whether we are living in times in which the belief in commonality is disappearing, slowly and surely. Perhaps only one trend is certain: like the modern statues of the gods and goddesses (as Hegel put it), *unser Knie beugen wir doch nicht mehr* before the republican god of the common good. Thus, all democracies, old and new, are left with only one democratic alternative: to embrace the difficult art of *judgement* in the philosophical sense.

237

Judgement, the publicly learned capacity to choose courses of action in public contexts riddled with complexity, is the democratic art *par excellence*. It relies neither on the rules of deduction and induction nor on the conjectural thinking of abduction. Judgement avoids flights of fancy as much as it shuns practical reason, which "reasons" by telling actors what to do and what not to do by laying down the law in the language of imperatives such as "always observe the principle of the common good." Judgement avoids categorical imperatives that instruct those who act, always to act in such a way that the criteria of their acts can become a general law. Judgement tacks between the unique and the general. It is neither "reflective" nor "determinant" (to use the highly questionable distinction drawn by Kant to describe decisions that derive general rules from the particular or derive the particular from the general, respectively). Judgement, instead, relies on the recognition that the practical choice of how to act in any context must be guided by the recognition of the *particularity* of that situation. This means giving recognition to its uniqueness or difference from what we are used to.

The need for democrats and democracies to recognize that they know that they do not know what is to be done, that decisions require judgements, and that judgements lie within the field of force between the particular and the general, are quintessential features of the democratic art of public judgement. This will rescue political judgement from accusations of arbitrariness – and from the lure of will-o'-the-wisp universals like "the common good" – that in practice tend always to produce either political peacockery or bovine arrogance, both of which sap democratic politics. Yet the problem of the "common good" principle is only one of the contemporary problems facing democratic politics. Other, less obvious, intellectual traps await Philadelphian republicanism. They must be emphasized, for they bring us to the cutting edge of contemporary thinking about democratic liberty. Two related examples of this spring to mind and point to the need to save the Philadelphia model of democracy by amending it.

One concerns the old republican defence of the right of men to bear arms. The original Philadelphian model had a geopolitical vision. Powerfully challenging the prevailing Westphalian system of international relations, it was driven by the desire to avoid the emergence of another Europe, which was seen to be racked by hierarchy, balance-of-power politics, and constant wars between and within states. The Philadelphia model not only called for balancing and dividing power within the two-tiered system of state institutions, including its policing and war-making powers (symbolized by the subdivision of powers of foreign affairs and military command, between the president and a divided Congress); the new republic also sought to avoid the mistakes of old Europe by maintaining a citizens' militia to ensure that the central government was prevented from waging unpopular foreign wars or perpetrating violence against its own citizens. Hence, the Second Amendment: "A well-regulated Militia, being necessary to the security of a free State, the right of the people to keep and bear Arms, shall not be infringed."

In practice, this strange republican premise has proved to be devilish. It cavorts with the enemies of civility. Contemporary republicans correctly warn that civic solidarity is today at breaking point. Yet most do not see that their own traditional formula for dealing with state violence – arming citizens – contradicts the latter-day call for their non-violent empowerment. As I have argued in *Reflections on Violence*, the problem of violence should be at the heart of contemporary political thinking, if only because all known forms of civil society are plagued by endogenous sources of incivility.[4] Civil societies, ideal-typically conceived, are complex and dynamic webs of social institutions in which the opacity of the social ensemble – citizens' inability to conceive, let alone grasp, the totality of social life – combined with the chronic uncertainty of key aspects of life – employment and investment patterns, who will govern after the next elections, the contingent identity of one's self and one's household – make their members prone to stress, anxiety, and revenge. All modern civil societies are more or less caught in the grip of what Heinrich von Kleist called the "fragile constitution of the world" (*die gebrechliche Einrichtung der Welt*), and such fragility – combined with social discrimination and the increasing availability and cheapness of weaponry – increases the probability that the customary moral sanctions and restraints upon the resort to violence can be rejected or avoided by some of their members. Republicanism is intellectually unhelpful in coming to terms with this trend. It is also ill-equipped to deal with a not unrelated problem facing many old and new democracies – the problem of incivility caused by indifference. Indifference abounds within actually existing civil societies. A growing number of citizens' everyday contacts are contacts with strangers – that is, with people whom we expect never to deal with again. Neighbourliness is threatened by this trend, which may well be irreversible, which is another reason why the temptation of incivility – using insulting words and even knives and guns to resolve tensions with strangers – is rising,

239

oiled by republican talk of citizens bearing arms. The implication is clear: the republican defence of liberty necessitates objections to the republican Second Amendment, which in turn requires active gun control, including greater efforts to police the dramatic spread of private police forces in the name of the right to bear arms.

It is true that the Philadelphia model of democracy bravely tried to ameliorate incivility by emphasizing citizens' duties towards *the public*. That meant not only being civil towards others but also being committed to a non-violent public sphere of reasoned debate and information, circulated among citizens by the printing press. The principle was summarized in the famous words of Thomas Jefferson in 1787: "Were it left to me to decide whether we should have a Government without Newspapers, or Newspapers without a Government, I should not hesitate a moment to prefer the latter."

How viable is this republican ideal of the public sphere, whose purpose is to monitor the power of government and so prevent it falling into the arms of corruption? The public sphere principle certainly stands behind most latter-day republicans' mistrust of commercialized media, television "infotainment" in particular, and draws upon the contemporary debate about the use of technology to allow citizens to filter out unacceptable TV programmes, the argument about Hollywood violence, and the debate about regulating the Internet. It also underpins the "public journalism" movement, as expounded by James Fallows, which seeks to draw a vulgarized media back towards more serious public issues and transform networks of communications into proper organs of "the public sphere."[5]

The main problem with this vision is not its questionable presumption that public life is dying but, rather, its failure to see that we are living in times in which public life and its corresponding spatial frameworks of communication are in a state of upheaval. The old hegemony of state-structured territorially bound public life mediated by radio, television, newspapers, and books is rapidly eroding. In its place we see the development of a multiplicity of networked spaces of communication that are not tied immediately to territory and which irreversibly fragment anything resembling a single, spatially integrated public sphere. The vision of a republic of citizens striving to live up to some "public good" is thus obsolete. Public life today is subject to structural transformations, not as Habermas defined them in *Strukturwandel der Offentlichkeit* but in the quite different sense of a developing and complex mosaic of differently sized, overlapping, and networked public spheres.

Although these public spheres emerge within different milieux in the nooks and crannies of civil societies and states, each is an interest-ridden stage of action that displays the essential characteristics of a public sphere. A public sphere is a particular type of spatial relationship between two or more people, usually connected by a certain means of communication – television, radio, satellite, fax, telephone, e-mail – in which non-violent controversies erupt, for a brief or more extended period of time, concerning the power relations operating within their given milieu of interaction and/or the wider milieu of social and political structures within which the disputants are situated. Public spheres are the sites of the quintessential democratic attitude – *diffidenza* (Eco), the constant attitude of healthy suspicion of power. Within public spheres, citizens name the unnameable, point at frauds, take sides, start arguments, try to redefine the world, and stop it going to sleep. As citizens, they learn about the world; engage in controversies over who should get what, when, and how; and thereby help to ensure, within both the state and civil society, that nobody privately "owns" power. Public spheres in this sense never appear in pure form and rarely in isolation. Although they typically have a networked, interconnected character, contemporary public spheres have a fractured quality which is not being overcome by some broader trend towards an integrated public sphere. The examples below illustrate their heterogeneity and variable size, and that is why I choose, at the risk of being misunderstood, to distinguish among three ideal-types of public sphere.

Micro-public spheres, evident within social-movement networks and the advanced communication systems of local governments, are spaces in which there are dozens, hundreds, or thousands of disputants interacting usually at the sub-nation-state level. *Meso-public spheres*, mediated by large-circulation newspapers such as the *New York Times* and *Le Monde*, and electronic media such as the BBC, RAI, and the four American networks, normally comprise millions of people interacting at the level of the nation-state. *Macro-public spheres* crystallize around global media events (such as the Tiananmen Square crisis and the recent Russian elections) and the Internet, and normally encompass hundreds of millions – and even billions – of people enmeshed in disputes at the supra-national and global levels of power.

It might be objected that the attempt to categorize contemporary public life into spaces of varying scope or "reach" is mistaken on both empirical and normative grounds. Empirically speaking, it could

241

be said that contemporary publics are not discrete spaces, as the categories of micro-, meso-, and macro-public sphere imply; rather, they resemble a modular system of overlapping networks characterized by the lack of differentiation among spheres. Certainly, the concept of modularization is helpful in understanding the complexity of contemporary public life, but this does not mean that the boundaries among variously sized public spheres are obliterated completely. On the contrary, modular systems thrive on internal differentiation, whose workings can thus be understood only by means of ideal-typical categories that highlight those systems' inner boundaries.

The triadic distinction among differently sized public spheres can also be contested on normative grounds. During the early years of the twentieth century, at the beginning of the broadcasting era, John Dewey's *The Public and Its Problems* famously expressed the complaint that modern societies are marked by the fragmentation of public life:[6] "There are too many publics and too much of public concern for our existing resources to cope with," wrote Dewey. "The essential need," he added, "is the improvement of a unified system of methods and conditions of debate, discussion, and persuasion, *that* is the problem of the public." This neo-republican appeal – repeated more recently by Robert Bellah, Michael Sandel, and others – fails to see that the structural differentiation of public spaces is unlikely to be undone in the coming decades.[7] The continued use of "the" public sphere ideal is therefore bound to empty it of empirical content and to turn the ideal into a nostalgic, unrealizable utopia. The Philadelphia ideal of a unified public sphere and its corresponding vision of a republic of citizens striving to produce "public opinion" and to live up to some "public good" are badly in need of rethinking. Unless it is revised, the continued talk of "the public sphere" could even have potentially *undemocratic* consequences. Why? Because the old republican supposition that all power disputes can ultimately be sited at the level of the territorially bound nation-state is obsolete: it is a remnant from the era of revolutions against empires and nation-state-building and the corresponding struggles of states' inhabitants to widen the franchise – and, hence, to direct public controversies primarily towards the operations of the sovereign state itself.

Our times are obviously different, and not only because of the "scattering" of political power, commerce, and communication below and beyond the reach of many states. Precisely because of this trend, the act of opinion-making and voting in periodic general elections is gradually losing its power to determine things. Unlike the Philadelphians, we live in the era of the universal franchise; the issue of who is entitled to vote has largely been settled. From here on, a central issue for the freedom-loving politics of citizenship is thus no longer who votes but *where* people vote. The question, in short, is whether republicans can successfully argue for citizens taking themselves into the uncharted waters of *post-republicanism* by developing forms of public life and self-government in transnational domains such as the United Nations, in the North American Free Trade Agreement (NAFTA), and in subnational or local arenas such as households, the school board, offices, and neighbourhoods. Their success in extending the frontiers of democracy will, in turn, determine the success of the Philadelphians' own founding objectives – life, liberty, and the pursuit of public happiness.

Notes

1. See Michael Sandel, *Liberalism and the Limits of Justice* (Cambridge: Cambridge University Press, 1982); Michael Sandel (ed.) *Liberalism and its Critics* (New York: New York University Press, 1984).
2. See Niklas Luhmann, *Social Systems* (California: Stanford University Press, 1995); *Essays on Self-Reliance* (New York: Columbia University Press, 1990); *Observations on Modernity* (California: Stanford University Press, 1998).
3. See Giovani Sartori, *Democratic Theory* (New York: Greenwood Press, 1973); *The Theory of Democracy Revisited* (London: Chatham House, 1987).
4. John Keane, *Reflections on Violence* (London: Verso Books, 1996).
5. James Fallows, *Breaking the News: How the Media Undermine Democracy* (London: Vintage Books, 1997).
6. John Dewey, *The Public and Its Problems* (Columbus, Ohio: Ohio University Press, 1954).
7. Robert N. Bellah, *The Broken Covenant: American Civil Religion in Time of Trial* (Chicago: University of Chicago Press, 1992); R. N. Bellah, *The Good Society* (London: Vintage Books, 1992); R. N. Bellah, *Habits of the Heart: Individualism and Commitment in American Life* (Berkeley, California: University of California Press, 1985).

15

Democracy at the United Nations

Daniele Archibugi

A "third wave" of democratization has begun. In the early 1990s, many countries embraced democratic systems for the first time. Other countries have returned to democracy after years out in the cold. Entire populations have been lining up to take part in the most definitive ritual of all democratic systems – free elections. In Chile, South Africa, Czechoslovakia, Hungary, Russia, Cambodia, and other parts of the world, citizens have been waiting, sometimes for hours or days on end, to exercise their right to elect their own leaders.

These epoch-making events have led many observers to believe that democracy exists solely within nations and not between nations. Hence, the speculation regarding the "end of history" and of the irrelevance of transforming international relations. The most optimistic observers – or perhaps those least aware of the cyclical nature of history – have argued that all international problems would be solved if every country adopted a democratic system. Some have even forecasted that, by a certain year, the process of democratization will be completed, with all countries of the world having turned to elective political systems of government. However, while an extension in the number of countries ruled according to democratic principles is not only desirable but, from the perspective of the latter years of the twentieth century, highly probable, it is difficult to judge the validity of these statements.

In fact, the events of the 1990s have shown that merely enlarging the community of democratic nations does not, by itself, lead to a peaceful and just international system: the Gulf War and the genocide in Somalia and Rwanda occurred after the collapse of the Berlin

Wall; the achievement of democracy in the Soviet Union and Yugoslavia also led to an outbreak of violence and civil wars. Therefore, the question arises whether, while democracy leaps forward at the national level, it can blossom at the international level in such a way as to help ameliorate the trends in conflict of the post-Cold War world.

The United Nations is the most complex and ambitious international organization that has ever existed with an ethos of democracy among nations. However, the organization itself is not democratic, by any standard. Since its inception in 1945, it has been governed, instead, by four great hypocrisies.

The first is the hypocrisy which lies behind the Western democracies. The United States, Great Britain, and France, the inspiring forces behind the United Nations, founded the organization in order to extend the democratic values of their own domestic political systems to the international sphere. Yet, these same democratic nations had no scruples about appropriating the power to block any security-related decision and endowing themselves with the imperial privilege of being permanent members of the Security Council with broad powers of veto.

The second hypocrisy originated in the countries of Eastern Europe, led by the Soviet Union. They demanded that the very term "democracy" should have no mention in the UN Charter. The term, it seemed, held unwelcome connotations of threatening ideological values. For years, the word "democracy" was absent from all official UN documents.

The third hypocrisy has come from third world governments. While having continually accused the United Nations of not representing the needs and aspirations of the weaker states, the majority of these same governments have failed to apply the principles of democracy to their own citizens. In fact, third world governments have been among those guilty of denying the most basic human rights and needs to their own subjects.

The fourth hypocrisy brings us again to the democratic countries of the West. These nations have been the most visible and vociferous champions of democracy throughout the world while, periodically, indulging in illegal international activity. On many occasions, for example, they have overturned legitimate governments in the third world, replacing them with puppet regimes. Far from applying the values of democracy beyond their own national boundaries, these countries have placed their international policies and actions exclusively in the defence of their own national interests.

245

These four hypocrisies derive from a genuine dilemma: it is difficult to establish what democracy among states should consist of and to pinpoint a nexus between a country's domestic political regime and its foreign policy.

Countries with extremely democratic domestic systems, such as the United States and Israel, have illegally attacked much less democratic states, such as Viet Nam, Grenada, Panama, Syria, and Lebanon. These actions were no different from the foreign policy of totalitarian states, such as the Soviet Union's invasion of Hungary, Czechoslovakia, and Afghanistan. On other occasions, the Soviet Union appeared to be on the side of democracy: it supported the decolonization process and opposed apartheid in South Africa much more consistently than did many Western democratic states. Thus, the history of the first 50 years of the United Nations demonstrates that democracies do not necessarily behave democratically away from home and a totalitarian regime does not necessarily behave in a totalitarian way beyond its own frontiers.

In spite of these contradictions, democracy is emerging as a powerful international ethos. In order to ensure that this is not merely rhetorical, reform of the United Nations must be underpinned by democratic values. Former UN Secretary-General Boutros Boutros-Ghali conceptualized the meaning of international democracy in a number of articles and with the anticipated *Agenda for Democratization*. After *An Agenda for Peace* and *An Agenda for Development*, this is a further milestone in UN efforts for international legality and justice.

It should, however, be remembered that the question of democracy at the United Nations was raised by civil-society groups long before it became fashionable among diplomats and policy makers. The Campaign for a More Democratic United Nations, convened by Jeffrey Segall and Harry Lerner, raised these issues several years ago, together with a large number of peace and federalist movements in the United States and elsewhere. However, it is not self-evident what a "democratic" United Nations should be and how it should operate.

The terms "cosmopolitan democracy" or "transnational democracy" have been used by a group of scholars, including Richard Falk, David Held, Mary Kaldor, and myself, to help define the characteristics of a model of democracy that transcends state frontiers. Realist scholars and politicians would, of course, regard endeavours of this nature to be idle and useless: according to them, interests and the balance of power are the driving forces of international politics. As scholars, we are aware of this but believe intellectual design must play a significant role at a time when the structure of the Cold War has been abandoned yet there is still uncertainty about the complexion and structure of the international system. The Peace of Westphalia (1648), the Treaty of Utrecht (1712), the Congress of Wien (1814), the Conference of Paris (1919), and the San Francisco Conference (1945) were all influenced to some extent by thinkers who carefully elaborated ideas of a better international society, structure, and system.

The term "cosmopolitan democracy" defines democracy from three related viewpoints – democracy within states, democracy among states, and the democratic management of global problems. The United Nations could, and should, play a role in each of these perspectives, provided that it is appropriately reformed.

Democracy within member states

Despite the new wave of democratization in the 1990s, a large number of UN member states still do not have elected governments. When democratization is demanded, it should not be overlooked that the United Nations embraces both democratic and autocratic member states. Despite this, the United Nations still has an extremely useful role to play in fostering the transition from autocratic systems to democratic ones and in facilitating democratization in post-conflict societies. Multifunctional peace-keeping missions in Cambodia, Salvador, Mozambique, and other regions have been instrumental in establishing the modalities and institutions of democracy in those cases. Over the last five years, the United Nations has been called in to invigilate elections in more than 50 countries. These operations did not violate sovereignty in so far as they were based upon the consent of the host states.

Is it possible, however, for the United Nations to promote democracy within states without the explicit consent of the parties in contention? In reality, the organization has had to exercise caution in dealing with the domestic systems of countries. The principle of non-interference, the bedrock of international law and the United Nations, has effectively prevented any form of pronouncement on issues within the domestic jurisdiction of states. Yet the Universal Declaration of Human Rights is one form of "interference" that indicates that some issues are not within the absolute jurisdiction of sovereign states. All UN member countries have pledged to respect these rights and, by ratifying numerous conventions, have authorized the international community to see that they are upheld.

Here we find the major contradiction of the United Nations' legal basis: although it requires its members to accept noble principles – such as those in the Universal Declaration – it does not, and cannot, do much to enforce them. Apart from sporadic examples – such as the sanctions against apartheid in South Africa – UN action against the violations committed by governments against their own subjects has been ineffective and, perhaps, lenient.

There are, of course, good reasons to accept the principle of non-interference. Interference by a country in the internal affairs of other countries has been dictated more by self-interest than by concern for oppressed populations. Of course, a multilateral institution such as the United Nations is less likely to interfere in the internal affairs of states to the benefit of other ones. However, given the current institutional structure of the United Nations, some states have more power and can legally avoid censure or the consequences of interfering in the internal affairs of other less powerful states. For the time being, as an arbiter the United Nations is neither omnipresent nor impartial. To strengthen its functions, it needs to act both at the inter-state and at the global levels.

An essential aspect of democracy within a country is the manner in which decisions are made *vis-à-vis* the inhabitants of other countries – in short, foreign policy. Of all types of public policy, foreign policy tends most to escape the net of democratic control. Even in the countries with the oldest democratic traditions, the work of foreign and defence ministries is continually veiled in secrecy, keeping citizens unaware of their own country's real objectives and the means used to achieve them. All governments believe that it would be detrimental to the "vital interests" of the nation to make foreign-policy decisions public or to have a public input into the process. This is why foreign policy everywhere is the preserve of narrow diplomatic circles; yet a state cannot be wholly democratic unless its foreign policy decisions are also put under the control of citizens.

Thus far, there has been little potential in the UN system to take into account how foreign-policy decision-making is formulated and elaborated by its members. If an autocratic government decides to invade a neighbouring country, the international community considers all the inhabitants of the country responsible for it, even when they have been the victims, rather than the authors, of the action. In principle, this should induce the peoples of each nation to take responsibility over the foreign policy of their governments. This is, for example, the reason why Immanuel Kant, in his celebrated perpetual peace project, argued in favour of a union of countries with a constitutional basis:

> If, as is inevitably the case under this constitution the consent of the citizens is required to decide whether or not war is to be declared, it is very natural that they will have great hesitation in embarking on so dangerous an enterprise.

Contrary to the Kantian ethos, the United Nations has not used any discrimination in relation to the internal regimes in accepting new member states. This implies that the foreign policy of its members is beyond the control of public opinion and therefore does not benefit from domestic input.

Democracy among states

As far as relations among states are concerned, the United Nations has endorsed the principle of equality. This is a formal principle, since all countries possess different degrees of political, economic, and military power. Furthermore, even in the constitutional system of the United Nations, some countries are "more equal than others." This is obvious when we remind ourselves that only five are permanent members of the Security Council. In fact, the United Nations is based on a two-tier structure – the General Assembly, with formally equal nations, and the Security Council, with a handful of oligarchic governments. To strengthen democracy in inter-state relations, both parties would be required to reform.

The existence of a permanent membership and veto in the Security Council contradicts two basic principles of democracy – elective appointment in executive bodies and the majority rule. Yet, however undemocratic it is, we must accept it because the permanent members are those with the greatest military power in the world. Without it, strategic decisions would be made in other places, such as superpower summits, which are not transparent and therefore are even less democratic than the Security Council.

Much of the debate on UN reform has concentrated on the Security Council in order to balance the requirements of representativeness and efficiency. The proposals of the majority governments have been highly disappointing: many have tried to acquire privileges for themselves rather than to limit the use of the veto power. The debate has reflected the desire for the extension of privileges rather than their limitation. Inevitably, it has been impossible to achieve any agreement, for the simple reason that a privilege accorded to everybody is no longer a privilege.

At this stage it is difficult to predict if, when, and how the Security Council will be reformed. The interests of "the peoples" would be to limit the use of the veto to issues concerning security and the use of force, and by including regional organizations, such as the European Union, the Organization of African States, and the Arab League, in addition to single governments. This will force governments to negotiate and reach a common position at the regional level first. It is unlikely, however, that governments would support a reform that limits their authority and prestige.

The other principal inter-state institution of the United Nations, the General Assembly, has been a tribune for world governments to express their opinions. Yet the effective powers of the institution have been negligible. The principle "one state, one vote" is not necessarily a democratic one: countries such as Malta or Luxembourg have the same electoral weight as China, India, or the United States.

There is a trade-off between the powers of the General Assembly and its electoral norms in its decision-making. An enlargement of the powers of the General Assembly would require it to weigh votes according to population, income, and the military force of each state. Developing democracy among states means defending the independence of the weakest, but also seeing that general decisions are taken with the consent of the governments who represent the majority of people living on the planet.

The United Nations, no less than the League of Nations, was designed to solve bilateral controversies among states peacefully. The International Court of Justice was to act as an arbiter among the contending parties. Unfortunately, the fact that only a few states have fully accepted its jurisdiction has severely hampered the function of the World Court. Democratic states, including the United States, have so far failed to accept and obey international judicial authority.

In the long term, the membership of the United Nations must be linked to the acceptance of its main judicial institution. To save the concept of international democracy from being an empty gesture, all states – with the established democracies leading the way – should be prepared to accept unilaterally the jurisdiction of the Court.

The democratic management of global problems

A key feature of the post-Cold War era is the new global agenda of problems whose solution is not specific to any state or set of states. Environmental issues, the spread of AIDS, the protection of fundamental human rights: these are all problems insoluble by any single government working alone. The United Nations has raised public awareness of such issues through a series of thematic conferences, such as the Earth Summit in Rio (1992), the Cairo conference on demographic growth (1994), and the Copenhagen conference on human development (1995). Non-governmental organizations have also made a significant contribution, demonstrating that global problems cannot be solved in an exclusively intergovernmental realm.

But the United Nations is essentially still an intergovernmental organization. Whilst "the peoples" are invoked in the preamble to the Charter, they are still excluded from the organization's decision-making processes. The toughest challenge facing the United Nations over the next half-century will be to open the doors of its building to the peoples of the earth. Peace and federalist movements have for long advocated the creation of a Second UN Assembly that would represent world citizens rather than their governments. The European and Canadian parliaments have officially supported this proposal. This could be the first step towards a truly global democratic system, just as national parliaments have been for the achievement of democracy within states. The full achievement of democracy at the United Nations will require that individuals be given direct political input into the global political process, thereby giving dignity and respect to the citizens of the world. Suffrage is the most direct method to accomplish this.

A number of transitory steps have been suggested to achieve an elected Second UN Assembly. For the time being, it is unrealistic to suggest that such a body could be given much power if it is to be directly elected. One proposal seeks to establish a Peoples' Assembly as a consultative body for the General Assembly and other UN bodies. As a starting point it has also been proposed that national parliaments appoint some of their members of parliament as representatives of the Peoples' Assembly; this was, for instance, the route taken by the European Parliament before its members were directly elected.

There are, however, global problems and issues that go well beyond the mere representation of peoples. Under what circumstances are the institutions of the international community justified in interfering coercively in the domestic affairs of individual states? And what is the UN's role on such occasions?

In the first place, the United Nations must uphold the protection of human rights. The General Assembly is in the process of deciding whether to create an international criminal court, whose duties would be comparable to those of the tribunals set up in response to the crimes against humanity committed in the former Yugoslavia and Rwanda. Unlike those ad hoc tribunals, this court would be permanent. In this way, the United Nations would make an important contribution to the protection of individual rights. In so far as it would have jurisdiction over violations against individual rights committed by other individuals, the international jurisdiction would be identical to the criminal jurisdiction existing within a country. Wherever national jurisdiction proved incapable of performing its duties (for example, because the alleged perpetrators of crimes are also the holders of executive power), international jurisdiction might be able to step in and play a substitute role.

It is, however, highly unlikely, even if this new court were to be installed in the short term, that it would be able to count on the coercive power necessary to enforce its sentences. Yet, the sentence of an independent judicial body would, in itself, be an important delegitimation of rulers guilty of crimes against humanity: it would, in short, be a first and very important step towards democracy within states.

Yet, are there cases in which the United Nations has the right and duty to intervene, using force if necessary, in a state's domestic affairs? The only situation in which this is legitimate is to prevent and stop acts of genocide. If people are essentially the constituency which the United Nations represents, then they must be collectively capable of preventing the genocide amongst themselves. The United Nations has to be capable, willing, and authorized to intervene promptly and effectively to defend civilian populations threatened with extermination. This obviously demands a total rethinking of the role of peace-keeping. Until the late 1980s, the UN peace-keeping force was a diplomatic support structure for containing local conflict and minimizing superpower confrontation. Experiences in the 1990s – in particular in the former Yugoslavia, Somalia, and Rwanda – show that the methods and principles underlying peace-keeping need to be reviewed substantially if acts of genocide are to be prevented effectively.

As for the physiology of domestic systems, I believe that the

United Nations must be very cautious about assuming prerogatives in which there is an element of arbitrariness. Robespierre warned against the desire to make peoples happy against their will. Paraphrasing him, I suggest that, by the same token, governments – the most powerful, first and foremost – need to be warned against making nations democratic against their wishes. It is always hard, sometimes impossible, to distinguish sincere love for the good of others from policies in defence of national interest.

From a historical point of view, the last 50 years show that democracy within nations has to be developed endogenously. Western democratic countries did almost nothing to fuel democracy in Eastern Europe: as the former began to set an example, the peoples of the East did everything in their power to overthrow their autocratic regimes.

The three dimensions of democracy I have outlined here are closely interrelated. Only if legitimate supranational institutions dig furrows of influence – even interference – into the domestic affairs of states will it be possible to reinforce the authority of one government in its dealings with those more powerful.

At the end of the twentieth century, democracy has proved to be the victorious political system. Unfortunately, its victory is still largely incomplete, in so far as it has failed to extend to international relations. The United Nations is the crossroads of democracy outside national frontiers. Working jointly to achieve democracy within states, in interaction between states and in global problems, it can make a tangible contribution to the development of democracy on our planet. During the celebrations for the United Nations' 50th anniversary, democracy was often invoked by governments and diplomats. Ironically, the very same governments have ignored the proposals and aspirations of global civil society to achieve anything resembling real democracy. Now, as we move forward into the twenty-first century, it is more important than ever to organize and create specific reforms towards the democratization of the United Nations.

Further Reading

Archibugi, Daniele, and David Held (eds) 1995. *Cosmopolitan Democracy: An Agenda for a New World Order*. Cambridge: Polity Press.

Barnaby, Frank (ed.) 1991. *Building a More Democratic United Nations*. London: Frank Cass.

Bonanate, Luigi. 1995. "Peace or Democracy?" In Daniele Archibugi and David Held (eds), op. cit.

Boutros-Ghali, Boutros. 1995. "Democracy: A Newly Recognized Imperative."
Global Governance 1: 3–11.

Falk, Richard. 1995. "Appraising the UN at 50: The Looming Challenge." *Journal of International Affairs* 48.

Held, David. 1995. *Democracy and the Global Order*. Cambridge: Polity Press.

Huntington, Samuel. 1990. *The Third Wave: Democratization in the Late Twentieth Century*. Norman: University of Oklahoma Press.

Kaldor, Mary. 1990. *The Imaginary War. Understanding the East–West Conflict*. Oxford: Blackwell.

Russett, Bruce. 1991. *Grasping the Democratic Peace*. Princeton: Princeton University Press.

Segall, Jeffrey, and Harry Lerner (eds) 1992. *Camdun-2: The United Nations and a New World Order for Peace and Justice*. London: Camdun.

16

A meditation on democracy

Bernard Crick

Democracy is both a sacred and a promiscuous word: we all love her but she is hard to pin down; everyone claims her but no one actually possesses her fully. A moment's thought will remind us why this is so.

Different usages

Historically, there have been four broad usages. The first is found with the Greeks, in Plato's attack on it and in Aristotle's highly qualified defence: democracy is simply, in the Greek, *demos* – the mob, the many – and *cracy*, meaning rule. Plato attacked this as being the rule of the poor and the ignorant over the educated and the knowledge-able, ideally philosophers. His fundamental distinction was between knowledge and opinion: democracy is rule, or rather the anarchy, of mere opinion. Aristotle modified this view rather than rejecting it completely: good government was a mixture of elements, the few ruling with the consent of the many. The few should have *aristoi*, or the principle of excellence, from which the ideal concept of aristoc-racy derives. But many more can qualify for citizenship by virtue of some education and some property – both of which, Aristotle thought, were necessary conditions – and so must be consulted and can, indeed, even occasionally be promoted to office. He did not call his "best possible" scenario democracy at all, rather *politea* or polity, a politi-cal community of citizens deciding on common action by public debate. But democracy could be the next best thing in practice if it observed "ruling and being ruled in turn." As a principle unchecked by aristocratic experience and knowledge, however, democracy was based upon a fallacy: "because men are equal in some things, they are equal in all."

The second usage is found in the Romans, in Machiavelli's great *Discourses*, in the seventeenth century English and Dutch republicans, and in the early American republic: good government is mixed government, just as in Aristotle's theory, but the democratic popular element could actually give greater power to a state. Good laws to protect all are not good enough unless subjects became active citizens making their own laws collectively. The argument was both moral and military. The moral argument is the more famous: both Roman paganism and later Protestantism had in common a view of man as an active individual, a maker and shaper of things, not just a law-abiding well-behaved acceptor or subject of a traditional order. (It was this disjunction that so concerned the late Maruyama Masao in all his major essays on modernism and traditionalism.)

The third usage is found in the rhetoric and events of the French Revolution and in the writings of Jean Jacques Rousseau: everyone, regardless of education or property, has a right to make his or her will felt in matters of state. Indeed, the general will or common good is better understood by any well-meaning, simple, unselfish, and ordinary person based upon their own experience and conscience than by the over-educated living amid the artificiality of high society. This view can embrace the liberation of a class or a nation, whether from oppression or ignorance and superstition, but it is not necessarily connected with individual liberty. (In the European eighteenth and nineteenth centuries, most people who cared for liberty did not call themselves democrats at all: they were constitutionalist or civic republicans, or, in the Anglo-American discourse, "Whigs.") The general will could have more to do with popularity than with representative institutions. Napoleon was a genuine heir of the French revolution when he said that "the politics of the future will be the art of stirring the masses." His popularity was such, playing on both revolutionary and nationalistic rhetoric, that he was able for the very first time to introduce mass conscription, that is, to trust the common people with arms; the autocratic Hapsburgs and Romanovs had to be most careful to whom and where they applied selective conscription.

The fourth usage of democracy is found in the American constitution and in many of the new constitutions in Europe in the nineteenth century and in the new West German and Japanese constitutions following the Second World War. It is also reflected in the writings of John Stuart Mill and Alexis de Tocqueville: that all can have citizenship if they care, but they must mutually respect the equal rights of fellow citizens within a regulatory legal order that defines, protects, and limits those rights.

What is most ordinarily meant today by "democracy" in the United States, Europe, and Japan is, ideally, a fusion (but quite often a confusion) of the idea of power of the people and the idea of legally guaranteed individual rights. The two should, indeed, be combined, but they are distinct ideas, and can prove so in practice. There can be, and have been, intolerant democracies and reasonably tolerant democracies. Personally, I do not find it helpful to call the system of government under which I live in the United Kingdom "democratic"; I prefer to discuss how the actual system could be made more democratic, just as others once feared that the democratic element was becoming too powerful. Sociologically and socially England is still, in many ways, a profoundly undemocratic society (Scotland and Wales somewhat more democratic), certainly when compared with the United States. But even in the United States there is now little citizenship or positive participation in politics in the republican style of the early American Republic. Of course, people vote in formal elections, but, between elections, talk of – and active participation in – politics rates far, far lower than the most favoured national activity, shopping.[1]

Democracy not the main concept

When considering the present nature and problems of democracy, what we often mean to talk about is something prior to either ideal or empirically observed definitions of democracy – politics itself. Here we all must have something to say. Politics is too important to be left to politicians. Politicians are too busy and preoccupied with – in the broad perspective of human history – short-term advantages and actions, with winning the next election, so others must speculate and try to do their long-term thinking about civilized humanity for them. Thought and action must go together, not merely if the political tradition is to be preserved but also, since the need is pressing, if it is to be extended. By political tradition I mean simply the activity of resolving disputes and determining policy politically – that is, by public debate among free citizens. Although this activity is one of the most important inventions of human civilization, it is now taken for granted or even regarded – because of the actions of particular politicians – as a debased or even dangerous activity. Its beneficial application is neither universal nor universally understood; or, even if understood, it is not always desired.

The political tradition may be the world's best hope, and perhaps its last hope as we see long-term problems begin to accumulate that could destroy (the phrase does have meaning) civilization as we know it. If political solutions – or, more likely, political compromises – are not found, power blocks will struggle harder and more ruthlessly and competitively, in a world of increasing demands and of diminishing resources, to maintain the standard of living of at least a voting majority of their own loyal inhabitants. And it is almost fatuous to recall that the misapplication of scientific and industrial technology gives us unique opportunities for mutual destruction. The two world wars of the twentieth century should have been a perfectly adequate demonstration of this, but could yet prove an inadequate premonition of the shape of things to come. During the Cold War, the fear of global nuclear destruction perhaps took the minds of most political leaders and thinkers off other, slower, global threats. And politically, the post-war era has seen some good reasons for political optimism about the internal affairs of states. The collapse of Soviet power through sheer inefficiency, the somewhat similar decline of military regimes in Southern Europe and South America, some relaxation of despotism in China, and signs of civic stirring even in the bloody anarchy of sub-equatorial Africa, are some such indicators. The myth of the superior efficiency and the invincibility of totalitarian and autocratic states has been exploded.

However, the collective inability of democratic states to act together by political agreement to deal with real and vital common problems has been amply demonstrated also. The response to the bloody break-up of the Yugoslavian Federation, let alone failure so far to achieve effective cooperation to prevent degradation of the environment of the whole planet, are illustrative. Take also the case of nuclear weapons: the threat of deliberate two-bloc world war now seems happily (if somewhat fortuitously) gone, yet the ability of the so-called great powers to prevent the spread of nuclear bombs to less stable regimes is now diminished almost to the point of impotence. Some of this impotence arises, of course, from the inability or unwillingness of political leaders in democracies (one in particular) to educate and change public opinion (precisely what Aristotle feared about democracies).

The invention, and then the tradition, of governing by means of political debate among citizens has its roots in the practices and thought of the Greek *polis* and the ancient Roman republic. So its political rule could be said to be as "Western" or "European" in its origins, and yet as universal in its application, as natural science. But the origins of even such powerful and influential traditions of activity do not endow the descendants of its progenitors with special wisdom – indeed, sometimes it gives them a false sense of superiority and dangerous overconfidence. The general ideas of political rule and of the natural sciences and attendant technologies are not bound to any one culture: they have spread universally, both as power-driven exports and as eagerly sought-after modernizing imports. The results, of course, vary greatly in different cultural settings and by the accidents of contingent events, but there is more in common now between such societies than in the pre-political, pre-scientific, and pre-industrial world. The Eastern world may, and almost certainly will, produce variants of the "democratic" (or, as I prefer to say, "political") tradition, from which the West may learn. This has already happened in technology. But, it is fair to say, the West does not stand still entirely. That the concept of citizenship was only fairly recently extended to women is no small matter – full civic equality is still far ahead, and the consequences of this are as likely to be as great in the future as they are still unclear in the present. Now this elevated view of politics may surprise our fellow citizens, who form their idea of "the political" from what they read in their national newspapers about the behaviour, in all respects, of actual politicians. Indeed, one must ask if such politicians are the friends or the foes of good government. Certainly, they are (to use a favourite word of Hannah Arendt's) thoughtless about the consequences in terms of public example of how they practise politics and behave themselves, which is part of politics.

The nature of the political

More than 30 years ago I wrote a book called *In Defence of Politics*, which has remained in print ever since and has been translated into many languages, including Japanese (thanks to the aforementioned Maruyama Masao). But it received very few reviews by my then academic colleagues in Britain. That did not dismay me, for I had aimed the book at the intelligent general reader, and it has been called, if only by the publishers, "a modern classic."[2] What does dismay me is that during the last 30 years there has been a continuing decline in book publishing of serious political thinking aimed at, and read by, the public, despite all the troubles and unexpected opportunities of our times.[3] Coherent political thinking can be all but abandoned by party leaders, debased and too often reduced to sound-bites uttered with a coached sincerity, but with no well-grounded justifications advanced for the fragments of general principles somewhat (or almost wholly) opportunistically advanced. Sincerity stands in for reasoning and, when politics is discussed, even by intelligent ordinary people, it is more often in terms of personalities than of principles and of appeals to immediate self-interest rather than to long-term mutual or public benefits. Only a few columnists and editorial writers in some quality newspapers keep up the once-prevalent tradition of intelligent and reasonably open-minded public debate and speculation.

However, the academic discipline of political thought has thrived as never before, both as the history and contextualization of ideas and as the analysis of meaning and implications of concepts in current use – freedom, equality, justice, sovereignty, nation, individualism, community, and so on. But this advance has been almost wholly internalized within the academy. Most academic writing on politics and the problems of democracy can be seen, sometimes rather generously, as contributions to the advancement of knowledge, as well as to the individual's reputation and promotion prospects, but few seem interested in diffusing this knowledge to the public, or are able to do so. Faults on both sides can be found: it is all too easy to make a career by writing about politics – "researching" is now the term more used – and yet for the product to remain wholly within the ivory tower, unknown to the public. The irony of doing this for the study of politics escapes most of the denizens of the castle. We are often rather like those student leaders of the 1960s, who proclaimed their solidarity with the working class and "the people" in a Marxist terminology understandable only to those among "the people" who had a degree in social science at a new university. But, on the other hand, the media take very few steps to discover and use the academic product. In Britain, only the talents of experts on electoral statistics are regularly courted. The idea is strange, that there is a tradition of political thinking and knowledge as relevant to the problems of the modern world as economic theory and one historically more important. Political considerations are far more often held to interfere with economic reasoning than the contrary.

The thesis of my *In Defence of Politics* was all too easy, even if challengingly simple. It spoke of making some "platitudes" pregnant: that politics is the conciliation of naturally different interests, whether these interests are seen as material or moral, usually both. I wrote in the Aristotelian tradition. There is a famous passage in Aristotle's *Politics* where he suggests that the great mistake of his master Plato was in writing about ideal states as if to find a single unifying principle. Rather,

... there is a point at which a *polis*, by advancing in unity, will cease to be a *polis*; but will none the less come near to losing its essence, and will thus be a worse *polis*. It is as if you were to turn harmony into mere unison, or to reduce a theme to a single beat. The truth is that the *polis* is an aggregate of many members.

Not all societies are organized and governed according to political principles. Most governments in history have suppressed public debate about policy, far preferring to encourage "good subjects" rather than good or active citizens. But this has become more and more difficult in the modern world. Yet it is not just so-called political ideologies that threaten free politics: nationalism and religion can do so also. These forces are sometimes reasonably tolerant, at other times intensely intolerant. Although politics is not necessarily threatened by strong religious belief, sometimes not even when there is a dominant religion, some beliefs and practices stifle or threaten free politics and the open expression of contrary views. But some secularists also can see politics as inherently disruptive of social order. "The country could be run better without all this politics." And many must sympathize with Joseph Goebbels' axiom: "Politicians perpetuate problems; we seek to solve them."

So political rule, I argued, existed before democratic government. It is logically prior to "democracy," unless by that term we mean, rather fatuously, "everything we would like," rather than a component of good government, a concept of majority opinion and power that is not always compatible with liberty and individual rights. Some dictatorships, for instance, have been (and are) genuinely popular, resting on majority support, and the stronger for it. Both historically and logically, politics is prior to democracy. We may want to fill the cart full of good things that everyone wants and feels they need, but the horse must go out in front. Without order there can be no democracy, and without politics even democracy is unlikely to be just.

Leaning on Aristotle

So I argued – still leaning on old Aristotle against the over-sophistication of modern social science, whether in the Marxist or the modern American variety – that politics rests on two preconditions, a sociological and a moral. The sociological is that civilized societies are all complex and inherently pluralistic, even if and when the injustices of class, ethnic, and gender discriminations will vanish or diminish. The moral aspect is that it is normally better to conciliate differing interests than to coerce and oppress them perpetually, or to seek to remove them without consent or negotiated compensation. While much political behaviour is prudential, there is always some moral context: some compromises are wrong to make, and some ways of coercion or even of defence are too cruel, disproportionate, or simply too uncertain. A nuclear first strike, for example, even against a nuclear power, could not reasonably be called political behaviour – even against Baghdad. Hannah Arendt was wiser than Clausewitz and Kissinger when she said that violence is the breakdown of politics, not its "continuance by other means."

So it was easy for me to argue that it is always better to be governed politically, if there is any choice in the matter. The thesis did not seem so banal or simple-minded at the time because there was sustained contrast, explicitly and implicitly, between political rule and totalitarian rule. The simple could then appear both profound and important. But with the breakdown of Soviet power and the old pull towards a binary system, the whole world has become more complicated. Previously existing contradictions in the so-called "free world" have both come to the surface and grown more acute. The concept of the "free world" begs far too many questions, makes too many assumptions. It is a highly complex concept, whose components need unpacking and testing carefully for quality, and is too often self-righteous and propagandistic in use. But the concept of politics certainly implies freedom and its widespread practice depends upon it.

Just as totalitarian rule and ideology can break down internally, so, too, can political rule; and political prudence can prove inadequate. I gave such situations little serious attention in the *In Defence of Politics*. Since then, I have studied such situations in books, documents, and newspapers and by talking to people on the ground in Northern Ireland, South Africa, and Israel/Palestine. Each of these is very different in detail but they share a problem in common. They can be used symbolically as examples of the general problem of the adequacy of "mere politics" when people enjoy some kind of a political tradition yet refuse any talk of compromise because they feel that their very identity is at stake if they give any ground.

The justification of politics in terms of the negation of totalitarianism is all too easy. The mundane could be made melodramatic in terms of contrast. The "defeat" of the USSR and the "victory" of the West also appeared to imply the rejection, and then the demise, of ideology. I took ideology to be not any set of specific ideas about particular things (say beliefs and doctrines) but secular claims to comprehensive explanation and policy. Old autocracies, however bigoted, bloody, and cruel, had limited aspirations – usually just for the ruling class to stay in power and so sleeping dogs could lie if they paid their taxes and doffed their hats. But some modern autocracies earned the new name because they saw the need to mobilize the masses, to make sleeping dogs bark (and even sing) in unison, to attempt to achieve the revolutionary objectives of an ideology. But ideology did *not* vanish with the demise of Communist power and its universalistic pretensions. Political prudence and pragmatism did not take over. Rather, there emerged the rapid – almost wildfire – spread of the belief that more or less unrestrained market forces cannot be resisted and will resolve all major problems on a global scale.

Ideologies and politics

Hannah Arendt, in her great book *The Human Condition*, remarked that there have only ever been two kinds of comprehensive ideologies claiming to hold the key to history – the belief that all is determined by *race* and the belief that all is determined by *economics*. Both racism and economicism are incidentally distinctive modern beliefs: before the late eighteenth century the world could get by without such enormous secular claims, and not even religions claimed to explain everything. Arendt pointed out that economic ideology took two rival forms – Marxism and *laissez-faire* – and yet the belief that there must be a *general system* had a common origin and linked them more than their disciples believe. The missionaries and the advocates of market ideology in the former Soviet bloc now denounce political interventions in the economy almost as fiercely as did the old totalitarians, although, fortunately, they are still subject to some political restraints and a few residual colonial inhibitions. In the party

263

politics of Britain, many people rightly rail against the excesses of privatization, the diminishment of public welfare, and the attacks of a government on the very concept of a *res publica* or a public interest. Governments can seek to distance themselves from any responsibility for guiding Adam Smith's hidden hand by which the free market becomes the public interest. But, in a broader perspective, the degree of political restraint upon the children of Hayek – the Reagans and the Thatchers – is also remarkable: they have done to us, for good or evil, much less than they know they ought to have done; and that is because of "irrational political factors," thank God!

Prices cannot be sensibly determined except by market mechanisms; the final breakdown of Soviet planning proved that. And capitalism is an international system whose imperatives can be ignored only at a fearful price, as in North Korea and Cuba. But it does not then follow that price must determine every human relationship, least of all the civic. Man is citizen as well as consumer. There is (or was) public and family morality, strong cultural restraints on the exercise of both economic and political power. New lines of demarcation and mutual influence between the polity and the economy need examining closely. If people see themselves purely as consumers they will lose all real control of government. Governments will then rule by bread and circuses, even if not by force; and torrents of trivial alternatives will make arbitrary and often meaningless choice pass for effective freedom. For all the absolutist rhetoric, in reality at least a degree of welcome confusion reigns. Only the two extreme positions of All-State or All-Market are untenable; there is a lot of space between. Political and economic factors and principles interact with each, limit each other; but neither can live for long without the other.

Of course, it was always foolish in the light of history to think that the end of the Cold War – a quite sudden event that neither prophets nor social scientists expected – would by itself lead to peace, prosperity, and freedom. And what new democracy has emerged looks much more like Schumpeter's view of democracy as a competitive electoral struggle between party élites – in his *Capitalism, Socialism and Democracy* of 1942 – than the old republican ideal of active and participatory citizenship.

In contrast to even the best democratic practices of today, consider a passage that used to be worrying to autocrats and élites in Europe, and a source of inspiration to their opponents, especially the American Republic founding fathers. The Periclean oration of the fifth century B.C. in Athens would once have been read by almost everyone who read books at all:

Our constitution is called a democracy because power is in the hands not of a minority but of the whole people. When it is a question of settling private disputes, every one is equal before the law; when it is a question of putting one person before another in positions of public responsibility, what counts is not membership of a particular class, but the actual ability which the man possesses. No one, so long as he has it in him to be of service to the state, is kept in political obscurity because of poverty. And, just as our political life is free and open, so is our day-to-day life in our relations with each other. We do not get into a state with our next-door-neighbour if he enjoys himself in his own way, nor do we give him the kind of black looks which, though they do no real harm, still do hurt people's feelings. We are free and tolerant in our private lives; but in public affairs we keep to the law. This is because it commands our deep respect....

Here each individual is interested not only in his own affairs but in the affairs of the state as well: even those who are mostly occupied with their own business are extremely well-informed on general politics – this is a peculiarity of ours: we do not say that a man who takes no interest in politics is a man who minds his own business; we say that he has no business here at all. We Athenians, in our own persons, take our decisions on policy or submit them to proper discussions: for we do not think that there is an incompatibility between words and deeds; the worst thing is to rush into action before the consequences have been properly debated....[4]

Historians now assert that Pericles was a demagogue, a kind of democratic dictator. But the point is what the demagogue said, the lasting ideal he invoked, not what he did or why he said it.

Notes

1. Seymour Martin Lipset does not put it quite so bluntly in his recent magisterial survey, *American Exceptionalism: A Double-Edged Sword* (New York and London: W.W. Norton, 1996), but the figures and attitude surveys that he reports lead to this conclusion.
2. *In Defence of Politics*, 4th edition (London: Penguin, 1992), first published by Weidenfeld and Nicolson 1962, and in the USA by the University of Chicago Press.
3. In fairness, I think this is less marked in the United States than in Britain, Germany, and France. The larger American market, of course, makes this possible, but also in the United States there are more serious journalists with resources and assistants for "research," able to gut the best academic literature.
4. From Thucydides, *The Peloponnesian War* (London: Penguin, 1954), pp. 117–118.

Contributors

Daniele Archibugi is a researcher at the Italian National Research Council in Rome and a Senior Research Associate at the University of Cambridge. He is an adviser to the Organization for Economic Cooperation and Development, to the European Commission and to various UN agencies. Dr. Archibugi is the Coordinator of the European Network on the Political Theory of Transnational Democracy.

Jean Blondel is currently an external professor at the European University Institute in Florence and Visiting Professor at the University of Siena. He holds honorary doctorates from the universities of Salford, Essex, Louvain la Neuve, and Turku. Professor Blondel started the European Consortium for Political Research in 1969 and directed it for ten years. He is also a current member of the Royal Swedish Academy of Sciences and the Academia Europaea.

Bernard Crick is Literary Editor for the *Political Quarterly*. He is also Professor Emeritus of Politics at Birkbeck College London and Honorary Fellow of the University of Edinburgh. He has been Chairman of the Hansard Society's commission on Political Education in Schools and joint Chairman of the British South Africa Conference during the three years of transition. Professor Crick has worked extensively in Northern Ireland on conciliation projects, and has been active in the Scottish devolution movement.

Saad Eddin Ibrahim is Professor of Political Sociology at the American University in Cairo, Secretary-General of the Egyptian Independent Commission for Electoral Review, and President of Cairo's Union of Social Professors. He is also chairman of the Ibn Khaldoun Center for Development Studies and a member of the World Bank's Advisory Council for Environmentally Sustainable Development. He is a recipient of the Jordanian Order of Independence Award and has written many books on the Middle East.

Takashi Inoguchi is Professor of Political Science at the Institute of Oriental Culture of the University of Tokyo. Until recently he was Senior Vice-Rector of the United Nations University. Professor Inoguchi has occupied research and/or teaching positions at the Université de Genève, Harvard University, Australian National University, University of Delhi, and Johns Hopkins University. Amongst his recent publications are *Japanese Politics Today*, *The Vitality of Japan*, *North-East Asian Regional Security*, *United States–Japan Relations and International Institutions After the Cold War*, and *Global Changes: An Analysis*.

Elihu Katz is Professor of Communication at the Annenberg School for Communications at the University of Pennsylvania. He is Emeritus Professor of Sociology and Communications at the Hebrew University of Jerusalem, and Scientific Director of the Guttman Institute of Applied Social Research. Dr. Katz was founding director of Israel Television and is a winner of the McLuhan–Teleglobe Canada Award, the Burda Prize in media research, and the Israel Prize.

John Keane is Professor of Politics at the University of Westminster and Director of the Centre for the Study of Democracy. Educated at the universities of Adelaide, Toronto and Cambridge, he has been awarded many scholarships and prizes. In 1992 he was elected a Fellow of the Royal Society of Arts. He has written numerous books, including *The Media of Democracy* (which has been translated into 16 languages), and is a frequent contributor to various media.

Juan J. Linz is Sterling Professor of Political and Social Science at Yale University. He holds degrees in Law, Political Science and Sociology, and has contributed to books on authoritarianism, fascism, political parties, nationalism, and religion. In 1987 he was awarded the Premier Principe de Asturias de Ciencias Sociales and in 1996 the Johan Skytte Prize in Political Science.

267

Ian Marsh is an Associate Professor at the Australian Graduate School of Management. He was educated at the University of Newcastle (New South Wales, Australia) and Harvard, and has held visiting positions at Keio University in Tokyo and the European University in Florence. Professor Marsh's most recent publication is a study of Australia's political and economic future entitled *Beyond the Two Party System: Political Representation, Economic Competitiveness and Australian Politics.*

Edward Newman is a Lecturer in International Relations at Shumei University in Japan, and his research interests are in global governance and foreign policy issues. Dr. Newman's recent publications include *The UN Secretary-General from the Cold War to the New Era: a Global Peace and Security Mandate?*

Claus Offe is Professor of Political Sociology and Social Policy at the Humboldt University, Berlin. He has been a visiting professor at the New School for Social Research in New York, and the Institute for Advanced Study in Berlin. Between 1976 and 1982 Professor Offe was a member of the Joint Committee on Western Europe, Social Science Research Council, and has also held Fellowships at six different universities.

Bruce Russett is Dean Acheson Professor of International Relations, and Director of United Nations Studies, at Yale University. He is also Editor of the *Journal of Conflict Resolution*, and a former president of the International Studies Association and Peace Society. He has published a substantial number of articles and books, of which the most recent is *Grasping the Democratic Peace: Principles for a Post-Cold War.*

Philippe C. Schmitter has been on the Stanford University faculty since 1986. He formerly taught at the University of Chicago and has held many visiting appointments. Dr. Schmitter has been the recipient of numerous professional awards and fellowships, including a Guggenheim in 1978, and has been Vice-President of the American Political Science Association.

Mihály Simai is currently a research professor at the Institute for World Economics of the Hungarian Academy of Sciences and the

Director of Graduate Studies in International Economics and Business Relations in the Budapest University of Economics. He is also a former Director of UNU/WIDER, and former member and Chairman of the UNU Council.

Alfred Stepan is Gladstone Professor of Government and Fellow, All Souls College, University of Oxford. Until recently he was President and Rector of the Central European University in Budapest and Prague. Dr. Stepan is the co-author of *Problems of Democratic Transition and Consolidation: Southern Europe, South America and Post-Communist Europe*, and the author of *Rethinking Military Politics: Brazil and the Southern Cone*; *The State and Society: Peru in Comparative Perspective*, and *The Breakdown of Democratic Regimes*.

J.A.A. Stockwin has been Nissan Professor of Modern Japanese Studies and Director of the Nissan Institute of Japanese Studies at the University of Oxford since 1982, and Fellow of St. Antony's College, Oxford. Between 1994 and 1995 he was President of the British Association of Japanese Studies. He is author of a number of books on Japanese politics and is engaged in a long-term study of political change and reform in Japan.

Index